WOMEN TALK BACK TO SHAKESPEARE

This study explores more recent adaptations published in the last decade whereby women—either authors or their characters—talk back to Shakespeare in a variety of new ways.

"Talking back to Shakespeare", a term common in intertextual discourse, is not a new phenomenon, particularly in literature. For centuries, women writers—novelists, playwrights, and poets—have responded to Shakespeare with inventive and often transgressive retellings of his work. Thus far, feminist scholarship has examined creative responses to Shakespeare by women writers through the late twentieth century. This book brings together the "then" of Shakespeare with the "now" of contemporary literature by examining how many of his plays have cultural currency in the present day. Adoption and surrogate childrearing; gender fluidity; global pandemics; imprisonment and criminal justice; the intersection of misogyny and racism—these are all pressing social and political concerns, but they are also issues that are central to Shakespeare's plays and the early modern period.

By approaching material with a fresh interdisciplinary perspective, *Women Talk Back to Shakespeare* is an excellent tool for both scholars and students concerned with adaptation, women and gender, and intertextuality of Shakespeare's plays.

Jo Eldridge Carney is a Professor of English at The College of New Jersey where she teaches courses in early modern studies, folk and fairy tales, and contemporary literature.

NEW INTERDISCIPLINARY APPROACHES TO EARLY MODERN CULTURE : CONFLUENCES AND CONTEXTS

Series Editors:
Carole Levin, levin829@yahoo.com
Marguerite Tassi, tassim@unk.edu

This interdisciplinary series publishes manuscripts from a wide range of fields, including but not limited to literature, history, art history, musicology, philosophy, religion and political science, in order to cultivate a truly multifaceted understanding of the early modern period. This series offers innovative scholarship that models interdisciplinary methodologies to emerging scholars and students and publishes books that show how paradigm shifts in knowledge happen when disciplines cross-fertilize and share the fruits of their labor.

Kingship, Madness, and Masculinity on the Early Modern Stage
Mad World, Mad Kings
Edited by Christina Gutierrez-Dennehy

Women Talk Back to Shakespeare
Contemporary Adaptations and Appropriations
Jo Eldridge Carney

WOMEN TALK BACK TO SHAKESPEARE

Contemporary Adaptations and Appropriations

Jo Eldridge Carney

Routledge
Taylor & Francis Group

LONDON AND NEW YORK

First published 2022
by Routledge
2 Park Square, Milton Park, Abingdon, Oxon OX14 4RN

and by Routledge
605 Third Avenue, New York, NY 10158

Routledge is an imprint of the Taylor & Francis Group, an informa business

© 2022 Jo Eldridge Carney

DOI: 10.4324/9781003166580

British Library Cataloguing-in-Publication Data
A catalogue record for this book is available from the British Library

Library of Congress Cataloging-in-Publication Data
Names: Carney, Jo Eldridge, 1954- author.
Title: Women talk back to Shakespeare : contemporary adaptations and appropriations / Jo Eldridge Carney.
Description: Abingdon, Oxon ; New York : Routledge, 2022. |
Series: New interdisciplinary approaches to early modern culture: confluences and contexts | Includes bibliographical references and index.
Identifiers: LCCN 2021020109 (print) | LCCN 2021020110 (ebook) |
ISBN 9780367763527 (paperback) | ISBN 9780367763510 (hardback) |
ISBN 9781003166580 (ebook)
Subjects: LCSH: Shakespeare, William, 1564-1616--Adaptations--History and criticism. | English literature--Women authors--History and criticism. |
Feminism and literature--English-speaking countries. | Women and literature--English-speaking countries. | LCGFT: Literary criticism.
Classification: LCC PR2880.A1 C37 2022 (print) | LCC PR2880.A1 (ebook) |
DDC 822.3/3--dc23
LC record available at https://lccn.loc.gov/2021020109
LC ebook record available at https://lccn.loc.gov/2021020110

ISBN: 978-0-367-76351-0 (hbk)
ISBN: 978-0-367-76352-7 (pbk)
ISBN: 978-1-003-16658-0 (ebk)

DOI: 10.4324/9781003166580

Typeset in Bembo
by Taylor & Francis Books

For Ruby, who talks back in all the best ways

CONTENTS

ACKNOWLEDGEMENTS

An earlier version of Chapter 1 appeared in *Borrowers and Lenders: The Journal of Shakespeare and Appropriation* 9.1 (2014).

Librarians are essential to any academic project, but when much of a book is written during a pandemic the work they do is even more valuable. I am enormously grateful to Dean Taras Pavlovsky and the entire staff of The College of New Jersey Library, and especially Dina Carmy, Bethany Sewall, and David Murray for their efforts in ensuring we all had the resources we needed for our scholarship and our teaching in this challenging year. Thank you also to the accommodating and cheerful staff at the Hopewell branch of the Mercer County Library.

Thank you to the wonderful TCNJ students who were willing to "talk back" and help me work through many of these ideas in our seminars: Paige Barmakian, Nicole Beagin, Shannon Cassaro, Jaime Corrigan, Daniel Hitchen, Rachel Howanich, Britta Koep, Angela Lengner, Cassidy Mansmann, Ally McHugh, Lauren Muccilli, Erin Murray, Catie Nadler, Carlie Pressler, Sarah Reynolds, Amanda Riccitelli, Angelica Rocco, Princy Shah, Courtney Shein, Destiny Valerio, Kattlyn Vasquez, and Madeleine Zurcher. I hope you will recognize traces of our vigorous discussions and healthy disagreements in these pages.

Michelle Ordini's incredible management of the English Department makes it possible for all of us to do our work better and thanks can never be enough for all that she does. Thank you to Eleanor Mackay Carney, Silas Jones, and Carter Wells for their research assistance and support, to Mindi McMann for her expert and thoughtful advice on sections of the book, and to David Blake for his steady encouragement. Thank you to Dean Jane Wong and TCNJ for research support, and to Isabel Voice and Laura Pilsworth at Routledge for making this such a pleasant process.

My deepest debt is to Carole Levin, my dear friend of many decades, who has encouraged this book from the beginning and gave useful feedback throughout. Carole's reputation as a scholar who cares deeply about advancing the work of others is well-deserved, and I have been so fortunate to be on the receiving end of her extraordinarily generous mentorship and friendship. To both Carole and Marguerite Tassi, co-editors of this new series, New Interdisciplinary Approaches to Early Modern Culture: Confluences and Contexts, thank you for your support on this project and for initiating a series that will allow more innovative and interesting work to join the scholarly conversation.

INTRODUCTION

In the summer of 2016, Supreme Court Justice Ruth Bader Ginsburg delighted her fans—and many of Shakespeare's—by presiding over a mock trial in connection with a production of *The Merchant of Venice*. In Shakespeare's play, Portia disguises herself as a male scholar to decide Shylock's legal claim; over four hundred years later, Justice Ginsburg traveled to Venice where she played herself, as she and four other judges heard the arguments and then delivered a ruling dramatically opposed to what Shakespeare's Portia had determined. Portia is sent to law school, Antonio's loan is repaid, Shylock's property is restored, and the Jewish moneylender's sentence to convert to Christianity is overturned. Ginsburg added, with her characteristic wit, that "after four centuries of delay in seeking payment, we think that Shylock is out of time in asking for interest."

This event was all in good fun, and not the first time that Justice Ginsburg ruled over Shakespeare-inspired trials. But it was also a moment in which Ginsburg, the second woman to be appointed to the United States Supreme Court, offered a stern revision to a play often criticized for its anti-Semitism and injustice. Festive airs aside, Ginsburg was explicitly talking back to Shakespeare.

"Talking back to Shakespeare," a term common in intertextual discourse, is not a new phenomenon. For centuries, women writers—novelists, playwrights, and poets—have responded to Shakespeare with inventive and often transgressive retellings of his work. In the 1980s, a substantial body of feminist criticism emerged that scrutinized representations of gender in Shakespeare's plays as well as in the various adaptations and intertextual borrowings by women. Marianne Novy's *Women's Revisions of Shakespeare* (1990) explored how nineteenth-century authors including Charlotte Bronte, Emily Dickinson, and George Eliot incorporated and rewrote Shakespeare in their poetry and fiction; Novy's *Transforming Shakespeare: Contemporary Women's Revisions in Literature and Performance* (2000) and Julie Sanders' *Novel Shakespeares* (2001) turned to twentieth-century revisions by women writers such as Kate Atkinson, Angela Carter,

DOI: 10.4324/9781003166580-1

Rita Dove, Gloria Naylor, Jane Smiley, and Marina Warner. Along with Novy and Sanders, the work of scholars Christy Desmet, Peter Erickson, Daniel Fischlin, Andrew Hartley, Alexa Huang, Sujata Iyengar, Margaret Jane Kidnie, Gordon McMullan, Elizabeth Rivlin, Ayanna Thompson, and many others, demonstrates that the creative and scholarly work of women "talking back to Shakespeare" has continued to evolve along productive parallel lines.

Thus far, feminist scholarship has examined creative responses to Shakespeare by women writers through the late twentieth century. This study explores more recent adaptations published in the last decade or so in which women—either authors or their characters—talk back to Shakespeare in a variety of new ways. "Talking back" typically implies a rebuke to an authoritative position, but it can also be a less accusatory impulse to continue a conversation. The works considered here are not all unmitigated critiques of Shakespeare's plays but they do insist on a re-examination of their aesthetic and ideological terms, and they invite a dialogue in which women and Shakespeare can talk back—and forth—with each other.

Since the beginning of the twenty-first century, innovative works by female actors, directors, and writers have continued to challenge conventional Shakespearean notions of gender and genre. Theatrical productions with all-female casts have flourished, most notably the London Donmar Warehouse "Shakespeare Trilogy" (2012–2015)—*Henry IV, Julius Caesar,* and *The Tempest*—with Phyllida Lloyd as director and Harriet Walter in the lead roles. Glenda Jackson's self-described "postgender" portrayal of King Lear in London (2016) and New York (2019) elicited widespread enthusiasm. In other cross-gender performances, Helen Mirren was cast as Prospera in director Julie Taymor's film *The Tempest* (2010). In literature, poet Jen Bervin recreated several of Shakespeare's sonnets with *Nets* (2004), her collection of erasure poems. And Jillian Keenan's *Sex With Shakespeare* (2016), while not the first memoir celebrating Shakespeare's emotional and physical impact, is arguably the most transgressive.

Women Talk Back to Shakespeare focuses specifically on transpositions of Shakespeare's plays into a variety of genres under the umbrella of fiction. Six of the works are by women writers: a historical novel, a libretto, a post-apocalyptic novel, a post-colonial novel, and two adaptations commissioned by the Hogarth Shakespeare Project. The seventh, a time-travel genre-bending novel by a male author that prioritizes the female voice, is arguably the most explicitly feminist of these works. These prose narratives share a creative engagement with Shakespeare, but there is nothing homogenous about the forms they adopt or about the subjects they embrace. Individually and collectively, this newest generation of adaptations expands our notions about how women can continue their dialogue with Shakespeare across the centuries.

The scholarly discourse on adaptation, appropriation, and intertextuality is rich, extensive, and often productively contested. Julie Sanders' distinction between adaptation and appropriation offers a useful departure point: whereas adaptation "signals a relationship with an informing source text or original" that is clearly recognizable, appropriation "frequently affects a more decisive journey away from the informing source into a wholly new cultural product and domain" (*Adaptation* 26). The works discussed in this book occupy various positions on the spectrum from explicit adaptations to more experimental appropriations, but since they all have a clear intertextual relationship with their Shakespearean sources, the term adaptation is broadly applied—along with retellings, revisions, and rewritings—to describe the works produced in the adaptational process. Adaptation theory has emerged as a robust field of critical inquiry in its own right, though still peripheral to more established forms of literary criticism. Popular culture lags even further in absorbing some of the most fundamental tenets of current adaptation discourse even as actual literary retellings across media appear at a prodigious rate. While adaptation theory has predominantly involved the transposition from literary texts to film, other modal relationships—as in this case, from drama to fiction—are increasingly being explored.

Women Talk Back is grounded in four major principles of current adaptation theory. The first—the most obvious but critical—is a repudiation of fidelity criticism, which judges adaptations worthy according to how faithfully they replicate their sources. The second argues that adaptations can freely and productively transpose their sources from one genre to another. The third recognizes that adaptations often involve ideological critiques of their source text, as suggested, in part, by the framework of "women talking back." Finally, adaptations are not unidirectional but can instead invite a return to and a re-evaluation of the source text. This book encourages a space in which women writers and readers in the twenty-first century talk back to Shakespeare and then he and his readers talk back to and with them in turn.

First, adaptation studies today have moved far beyond former critical orthodoxies of fidelity criticism, which measured a new work according to its proximity to the "original" and the faithfulness of its reproduction. Fidelity criticism assumed that the source text was the superior entity that the adaptation needed to live up to; now, while still acknowledging a debt and a connection to the previous works, adaptations are seen as creative productions in their own right whose worth are not dependent on their degree of replication. As Linda Hutcheon points out, "an adaptation is a derivation that is not derivative—a work that is second without being secondary" (9). And yet, anecdotal reactions and book, film, and theatre reviews are often rife with indignation when a source work is not faithfully reproduced. Thomas Leitch reminds us that "Fidelity, widely execrated within the field as a criterion for the success or failure of an adaptation, is just as widely adopted as a criterion outside the field" (8). Fidelity criticism seems to emerge with even more vitriol in the case of Shakespeare and his defenders who view any retellings of his work as unnecessary violations of sacred texts. The well-known fact that Shakespeare, that upstart crow, was himself a notorious plunderer of prior works and an adaptive genius matters not to fidelity purists. This study, however, reminds readers that "It is at the point of infidelity or departure that the most creative acts of adaptation take place" (*Adaptation* 24).

The second principle involves the transposition between genres—for most of the works in this study, from plays to novels. In spite of the fact that Shakespeare's works have resurfaced as comic books, graphic novels, musicals, operas, podcasts, television shows, and video games, there is still stubborn resistance against his plays reappearing in other genres, as evidenced by the lively response to the Hogarth Shakespeare Project. In 2014, as international fervor geared up surrounding the 450th anniversary of Shakespeare's birth and the 400th anniversary of his death, the Hogarth Press launched its plan to have Shakespeare's works retold by acclaimed and bestselling novelists of today. Hogarth's initial announcement was met with both eager anticipation and dismay. To date, seven novels have been published and the series appears to be concluding; these works have been subject to a wide range of criticism and praise, but for many, it is the entire enterprise that is suspect. The title of Adam Gopnick's *New Yorker* essay, for example—"Why Rewrite Shakespeare?"—signals the bias that follows:

> We apply our dutifully expansive moral imagination to the plays, and, while this makes them seem fuller to us, it brings us no closer to Shakespeare … a dramatic poet rather than a psychological novelist or a self-conscious critic of texts, and his imagination runs in broader, potent strokes that are not so much illuminated as belied by the inward-turning ironies of the modern psychological novel.
>
> *(87)*

Gopnick argues that the novel's emphasis on interiority detracts from Shakespeare's genius manipulation of bold characters and swift plot, while others object to the replacement of Shakespeare's rich metaphorical language with a modern idiom. Indeed, the creative possibilities allowed by a play and a novel are different, but this study accepts that with any change of modality the losses can be compensated by the gains—which is part of the delight we take in adaptations.

The third adaptive strategy of the works explored here is their challenge to Shakespearean aesthetic, ideological, or social norms. Adaptations are not inherently progressive: when they are simply works of homage or replication, they do little to resist the source narratives, but the adaptations considered here all question the plays' purported values and hierarchies to varying degrees. In most cases, that challenge is at least partially informed by a feminist approach. These revisions seek to reclaim space from a male-centered text for more visible and substantial roles for female characters, as articulated by Gérard Genette: "The revaluation of a character consists in investing him or her—by way of pragmatic or psychological transformation—with a more significant and/or more 'attractive' role in the value system of the hypertext than was the case in the hypotext" (158). Other revisionist strategies from a feminist perspective involve exposure of patriarchal prejudices, explicit condemnation of misogynistic behaviors, compensatory reallocation of positions of power, and a decided shift to female-centered narratives.

At the same time, this new generation of adaptations also interrogates a range of cultural beliefs and practices beyond the gender politics that the plays embody, even as they recognize the gap between early modern and contemporary contexts. Alongside gender inequality, these adaptations engage with issues of climate change, colonialism, ecological predation, economic inequality, global pandemics, mass incarceration, and racism—subjects that emerge from both the current moment and the plays that have engaged them. However, the serious ideological challenges that these works pose to Shakespeare should not negate the spirit of play that many of them possess: the author's pleasure in inventing the clever connective threads between the source text and the adaptation, as well as the reader's satisfaction in deciphering and recognizing them. As Sanders puts it: "the political aspect of 're-visionary' writing should never occlude the simultaneously pleasurable aspects of reading into such texts their intertextual and allusive relationship with other texts, tracing and activating networks of association ..." (*Adaptation* 10).

Finally, this study intends that these adaptations invite a mutual conversation with the Shakespeare plays they are re-envisioning. In his account of dialogizing adaptation studies, Jørgen Bruhn insists that

> Adaptation (be it from novel to film or between other media) ought to be regarded as a two-way process instead of a form of one-way transport ... we should study both the source and result of the adaptation as two texts, infinitely changing positions, taking turns being sources for each other in the ongoing work of the reception in the adaptational process.
>
> *(69)*

Borrowing an example of this dialogic process from an earlier but well-known Shakespearean adaptation, anyone who has read or seen Tom Stoppard's play, *Rosencrantz and Guildenstern are Dead*, and then revisited *Hamlet* would presumably find the absurdity and portent of the two lackeys—whom they may have previously dismissed—now difficult to ignore. These adaptations should initiate similar re-evaluations of the Shakespeare plays they draw on, even though those readings are not predetermined.

The first chapter examines Toni Morrison's *Desdemona* (2011), which explores the afterlife of the characters in *Othello*. Described as a combined concert and theatrical experience, *Desdemona* is a collaboration among writer Toni Morrison, theatre director Peter Sellars, and musician Rokia Traoré. Morrison's text, a series of monologues and dialogues spoken by an actress who plays Desdemona and channels various other characters, alternates with songs written and performed by Traoré, a renowned Malian singer and composer; the result, a hybrid narrative of words and music, disrupts the generic boundaries between the page and the stage. At the same time, Morrison's text fulfills her claim that Desdemona deserves a more complex and substantial portrayal than Shakespeare provided; *Desdemona* is a frank exploration of how the constraints on female behavior, community, and speech, along with what we refer to today as toxic masculinity and entrenched racism, lead to the tragic outcomes of *Othello*.

Elizabeth Nunez's *Prospero's Daughter* (2006) is the subject of the second chapter, a novel that interrogates the intersection of racism, class, and gender inequalities in *The Tempest*. While the novel follows the contours of Shakespeare's play closely, Nunez transposes her authoritarian protagonist Prospero and his subjects to Trinidad, where she grew up, just before it gained independence from British colonial control in 1962. This setting allows her to situate her narrative within the tradition of critical and performative interpretations that view the play through a post-colonial lens. Nunez's Prospero counterpart is no kindly patriarch or impressive magician but a stand-in for the cruel and exploitative British Empire: he wields his authority over his daughter, the islanders, and the landscape with an ironclad belief that he is spreading the gospel of British superiority. While Nunez depicts his acts with the unflinching criticism they deserve, she also imagines the people he has subjugated as allies who unite to challenge the environmental exploitation, misogyny, and racism he promotes, pointing to a more optimistic future than the one Shakespeare's play offers.

The focus of the third chapter is Margaret Atwood's *Hag-Seed* (2016), another take on *The Tempest*. While *Prospero's Daughter* responds to *The Tempest*'s foreshadowing of post-colonial politics, *Hag-Seed* turns to the play's meta-theatrical elements and spectacle. That Atwood would choose to revisit *The Tempest* with its elements of the magical and the illusory arts is in keeping with her more recent preoccupation with speculative fiction and futurism. *Hag-Seed* focuses on a theatre director named Felix who has been usurped from his role as artistic director of a Canadian theatre festival; he finds his opportunity for retaliation when he is hired to teach theatre to a group of prisoners and decides to lead them in a performance of an interactive version of *The Tempest*. This chapter explores how Atwood exposes the play's tensions between realism and the supernatural and between forgiveness and revenge. Finally, Atwood talks back to Shakespeare's iconic hold in the canon as she explores the moral and ethical imperatives of Shakespearean appropriations.

The fourth chapter turns to *The Gap of Time* (2015), Jeanette Winterson's retelling of *The Winter's Tale*. Winterson's was the first novel to be published in the Hogarth series and by her own account she was thrilled with the opportunity to revisit *The Winter's Tale*, which she refers to as her life-long talismanic text. The novel is set in London in the midst of the 2008 financial crisis; Winterson contemporizes the setting, characters, and plot of *The Winter's Tale* but maintains explicit parallels between the two worlds. As in her previous fiction, Winterson emphasizes the fraught and complicated human relationships of adulthood, the conflict between homosocial and heterosexual identities, the perils of social inequity, and most of all, the centrality of the "lost child" figure. In addition to asking us to reconsider the outcomes of *The Winter's Tale*, *The Gap of Time* challenges social and fictional adoption narratives in her more generous articulation of how family is constructed.

The fifth chapter examines Mark Haddon's *The Porpoise*, a rich retelling of *Pericles* that crosses back and forth among ancient, early modern, and contemporary periods. Shakespeare's play begins with the story of a princess sexually abused by her father; she is given no name and no voice and she is blamed for her complicity. In *Pericles*, this incest episode is the catalyst for the rest of the play but is otherwise ignored. Haddon claims that what intrigued him about the play was this marginalization and suppression of the female voice. *The Porpoise* exposes the intersection among social entitlement, male dominance, and female disempowerment—and then imagines ways to turn that world upside down by allowing the female characters control over their own narratives and the opportunity to seek revenge for the injustices they have suffered.

Given the global coronavirus pandemic, which began in 2019, *Station Eleven* (2014), the subject of the sixth chapter, is a timely and eerily relevant novel. While Mandel's other works are situated in the genre of contemporary crime fiction, this novel's affinity is with the flourishing post-apocalyptic genre—and with Shakespeare's *King Lear*. *Station Eleven* picks up where *Lear* ends, in a world of epic devastation. The novel begins with an actor playing Lear suddenly collapsing on stage, the first of many deaths as a global virus swiftly destroys most of the world's population within weeks. In the decades that follow, a precarious civilization is gradually rebuilt. *Station Eleven* does not overtly adapt *King Lear* but it centers on a group of survivors who travel the country performing Shakespeare's plays wherever they find other small communities. The novel is grounded in Shakespearean references and allusions, but more importantly, it explores the same metaphysical questions that *King Lear* asks regarding restoration and redemption in the aftermath of grand tragedy.

The final adaptation is Maggie O'Farrell's novel *Hamnet* (2020), a historical novel about the death of Shakespeare's eleven-year-old son Hamnet in 1596. Although *Hamnet* imagines a possible connection between the young boy's death and his father's play *Hamlet*, the focus is on the life of Shakespeare's family rather than the play itself—or its author. O'Farrell describes this as "the book she has wanted to write for thirty years" to reclaim more attention for Hamnet Shakespeare; in the process of writing the novel, she was also compelled to offer a revisionist portrayal of Anne Hathaway. A novel that adapts an actual chapter from history may seem to be an outlier in the company of direct literary adaptations, but historical records are also based on a legacy of texts and a particular interpretative lens. *Hamnet* talks back to Shakespeare by reaching through centuries of bardolatry and its concomitant appropriation of Anne Hathaway in a reconstruction of Shakespeare that is at once iconoclastic and humanizing.

Each chapter of this book is similarly constructed; the first half offers a reading of the Shakespeare source, focusing on the issues that are most critical in the adaptation, and the second half discusses the adaptation, with a backwards look at the source material. All of the discussions are grounded in the larger scholarly conversation about each pair of works; my intention is to provide a broad overview of the most relevant foundational and current scholarship that will, in turn, provoke further discussion and research. Unless otherwise noted, all citations from Shakespeare's plays are from Stephen Greenblatt's Norton 3rd edition.

While contemporary adaptations continue to question the problematic gender politics, racism, and social hierarchies of Shakespeare's plays, this new generation of works demonstrates an even more expansive notion about how authors and their characters can and must talk back to Shakespeare to engage with today's most pressing issues inside and outside literary boundaries. The privileged status that the Shakespearean canon has occupied does not protect it from authors who return to it again and again for creative inspiration and interrogation. A recurrent theme in all of the adaptations considered here is that it is no longer ethical to deify

Shakespeare or protect his works as sacrosanct. At the same time, the constant metamorphosis of Shakespeare's plays is seen as reciprocally energizing, for these works ensure an ongoing dialogue in the twenty-first century between Shakespeare and the women who talk back.

Further reading

Desmet, Christy, Andrew Hartley, and Georgianna Ziegler. "Appropriations." In *Shakespeare In Our Time*, eds. Dympna Callaghan and Suzanne Gossett. London: Bloomsbury Arden, 2016: 229–243.

Desmet, Christy and Robert Sawyer, eds. *Shakespeare and Appropriation*. London: Routledge, 1999.

Donadio, Rachel. "Ginsburg Weighs Fate of Shylock." *New York Times*. 7–28–2016.

Fischlin, Daniel. *Outerspeares: Shakespeare, Intermedia, and the Limits of Adaptation*. Toronto: U of Toronto Press, 2014.

Hartley, Andrew James. *Shakespeare and Millennial Fiction*. Cambridge: Cambridge UP, 2017.

Huang, Alexa and Elizabeth Rivlin, eds. *Shakespeare and the Ethics of Appropriation*. New York: Palgrave Macmillan, 2014.

Kidnie, Margaret Jane. *Shakespeare and the Problem of Adaptation*. New York: Routledge, 2009.

Leitch, Thomas. "Twelve Fallacies in Contemporary Adaptation Theory." *Criticism* 45. 2: 149–171.

McMullan, Gordan, Lena Cowen Orlin, and Virginia Mason Vaughan, eds. *Women Making Shakespeare: Text, Reception, and Performance*. London: Bloomsbury, 2014.

References

Bruhn, Jørgen. "Dialogizing Adaptation Studies." In *Adaptation Studies: New Challenges, New Directions*, eds. Jørgen Bruhn, Anne Gjelsvik, and Eirik Frisvold Hanssen. London: Bloomsbury Academic, 2013: 69–88.

Genette, Gérard. *Palimpsests: Literature in the Second Degree*, trans. Channa Newman and Claude Doubinsky. Lincoln: U of Nebraska Press, 1982.

Gopnick, Adam. "Why Rewrite Shakespeare?" *The New Yorker*. October 10, 2016: 86–88.

Greenblatt, Stephen, ed. *The Norton Shakespeare*, 3rd ed. New York: W. W. Norton and Company, 2015.

Hutcheon, Linda. *The Theory of Adaptation*, 2nd ed. New York: Routledge, 2012.

Leitch, Thomas, ed. *The Oxford Book of Adaptation Studies*. Oxford: Oxford UP, 2017.

Novy, Marianne. *Women's Revisions of Shakespeare*. Champaign: U of Illinois Press, 1990.

Novy, Marianne. *Transforming Shakespeare: Contemporary Women's Re-Visions in Literature and Performance*. New York: Palgrave Macmillan, 2000.

Sanders, Julie. *Novel Shakespeares*. Manchester: Manchester U Press, 2001.

Sanders, Julie. *Adaptation and Appropriation*, 2nd ed. New York: Routledge, 2016.

1

TONI MORRISON AND ROKIA TRAORÉ'S *DESDEMONA* AND WILLIAM SHAKESPEARE'S *OTHELLO*

On May 15, 2011 an innovative performance piece, *Desdemona*, premiered at the Akzent Theatre in Vienna, Austria. Billed as a combined concert and theatrical experience, *Desdemona* was created by three internationally known artists: writer Toni Morrison, theatre director Peter Sellars, and musician Rokia Traoré. Morrison's libretto, a series of monologues and dialogues spoken by an actress who played Desdemona and channeled various other characters from *Othello*, alternated with songs written and performed by Traoré, a renowned Malian singer and composer. After its initial staging, *Desdemona* was performed throughout Europe before traveling to New York and Berkeley, and finally London, where it was featured in the World Shakespeare Festival, part of the Cultural Olympiad of 2012.

In numerous interviews, Morrison, Sellars, and Traoré have described the conception of *Desdemona*. In short, Sellars once explained to Morrison that he found Shakespeare's *Othello* a thin play with stereotypical principal characters. Morrison convinced Sellars that there was more depth to Desdemona than productions had typically extrapolated, but she conceded that even Shakespeare had not allowed Desdemona to tell her full story. Sellars challenged Morrison to write that missing story and, after enlisting Traoré's participation in the project, an intermedial and transnational collaboration was born. Theatrical performances are ephemeral—there are some reviews and brief YouTube clips of *Desdemona* but no full-length video or audio recordings, without which we cannot provide a full analysis of the musical components or performance choices integral to the production. However, the text was published in 2012, allowing us to read *Desdemona* in conjunction with *Othello*.

Othello is one of Shakespeare's most frequently adapted works, as composers, filmmakers, novelists, poets, and other playwrights have been drawn to the play's doomed love story and its exposure of entrenched racial fault lines. Among the most significant cinematic adaptations in recent decades are Oliver Stone's 1995 film with Lawrence Fishburne as Othello, notable as the first major Hollywood film that cast an actor of

DOI: 10.4324/9781003166580-2

color in the lead role after centuries of portrayals in blackface; and, in 2006, Indian director Vishal Bhardwaj reframed *Othello* as a contemporary crime drama in the highly acclaimed film *Omkara*. In literature, Caribbean poet Derek Walcott's poem, first published in 1965, "Goats and Monkeys," and Sudanese novelist Talib Salih's 1966 novel, *Season of Migration to the North*, expose the heteronormative and racial oppression in *Othello*. Djanet Sears' 1997 play, *Harlem Duet*, is a time-traveling prequel that imagines an Othello who betrays his black wife for a white woman and examines the damaging consequences of internalized racism. In recent years, *Becoming Othello: A Black Girl's Journey*, a play that weaves autobiography with Shakespeare and features author Debra Ann Byrd in the role of Othello, radically subverts gender conventions. Another timely interface with *Othello* is the one-man play by Keith Hamilton Cobb, *American Moor*, about a black man's audition for the role of Othello before an egotistical, narrow-minded white director, an occasion that engenders a piercing exploration of racial prejudices in America.

Desdemona adds a unique contribution to the growing body of works engaging with *Othello* in its emphasis on the intersection of race with gender, religion, and social class; as a hybrid narrative of words and music, it pushes against aesthetic boundaries as well. Morrison's *Desdemona* is something so "wholly new" that its creators were not even sure what to name it, as Sellars explained in an interview, "A concert? A theatrical experience? We'll split the difference" (UC Berkeley Events). *Desdemona* is also an unusual addition to the body of *Othello* revisions because it is both prequel and sequel to Shakespeare's tragedy; it expands the temporal parameters of the play by imagining Desdemona's girlhood as well as her story from the other side of the grave, the "undiscovered country" Hamlet famously evokes. Morrison's reconstruction of Desdemona's world is a rich, lyrical narrative in itself, but it also explicitly engages with Shakespeare's articulation of Desdemona and with a subsequent tradition of critical and performative dismissals of her and the other even more marginalized female characters. As Sellars writes in the foreword to *Desdemona*, Toni Morrison's entire fictional oeuvre "honors the missing histories of generations whose courage, struggles, achievements, loves, tragedies, fulfillments and disappointments have gone unrecorded" (7). In this work, it is the lacunae in the histories of Desdemona, the other women in the play, both black and white, and Othello himself that Morrison is filling. In the liberating world of the afterlife she creates a space for them to talk with each other and, thus, to talk back to Shakespeare.

Othello and *Desdemona*: Synopses

For the purposes of adaptive comparison, it is necessary to provide brief synopses of Shakespeare's *Othello*, probably written in 1602–1603 and first performed in 1604, and the text of Toni Morrison's *Desdemona*, published in 2012.

Othello, one of Shakespeare's most well-known plays then and now, centers on the precipitous downfall of Othello, a great warrior and a Moor who is summoned to Venice to assist in its foreign affairs. Brabanzio, a revered senator, is impressed with Othello's military reputation and invites him to his home where he meets and falls in love with Desdemona, Brabanzio's daughter. Equally enamored, Desdemona elopes with Othello and her father is outraged to learn she got married without his permission, especially to a black man. Brabanzio's fury is fueled by Iago, one of Othello's officers, who is intent on destroying Othello. The cause of Iago's extreme hatred of Othello is one of the vexing questions of the play, though it seems in part due to jealousy that Othello gave another officer, Cassio, the job promotion that Iago thought he deserved.

The Senate overrules Brabanzio's complaint against Othello because they need him to fend off an impending Ottoman invasion. When a storm at sea prevents the Turkish attack, Othello, Desdemona, and the other Venetians are reunited in Cyprus, where Iago masterminds a plot to convince Othello that Desdemona is having an affair with Cassio. Othello demands tangible "ocular" proof and through a series of lucky coincidences; the unwitting cooperation of Roderigo, who is infatuated with Desdemona; and the reluctant help of his wife Emilia, Desdemona's lady-in-waiting, Iago manages to persuade Othello of Desdemona's guilt. At Iago's urging, Othello smothers Desdemona in her bed; its duration and its enactment directly on stage make it one of the most agonizing episodes of violence performed in a Shakespearean tragedy. Emilia discovers the murderous act just as Desdemona is dying; she alerts everyone that Othello has killed his wife, and when she realizes Iago's wrongdoing and exposes him as well, Iago stabs her and she dies next to Desdemona. Othello, then understanding his error, kills himself and also lies by Desdemona, first asking that the story of his life be honestly told. Iago is led off to his punishment but refuses to speak another word. The play ends, in the lament of one of the Venetian noblemen, with "the tragic loading of this bed."

Desdemona is a slim work, just fifty-seven pages of text by Morrison and song lyrics by Traoré. Desdemona's monologues and her dialogues with other characters are interspersed with songs by Sa'ran, the African woman referred to as Barbary in *Othello*. The work is divided into sections or scenes representing Desdemona's various soliloquies or conversations and the songs, and it takes place entirely in the afterlife. Morrison's text alludes to all of the major plot events of *Othello*, and in spite of its brevity, it also amplifies Shakespeare's narrative. In addition to Desdemona's account of her girlhood and her fractious relationship with her parents, she has conversations with Emilia, her serving woman and confidante, and with Sa'ran, whose counterpart is described as her mother's maid in *Othello*, although here she is Desdemona's nurse. There is also a brief interlude in which new characters are added to the narrative: the mothers of Desdemona and Othello meet and express their mutual grief over their children's fate. Finally, Desdemona speaks with Othello, and he too supplies a backstory of his boyhood, his experiences as a child soldier, and the war crimes he committed with his comrade, Iago. The play ends, if not in complete reconciliation, in an acknowledgement of mistakes and an increased understanding among the various characters.

Othello: Speak of me as I am

Shakespeare, himself an enthusiastic adapter, draws directly on at least two popular sources for *Othello*, neither of which originated in England. The skeleton of the plot comes from a tale in Italian author Giraldi Cinthio's popular collection, *The Hecatommithi*. Shakespeare focuses much more on the subject of race than Cinthio, and for that he likely drew on John Pory's 1600 translation of *A Geographical History of Africa* by Hasan ibn Muhammad al-Wezzan, known in England as Leo Africanus. A Muslim who was born in Granada and lived in Morocco, he was captured in 1518 by pirates in the Mediterranean and given as a "gift" to Pope Leo X in Rome where he was converted, perhaps forcibly, to Christianity and baptized with his captor's name. Most scholars agree that Shakespeare borrows some of the racial stereotypes that appear in *Othello* from Pory's inaccurate and sensationalized translation of the Africanus narrative and that Othello himself may have partially been inspired by al-Wezzan, though the differences between the two are as significant as the correspondences (Andrea 10–14 and Zhiri 176–180). Shakespeare's representation of race also reflects influences he absorbed by literary osmosis: many dramatic works that precede *Othello* include portrayals of racial stereotyping and, as Kim Hall points out, "Moors who frequented the Elizabethan stage and popular entertainment were overwhelmingly, stereotypically evil and male" (182). Another contemporary example that likely informed Shakespeare's representation of "Othello the Moor" was the diplomatic visit to London in 1600–1601—just a year or so before Shakespeare wrote *Othello*—of the Moroccan Ambassador Abd el-Ouahed and his entourage. Over the course of their six-month stay, Londoners responded to their guests with a combination of curiosity, suspicion, and xenophobia, and Shakespeare would surely have been aware of the presence of African visitors of such high degree and of the gossip surrounding them (Harris 32–35).

Although scholarship on *Othello* is extensive, only in recent decades have critics foregrounded the subject of racism so fundamental to the play, which previous considerations worked hard to erase. Long overdue discussions of race in all of Shakespeare's plays, but especially *Antony and Cleopatra*, *The Merchant of Venice*, *The Tempest*, and *Titus Andronicus*, along with *Othello*, have invigorated Shakespeare studies, for as Ayanna Thompson insists, "If you ask today in the 2020s if the concept of race existed for Shakespeare and his contemporaries, the answer is an emphatic yes … racialized epistemologies existed and were deployed" (*Cambridge Companion* 2). Against continued claims that "race did not exist in Shakespeare's cultural and creative imagination," (*Cambridge Companion* 1) many early modern scholars are currently turning to Geraldine Heng's monumental study, *The Invention of Race in the European Middle Ages* (2018). Heng argues that from the eleventh century through the Renaissance to the Enlightenment, "race has no singular or stable referent," and its manifestations were inconsistent and malleable, but they were always intended to mark the real and perceived differences between people: race was "a structural relationship for the articulation and management of human differences, rather than a substantive content" (19). *Othello*, a play in which the eponymous tragic hero is described more often as "the

Moor" rather than by his name and is repeatedly marked as "other" within Venetian society, is central to these discussions.

Othello begins with the daring elopement of a celebrity couple, the beautiful aristocratic white woman, Desdemona, and the admired, noble military leader, Othello the "Moor." But any suggestion that this will be a progressive love story is quickly overshadowed by Iago's vitriol and intended revenge. Iago, Othello's ensign, offers conflicting reasons to his underling Roderigo why he "hates the Moor," but he is clear about his goal to destroy him. In the streets outside of Brabanzio's house, Iago and Roderigo shout to him that his daughter has married Othello, reveling in a tirade of racialized slurs that sets the tone for the manifestations of racism that pervade the entire play. Never using Othello's actual name, they instead refer to him as "the Moor" and "the thick lips," and then describe the couple's marriage in terms of bestial coupling. They urge Brabanzio to imagine pornographically that an "an old black ram/ Is tupping your white ewe," that "your daughter and the Moor are now making the beast with two backs," and that Desdemona is "cover'd with a Barbary horse" and will reproduce animals. Brabanzio is enraged, not at Iago for his racist fear-mongering, but at Desdemona; her transgression in choosing her own husband is second only to her choice of a black man who will "degrade his lineage," as Joyce MacDonald puts it. Brabanzio agrees with the racist characterization of Othello so completely that he laments that her marriage to the reprehensible—but white—Roderigo would have been preferable: "Shared notions of racial standing and identity unite men more intimately than they can be separated by social gradation" (Macdonald 210). This racism displayed at the outset by Brabanzio, Iago, and Roderigo becomes the center of the play's tragedy, and it cannot be considered apart from Othello's marriage to Desdemona, his professional identity, and their social positions.

A play that describes the demise of an upper-class white woman nonetheless subject to patriarchal control, and a black man who is valued for his professional expertise but is still a suspicious outsider, immediately suggests the intersectional obstacles that their entwined narrative posits. Desdemona and Othello are both constrained by a dominant white male elite and share overlapping restrictions, yet the oppressive forces that threaten them individually are not identical and, indeed, are deployed to divide them. In other words, Othello is led to join in the endemic misogyny that undermines Desdemona, and Desdemona begins to reflect some of the racist views of Othello that her society promotes. Moreover, Othello himself comes to internalize the racist charges preying on him just as Desdemona engages in essentializing rhetoric against women.

Desdemona has been viewed as either a devoted, acquiescent wife or a bold, courageous woman who flouts conventional norms; interestingly, both sides have claimed as evidence Desdemona's unconditional love for Othello. In her survey of *Othello*'s theatrical history, Virginia Vaughan demonstrates that "before the arrival of feminist criticism, English-language critics had little to say about Desdemona," a minimization also found in stage productions (48). This neglect was due to "an aesthetic definition of tragedy [that] excluded most of her scenes as trivial" and an idealization of Desdemona that the text did not consistently support (66). Edward Pechter also describes Desdemona's legacy of theatrical misrepresentation:

> Whether celebrating or deploring it, the critical tradition has been remarkably consistent for two centuries in describing Desdemona as silent, submissive, and in a sense even complicit in her own murder. It is therefore worth noticing on what an unsubstantial foundation this massive interpretive edifice has been constructed.
>
> *(124)*

In recent decades, feminist scholarship and theatrical performances have largely sought to counter Desdemona's diminishment, even if she does not emerge as one of Shakespeare's most dynamic heroines.

The first we hear of Desdemona, however, certainly is daring: she defies her father, marries a black man, and insists on accompanying him to war. Furthermore, she fully participates in—and perhaps even initiates—their wooing. Othello explains that when Brabanzio invited him to share his adventurous travels and military exploits, Desdemona would "with a greedy ear/ Devour up my discourse." Observing her interest in his tales, Othello continued to narrate his "pilgrimage" and Desdemona was attracted to the romantic strangeness:

> My story being done,
> She gave me for my pains a world of sighs ...
> She wished she had not heard it, yet she wished
> That heaven had made her such a man. She thanked me,
> And bade me, if I had a friend that loved her,
> I should but teach him how to tell my story.
>
> *(1.3. 159–168)*

Othello's explanation that he won Desdemona by story-telling is delivered in front of the entire Senate to defend himself against Brabanzio's charges; thus, they become engaged listeners as well, and given the Duke's response—"I think this tale would win my daughter too"—they were as moved by Othello's tales as Desdemona and Brabanzio were.

What were these narrative marvels that Othello performed so effectively? He tells of being sold into slavery and later redeemed, of "disastrous chances/ Of moving accidents by flood and field/ Of hairbreadth scapes," of adventures through rough and surreal locales, "and of the Cannibals that each other eat/ The Anthropopaghi, and men whose heads/ Do grow beneath their shoulders" (1.3. 137–147). As Emily Bartels argues, he recounts these exotic stories at this point "as if to be a Moor were an asset and not (as Iago and friends would have it) a liability." The stories are obviously preposterous, "a generic catalogue of clichéd wonders that pop up in descriptions of a number of non-European worlds," from Pory's fictional introduction to Africanus' narrative, as well as other contemporary travel narratives (148–151). Lynn Enterline

also points out that Othello "eloquently defends himself in public by imitating a culturally significant classical precedent: Virgil's Aeneas" whose adventures almost any
early modern schoolboy's education would have found familiar (156). But these fantastic tales are precisely what a Moor would be expected to tell to please the crowd but
still demarcate his difference; expectations for a racialized "other" to entertain a white
audience have unfortunately had a long tradition. However, the self-deprecating and
disingenuous protestation "Rude am I in my speech" that Othello prefaces his
impressive performance with is rhetorically brilliant and demonstrates his control of
the situation, for he is fully aware that his role as raconteur as well as warrior is
necessary for his self-preservation.

In this courtship driven by story-telling, it is clear that Desdemona has fallen in
love with Othello's carefully constructed narratives, which may comprise some
elements of truth—his enslavement, his military exploits—but also include outlandish fabrications. Given the constraints of her conventional life, it is under-
standable that she would find these stories appealing; perhaps the worst to be said
of Desdemona at this point is that she is guilty of misreading, of confusing the tales
with the teller. Some critics have argued that her auditory role is a sign of passive
reception, but others have ascribed agency to Desdemona's listening. Heather
James, for example, claims that Desdemona's response to Othello's tales "reveals
how her emotions, through sympathetic audition, have become as strange and
wondrous as Othello's tale of heroic suffering ... Attentive, serious, lovesick,
greedy, [she] is ready to leap from representation to action" (376).

Desdemona's opportunity to take that action comes when she is summoned to
the Senate to answer her father's complaint that she was bewitched into marriage.
Seemingly unintimidated by the call to speak in an all-male public arena, she
acknowledges her love of her father but then commits to her new role as Othello's
wife: "But here's my husband/ And so much duty as my mother showed/ To you,
preferring you before her father,/ So much I challenge that I may profess/ Due to
the Moor my lord" (1.3. 184–188). She further insists on accompanying Othello to
his outpost in Cyprus. Later, when Iago, Emilia, and Desdemona wait on the island
for Othello's ship to arrive, Desdemona holds her own in a bantering conversation
with Iago about female stereotypical behavior.

Iago soon puts his revenge plan in motion: he contrives a drunken incident that
leads to Cassio losing his position as lieutenant and he persuades Emilia to steal a
handkerchief from Desdemona, a prized gift from Othello, to plant with Cassio as
proof of their adultery. The third prong of his master plot is Desdemona's agreement
to plead to Othello on Cassio's behalf, thinking that she is helping both men overcome their misunderstanding. But the multitasking Iago has meanwhile sown the
seeds of jealousy in Othello, and Desdemona's defense of Cassio infuriates Othello.
Desdemona's mistake at this juncture is another misreading: she misinterprets Othello's
annoyance with her interference as work-related stress, but she remains confident that
she is right to speak her mind. It is only when Othello begins to display signs of anger
that the spirited Desdemona becomes more docile and resigned. By the time Othello
confronts her about the missing handkerchief, a prized gift to her, she becomes

duplicitous herself, afraid to admit to the truth of its loss. But Othello's credibility is also now suspect, as he spins a tale for her of his gift's meaning:

> That handkerchief
> Did an Egyptian to my mother give.
> She was a charmer, and could almost read
> The thoughts of people. She told her, while she kept it
> 'Twould make her amiable and subdue my father
> Entirely to her love, but if she lost it
> Or made a gift of it, my father's eye
> Should hold her loathèd, and his spirits should hunt
> After new fancies.
>
> *(3.4. 51–59)*

To the enchanted powers of the handkerchief, Othello then adds sentimental value, claiming that it was his dying mother's bequest to his future wife. Othello's story is problematic on multiple levels. First, it is curious that he did not explain the handkerchief's import when he first gave it to Desdemona; as Michael Neill rightly claims,

> It is as though in his determination to endow the lost token with the overplus of significance he needs it to have, Othello has to invest it with a romantic narrative to match the glamour of his own "travailous history."
>
> *(30)*

However, his story is also more than a "romantic narrative," for it carries an ominous threat that the loss or repurposing of the gift will justify the husband's adulterous rejection of his wife. Furthermore, the origin story associates Othello with the very charges of magic and ensorcellment that he had denied when Brabanzio accused him of bewitching Desdemona. Finally, it is not certain that the story is even true, as later in the play Othello offers a different explanation of its history: "It was a handkerchief, an antique token/ My father gave my mother" (5.2. 223–224). Othello's stories that once seemed exotic are now dangerous and questionable. In contrast to the beginning of their relationship, Desdemona and Othello are not united by constructed fictions but divided by deliberate falsehoods, and the play thus pivots towards its seemingly inevitable tragic outcome.

Distraught and confused by her husband's anger, Desdemona turns to Emilia, her one available female ally. Shakespeare's tragedies are overwhelmingly male-centered; they feature instrumental female characters—Cordelia, Lady Macbeth, and Tamora, for example—but there are relatively fewer women than in the comedies. In *Othello*, there are three female characters present: Desdemona and Emilia, and Cassio's mistress Bianca, but she has no encounters with the first two women. Other women are mentioned only in passing—Desdemona's mother and her maid, Barbary, along with Othello's mother and the Egyptian charmer. If individual women are generally on the margins of masculine-driven tragedies, supportive female community is even less visible. The Celia–Rosalind, Beatrice–Hero, Portia–Nerissa friendships that energize the comedies are absent in the tragedies, though the relationship between Desdemona and Emilia has been seen as an exception.

Emilia, assigned to be Desdemona's lady-in-waiting while they are in Cyprus, would have helped her with personal tasks such as bathing and dressing; the intimacy of these encounters often led to personal confidences and close relationships. In the hierarchy of social positions, Emilia occupied a liminal status: she was neither a working-class servant nor quite Desdemona's equal. But because of her proximity to her aristocratic or royal mistress, the lady-in-waiting was a valued role and one that could produce loyal alliances. Emilia and Desdemona seem to be mutually supportive: Desdemona defends Emilia against Iago's misogynistic attacks and Emilia defends Desdemona against Othello's jealous outbursts. On the other hand, Emilia betrays Desdemona and makes a fatal contribution to the tragic outcome when she steals her handkerchief for Iago. Although Emilia was unaware of Iago's intentions, she suspects it cannot be for a good cause; moreover, she knows that Desdemona "so loves the token … that she reserves it evermore about her/ To kiss and talk to" (3.3. 310–312). When Desdemona frantically searches for the handkerchief and asks Emilia if she knows its whereabouts, Emilia also lies: "I know not, madam" (3.4. 17).

The most extended portrayal of their relationship is the so-called "unpinning scene" in which the two women converse while following Othello's orders that Desdemona undress and prepare for bed. This scene, often touted as a rare example of female camaraderie in a Shakespearean tragedy, was for centuries eliminated in performance because the frank dialogue between Desdemona and Emilia about female desire and sexuality did not conform to an image of idealized womanhood. Denise Whalen also explores the performance history of this scene, demonstrating that the differences between the 1622 quarto—which does not include most of 4.3—and the 1623 Folio text "reveal an inclination to suppress and restrain female agency." Whalen concludes that "the history of this scene in performance shows an unnerving disposition to still the female voice, which makes it all the more remarkable that Shakespeare wrote the scene at all" (508).

In recent decades, stage and film performances have typically restored this scene in which the two women discuss marriage, infidelity, and gender inequities with such frankness that some critics uphold it as an example of Shakespeare's proto-feminism. Emilia's angry outburst that men can be unfaithful with impunity while women are punished for the same deed is contrasted with Desdemona's more naïve doubt that women would "abuse their husbands/ In such gross kind" (4.3. 62–63). Against Emilia's saucy resentment and sexual banter, Desdemona's innocent questioning confirms her belief in the essential virtue of women. It is a rare moment of female candor in the absence of male intrusion.

Yet, their conversation also reiterates the dichotomous virgin/whore view of women that the private talk between two women seems to resist. As Leah Marcus argues in her analysis of this scene's inclusion in the Folio version, "by hammering away at the topic of sexual transgression within the context of marriage between a Venetian and a Moor, by scratching away at a wound and continually reopening it" these passages "helps to keep alive in the play an itch of sexual prurience" that reinforces the play's imaginary sexual misconduct (120). Furthermore, apart from what the two women discuss behind closed doors, their seemingly blunt conversation is marked by numerous retractions and digressions that indicate a significant "interplay of denial, repression and displacement" in which they often do not talk *to* each other and in fact displace the problems in their heterosexual relationships onto each other rather than on men (Boose 39–40). In *Othello*, it is difficult for female solidarity to stand up against the forces of masculine loyalty and domination. As Emilia admits to herself when she gives the handkerchief to Iago, "I nothing but to please his fantasy" (3.3. 316).

Homosocial bonds between men are also fraught but are more entrenched in the male-centered military context of the play. Even though Othello is an outsider by race he is in the boy's club by nature of his reputation as an accomplished general, or rather, an experienced mercenary. The military world is portrayed as inherently and structurally homosocial; women threaten to undermine this masculine stronghold, for when men traverse into the female realm of domesticity and effeminacy they jeopardize their warrior preparedness and social dominance. Indeed, in many of Shakespeare's plays, marital and martial commitments are shown to be incompatible. It may seem curious that when Othello is convinced that Desdemona is unfaithful, he launches into an elaborate and self-pitying "farewell to my profession" speech: "Farewell the plumed troops and the big wars/ That makes ambition virtue! O, farewell,/ Farewell the neighing steed and the shrill trump/ ... Pride, pomp, and circumstance of glorious war/ ... Farewell, Othello's occupation's gone" (3.3. 353–363). But because of Desdemona's assumed infidelity, he has been humiliated and has relinquished his claim to authority: if he cannot control a wayward wife, then his ability to command men is also in question.

Furthermore, the homosocial bond forged through the military brotherhood here crosses over into expressions of homoeroticism; as Melissa Sanchez puts it, Othello, "not Desdemona, is the play's primary object of desire ... Indeed, the word 'love' expresses the bonds between Cassio, Iago, and Othello at least as insistently as that between Othello and Desdemona" (126). This is manifest most visibly in Iago's obsession with both Othello and Cassio, which he expresses in terms of love and hate with equal frequency and vehemence. As evidence of Iago's repressed homosexuality, many scholars cite Iago's report to Othello that Cassio talked in his sleep when they were bedfellows:

> In sleep I heard him say "Sweet Desdemona,
> Let us be wary, let us hide our loves,"
> And then sir, would he grip and wring my hand,
> Cry "O sweet creature!" then kiss me hard,
> As if he plucked up kisses by the roots,
> That grew upon my lips, lay his leg o'er my thigh,
> And sigh, and kiss, and they cry "Cursèd fate,

That gave thee to the Moor!"

(3.3. 423–430)

The convergent uncertainties raised by Iago's account complicate several bound-aries: it seems quite likely that "honest Iago" is inventing this story as part of his arsenal of evidence for adultery. And in muddying the boundary between truth and fiction, he also blurs the line between heterosexual and homosexual desire and their objects. Iago's tale is one of a love quadrangle, for in it he and Cassio are joined by the invocation of both Desdemona and Othello. But any homoerotic feelings Iago harbors for Cassio or Othello are inseparable from how he views their various roles in their shared military enterprise. Robert Matz points out the inter-section between male same-sex desire and male political relationships and argues that "this desire cements these relationships but may also be invoked accusatorily to disrupt them" (261). When Othello reinstates Iago to his favor the oaths they make to each other conflate military loyalty and love: "Now art thou my lieutenant," Iago replies, "I am your own forever" (3.3. 495–496).

Many readings of the play have concentrated on the racist views expressed by Iago and Roderigo, but they are also the villainous characters of the play. More recent analyses have pointed to the fact that others, including Brabanzio, the Duke, and Emilia, who calls Othello "the blacker devil," also participate in racialized assumptions and behaviors, even if they are less explicit. Even Othello internalizes racist construc-tions of his identity: by the time he comes to kill Desdemona, he has convinced himself that her adultery with Cassio is because "I am black" and is embarrassed that his reputation is tarnished: "My name, that was as fresh/ As Dian's visage, is now begrimed and black/ As mine own face" (3.3. 267 and 391–393). His murder of Desdemona is preceded by juxtaposing his own blackness with "that whiter skin of hers than snow/ And smooth as monumental alabaster" (5.2. 4–5). As Ian Smith states, "The play dramatizes two different kinds of racial tactics—one explicit and direct, the other covert and invisible—that operate as complementary forms of active racial aggression" (110).

Iago is not solely responsible for inciting Othello's sense of inferiority but he is its prime architect—he is also the main instigator of Othello's misogyny. Critics some-times argue that this is a play about the failures of communication: if only Othello had asked Desdemona directly about his suspicions the truth would have emerged and the tragic outcome averted. But Othello did accuse Desdemona directly of being "false as hell" and called her "whore" and "strumpet," but then proceeded to ignore her vehement protestations of innocence. Othello also asks Emilia who, as her lady-in-waiting, would have been privy to Desdemona's intimate life about his wife's conduct. Emilia insists that Desdemona is "chaste, honest, and true," but Othello also dismisses Emilia as "a simple bawd"—the words of women are meaningless within the over-whelming misogyny in the play (4.2. 18–21).

A play that begins with an interracial union, signaling a more optimistic articu-lation of gender and race, ends up divided by those very forces. Heterosexual relationships are destructive, but so are male homosocial bonds, while female solidarity is ultimately insufficient. Othello, the celebrated general called upon to save Venice at the beginning of the play, dies by his own hand, disgraced and regretful. Before he stabs himself, he makes one deathbed request. A man whose own fictional constructions were so instrumental in his fortunes now asks that his own story be told:

> I pray you in your letters,
> When you shall these unlucky deeds relate,
> Speak of me as I am. Nothing extenuate,
> Nor set down aught in malice. Then must you speak
> Of one that loved not wisely but too well;
> Of one not easily jealous but, being wrought,
> Perplexed in the extreme; of one whose hand
> Like the base Judean, threw a pearl away
> Richer than all his tribe ...
>
> *(5.2. 345–353)*

The play ends with the nobleman, Lodovico, heading back to Venice to "this heavy act with heavy heart relate" (5.2. 382). It is unclear, however, how Lodovico will tell the tragic story of Othello and Desdemona—it is left to future retellings to relate these unlucky deeds.

Desdemona: Honest talk, not fantasy

Toni Morrison's literary career elicits descriptors of greatness: grand, monumental, prodigious. The range and quality of her work have earned her a long list of accolades and awards, with the Nobel Prize for Literature in 1993 perhaps the most notable for its recognition of her international impact. Morrison spent a decade as an editor at Random House and then turned to her own writing that includes children's literature, essays, short fiction, and eleven novels. Her most famous work, *Beloved*, won the Pulitzer Prize in 1988 and is a fictionalized account based on the life of Margaret Garner, an African-American woman in the mid-nineteenth century who killed her child rather than seeing her enslaved. This historic episode was also the basis of an opera, *Margaret Garner* (2005), for which Morrison wrote the libretto; like *Desdemona*, it is another example of both adaptation and intermedial collaboration.

Morrison's death in the summer of 2019 marked the loss of one of America's greatest writers and one who, in her literary and political life, consciously drew on the experience of being black in America and generously promoted the work of other black authors and their place in our literary culture, but did not want to be narrowly labelled "a black woman writer." Morrison's was a wise voice we need in this moment of extreme racial reckoning, but others, inspired by her legacy, are filling in that gap and reminding us to turn to the words she left behind. Many of those words seem remarkably prescient—or rather, what she said was always timely and some of us were perhaps not listening hard enough. This is certainly the case with Morrison's version of Desdemona, who is given more voice herself but also needs to attend more carefully to the expression of others.

Desdemona is not the only time Morrison has engaged with Shakespeare in her fiction. Malin LaVon Walther, for example, reads Morrison's *Tar Baby* as a "corrective counterpoint to Shakespeare's *Tempest*" (137), while Chris Roark demonstrates that in *The Bluest Eye* "Morrison uses *Hamlet* as a foil in order to critique ... the alienation imposed by Hamlet's 'soliloquy sense' of the self" (1). Perhaps even more important than tracing intertextual connections to specific Shakespeare plays is Morrison's larger project: "her trademark juxtaposition of African-American texts" with works considered canonical in order to "critique and reconstruct the assumptions, practices, and critical interpretations of Euro-American texts" (Walther 137).

In performance, one of *Desdemona*'s most visible challenges to Shakespearean drama is the superimposition of the text, prominently displayed on the background of the otherwise spare, dark stage. Because *Desdemona* was performed in multiple countries, this served the practical purpose of translation for the audience. Sellars may have borrowed this strategy of supertitles from his experience as an opera director, but in the world of Shakespearean productions, such a fusion of text and performance is unusual. In an essay on *Prospero's Books*, the avant-garde film based on *The Tempest*, Douglas Lanier discusses the tension between Shakespeare on the page and Shakespeare on the stage, the debate over whether the script or a theatrical production claims greater authority. For Lanier, *Prospero's Books* bridges this "familiar competition," confronting and transforming the burden of the book into a visually rich cinematic vocabulary (191–194). Similarly, Morrison's *Desdemona* successfully conjoins the lyrics boldly printed on the large backdrop with the words spoken by the actress playing Desdemona and the songs performed by Traoré. No single artistic element claims dominance.

The new, cultural product that Morrison creates, however, is not just a matter of expanding the generic boundaries of theatre, and my focus now turns primarily to the text itself. Morrison's initial interest in this project was driven by the characterization of Desdemona: she argued that the Desdemona of Shakespeare's play was richer and more substantial than in most stage and screen representations, or, as we have seen, discussions in literary criticism, but that she still deserved the amplification of character conferred by having a fuller narrative. Indeed, Toni Morrison's *Desdemona* is not the first example of an artistic reconfiguration of Desdemona. In addition to the many adaptations of *Othello*, there are others that focus on Desdemona specifically. Anne MacDonald's 1990 comedy, *Goodnight Desdemona (Good Morning Juliet)*, unites two of Shakespeare's familiar heroines and rescues them from their tragic demise. Paula Vogel's 1987 comedy, *Desdemona: A Play About a Handkerchief*, goes even further in creating an audacious Desdemona who loudly proclaims her sexual exploits. However, as Elizabeth Gruber points out, "Though *Desdemona* redresses the marginalization of female characters in Shakespeare's play, Vogel's text also offers a piercing critique of women's collusion in patriarchal structures" (2). Vogel's Desdemona professes to take control of her sexual desires but this independence does not prevent her tragic death. Both Vogel and MacDonald are interested in a spirited and transgressive response to the heterosexual politics of tragedy; Morrison's work, on the other hand, offers a more complex and expansive narrative, situating Desdemona within her own historical context and within the homosocial community of women alluded to in Shakespeare's play.

Morrison's chosen backdrop harkens back to Homer and Dante, but it evokes more than a temporary trip to the underworld. As Morrison herself explains, this was an artistically liberating strategy, for the timelessness of the afterlife, where "there is nothing to lose," allows for honest revelations, productive encounters, and genuine forgiveness. In the same interview, Traoré adds that composing musical dialogue to be sung "from the grave means you're beyond a place of fear ... you have the space to speak about things that are difficult to speak about in life" (UC Berkeley Events). Desdemona rejoices in the narrative freedom of the afterlife: "I exist ... between life on earth and life beyond it ... I exist in places where I can speak, at last, words that in earth were sealed or twisted into the language of obedience" (Morrison and Traoré 14). The setting, which Morrison argued was essential to the success of the project, offers an opportunity for human interaction and reconciliation that the genre of conventional tragedy does not accommodate.

The first strategy Morrison uses in creating a more substantial Desdemona is to allow her a childhood. In *Othello*, we meet Desdemona as a young woman of marriageable age, but we hear nothing of her girlhood except when she briefly mentions her mother's maid, Barbary. But in Morrison's work, Desdemona vividly describes her experiences growing up, her relationship with her parents and her nurse, and her attempts to construct and defend her own identity in a rigidly patriarchal world. Hearing about Desdemona's girlhood enlarges our notions of the adult woman she becomes and the choices she makes.

This work begins with Desdemona defiantly laying claim to her own selfhood: "My name is Desdemona," she declares in the opening line, but after explaining that her name means "misery," "ill fated," and "doomed," she rejects the connotations of the identity her parents gave her: "I am not the meaning of a name I did not choose." In refusing to accept the tragic implications that her name forecasts, Desdemona resists the circumscribed role dictated by both her parents and Venetian society:

> Perhaps my parents
> Believed or imagined or knew my fortune
> at the moment of my birth. Perhaps being
> born a girl I gave them all they needed to
> know of what my life would be like. That it
> would be subject to the whims of my elders
> and the control of men.
>
> *(13)*

While Desdemona is reflecting back from the vantage of adulthood, she understood even as a young girl that "Men made the rules, women followed them," a practice

Desdemona's mother and father willingly accepted: "My parents, keenly aware and approving of/ that system, could anticipate the future of a girl child accurately" (13).

Historians Sara Mendelson and Patricia Crawford describe the commonly shared gender prejudices of early modern parenting:

> In practice, a good deal of contemporary evidence supports the view that even before the birth of a child, elite parents felt differently about the prospect of a son or daughter. One preacher observed, "it is a greater blessing to have a sonne, then a daughter." More bluntly, the Italian Ochino remarked, "commonly we rejoice at the birth of Boyes, and grieve at the birth of Girles."
>
> *(80)*

As Mendelson and Crawford demonstrate, class concerns intersected with gender bias: "elite parents"—as Desdemona's were—often believed that daughters demanded a particular upbringing:

> Most girls remained with their families, where they were educated by their mothers. They were taught to behave differently from boys. They were to be more restrained, and to preserve their chastity. Bodily comportment for the two sexes was different. While a girl was cautioned about modesty before she was three a boy of the same age was urged to "take up his Coats, and piss like a Man."
>
> *(89)*

The duration of girlhood was also dependent upon class status. Lower class girls were often sent into service at a fairly young age, precipitating an earlier transition to adulthood. On the other hand, privileged daughters of aristocratic families were more likely to be kept home under their parents' supervision and control, or placed in the homes of other upper-class families. But as Desdemona's story demonstrates, privilege and protection equaled confinement.

In *Desdemona*, Senator Brabantio corresponds with Shakespeare's powerful Venetian citizen who wants to make a respectable marriage for his daughter: "His sole interest in me as/ I grew into womanhood was making certain/ I was transferred, profitably and securely,/ into the hands of another man" (20). But his role in this work is otherwise negligible, transferring more of the parental control to Desdemona's mother. In her influential essay, "Where Are the Mothers in Shakespeare?," Mary Beth Rose reminds us that mothers were minimally represented in Shakespeare's plays, which is often seen as an explanation for the unchecked and unleashed expressions of patriarchal control (301–302). But Rose also argues that an increased presence of Shakespearean mothers would not necessarily have mitigated the strictures of paternal rule over daughters: witness Lady Capulet's refusal to support Juliet's objections to marrying Paris. When Juliet begs her mother to intervene with her father, her mother dismisses her: "Talk not to me, for I'll not speak a word" (3.5. 202).

In *Desdemona*, Madame Brabantio adheres to the same code of wifely obedience as Lady Capulet, modeling proper female submissiveness for her daughter, educating her, but in womanly restriction:

> She taught me how to handle myself
> at table, how to be courteous in speech ...
> she did not tolerate dispute from a child, nor involve
> herself in what could be called my interior
> life. There were strict rules of deportment...
> And there was sensible
> punishment designed for each impropriety. Constraint was the theme of behavior.
> Duty was its plot.
>
> *(17)*

Desdemona's mother cares more about her appropriate outward behavior than her "interior life," recalling the thematic opposition between "being" and "seeming" in *Othello*, where the tragic outcomes are supported by characters' investments in appearance over reality. Morrison's Desdemona, however, often indulges in unseemly and sensuous play, though she is aware that "my desires, my imagination must remain hidden" (17). Not atypical in either early modern culture or drama is that Desdemona's mother participates in the oppressiveness of what Desdemona calls "that system."

In *Othello*, neither Desdemona's mother nor Othello's is present, though both of them are mentioned, and Desdemona and Othello "both speak lines that suggest fantasies of maternal love in the background of their own relationship" (Novy 94). Morrison restores these two women to her world and while their presence does not alter outcomes, it gives them a voice. In keeping with Morrison's emphasis on the female relationships and attempts to bridge difference, she includes a brief scene in which the mothers of the tragic lovers come together. Their meeting typifies the overarching pattern of *Desdemona* in which encounters between two characters begin by airing grievances and end, if not in forgiveness, at least in its potential. Madame Brabantio may have been a strict mother, but she is devastated by Desdemona's murder, just as Soun, Othello's mother, grieves her son's suicide. When Soun asks, "Are we enemies then?" Madame Brabantio replies, "Of course. Our vengeance is more molten than our sorrow." But when Madame Brabantio suggests that they kneel to pray, Soun counters with another idea:

> I come from a land wildly different from yours. A desert land pierced by forests of palm. There we obey nature and look to it for the language of the gods ... We build an altar to the spirits who are waiting to console us.
>
> *(27)*

Their gradual progress towards mutual respect is never sentimentalized; Morrison's characters only achieve a generosity of spirit because they are first permitted honest—though uncomfortable and painful—expression of their anger.

This tense movement towards reciprocal understanding also marks Desdemona's encounters with Emilia, Barbary, and Othello. At first, as Ayanna Thompson notes, Desdemona sounds "like many contemporary white liberals," who does not fully understand her privilege (*Desdemona* 502). Her confrontation with Emilia begins in harsh recrimination: as in *Othello*, Morrison's Emilia is brazen and pragmatic and Desdemona quietly self-righteous. Desdemona reminds Emilia, "You and I were friends,/ but didn't the man you knelt to protect run/ a gleaming sword through your survival strategies?" Emilia's rebuke reveals the fissures in their alleged friendship:

> And why did he? Because I befriended and
> supported you. I exposed his lies,
> you ingrate! That is your appreciation for my devotion to
> you? "My cloak, Emilia," "My night gown, Emilia."
> "Unpin me, Emilia. Arrange my bedsheets,
> Emilia." That is not how you treat a friend; that's how you treat a servant.
>
> *(43)*

But as Emilia explains that her hardened worldview resulted from the many disappointments in her life, she and Desdemona approach a semblance of sympathy for each other. Emilia tells Desdemona, "Like you I believed marriage was my salvation. It was not." Her marriage was filled with cruel lust rather than love, and "that passion generated nothing." Her childlessness was even more painful because she was herself an orphan. Desdemona replies sympathetically, "I wish I had known you when we were children ... You had no mother. I had no mother's love." When Emilia objects that "It's not the same," Desdemona apologizes: "You are right to correct me. Instead of judging, I should have been understanding" (44). Emilia is given the last word; after thanking Desdemona for her apology, she concludes with a lyrical description of a lizard she once saw that "shed her dull outer skin ... exposing that which had been underneath—her jeweled self," but she keeps the old skin in case she needs to camouflage "her true dazzle." Emilia cites this as a metaphor for her own survival skills, and her conclusion, "that little lizard changed my life" announces her insistence on being resourceful and resilient.

If Shakespeare's conversation between these two women is troubling for its circumlocutions, Morrison's rendering is equally disconcerting for its penetrating honesty. Morrison does not rush her characters to facile friendship; they ultimately achieve a measure of reciprocity, but only after fully expressing their trauma. While these truthful meetings give voice to the women individually, they also strengthen female bonds—in counterpoint to the representation of same-sex relationships in *Othello*, in which male allegiances overwhelm ties between women.

The trajectory from blame to empathy is particularly evident in Desdemona's first meeting with Barbary, the centerpiece of *Desdemona* in text and in performance. On stage, Barbary is the only other character physically present on stage besides the background musicians; while Desdemona speaks all of the other characters' parts by using different vocal registers, Barbary speaks her own lines as well as singing the lyrics of her own songs. In *Othello*, we hear of Barbary in 4.3, the "unpinning scene," when Desdemona reminisces in a foreshadowing of her own imminent death: "My mother had a maid called Barbary,/ She was in love, and he she loved proved mad/ And did forsake her. She had a song of 'Willow.'/ An old thing 'twas, but it expressed her fortune,/ And she died singing it. That song tonight/ Will not go from my head …" (4.3. 26–31). From this brief reference Morrison constructs an entire character and relationship, fusing northern Africa with Venice and, by extension, early modern England.

In *Desdemona*, Barbary is not her mother's maid but Desdemona's childhood nurse: "My solace in those early days lay with my/ nurse, Barbary" (18). Desdemona is thrilled when she sees Barbary in the afterlife and recalls the intimacy of their past together, for Barbary represented all that Desdemona's mother did not: comfort, generosity, pleasure, spontaneity. Serena Guarracino points out that "to the postcolonially attuned ear, this means that Desdemona, just like many other white children in later, colonial times, was raised by a black nanny who told her African stories and sang her African lullabies," for indeed, Desdemona explains how Barbary took care of her, braiding her hair, dressing her, entertaining her (65). But Sujata Iyengar also claims that "It is helpful to read Desdemona's memories of Barbary braiding her hair through Susan Bordo's moving essay about accepting and acknowledging the support of black caregivers and friends as she parents a black daughter when she herself is white." A collaborative experience, Iyengar compares to Morrison and Traoré as "co-mothers" of *Desdemona*, a play that "ultimately celebrates and commemorates women's love" (515). Desdemona is also grateful to Barbary for instilling a love of stories that revealed a world beyond corsets and drawing rooms:

> Barbary alone conspired with me to let my imagination run free. She told me stories of other lives, other countries, places where gods speak in thundering silence and mimic human faces and forms. Where nature is not a crafted, pretty thing, but wild, sacred and instructive. Unlike the staid, unbending women of my country, she moved with the fluid grace I saw only in swans and the fronds of willow trees.
>
> *(18)*

Guarracino argues that "This portrait of Barbary/Africa as a woman/land of communion with nature and 'primitive' freedom from social customs could not be more exoticizing" (65). Indeed, Morrison is eager to contrast Barbary's liberating influence on Desdemona with Madame Brabantio's restrictive mandates but, in establishing a Barbary/nature and Madame Brabantio/civilization paradigm, she may be reinforcing some of the binaries that she sought to undo in *Othello*.

If Desdemona misread her assumed friendship with Emilia, she misreads her relationship with Barbary even more egregiously:

> We shared nothing ...
> I mean you don't even know my name.
> Barbary? Barbary is what you call Africa.
> Barbary is the geography of the foreigner,
> the savage. Barbary? Barbary equals the
> sly, vicious enemy who must be put down
> at any price; held down at any cost for the
> conquerors' pleasure. Barbary is the name of
> those without whom you could neither live
> nor prosper.
>
> *(45)*

She explains that her real name was Sa'ran, but Desdemona, still insisting upon her romanticized view of their relationship replies, "Well, Sa'ran, whatever your name, you were my best friend." Sa'ran disagrees: "I was your slave ... I am black-skinned. You are white-skinned ... So you don't know me. Have never known me" (45–46). In his discussion of *Othello*'s relevance to our current moment of racial reckoning, Ian Smith reminds us that

> knowledge within America's racial divide is asymmetrical: blacks have always needed to know whiteness, its rules, discipline, and various forms of corporal punishments, while whiteness has been free of the burden of knowing anything about the cultural intimacies of blackness.
>
> *(108)*

Desdemona's ignorance about Sa'ran demonstrates this self-centered asymmetry.

When Shakespeare wrote *Othello*, "Barbary" was the English term for Northern African territories with which England had strained diplomatic and trade relations; Barbary was also used as a racial slur in popular culture and literature, as when Iago hysterically warns Brabanzio that his daughter is coupling with a Barbary horse. Kim Hall points out that

> All the usual associations with Barbary ... appear in *Othello*, but the most powerful link is clearly the maid Barbary, whose song Desdemona sings at the height of tension and danger in her marriage ... Given the English habit of naming black servants after geographical regions, it would not be far-fetched to think of Barbary as African.
>
> *(260)*

Lenore Kitts explains that as Sellars imagined *Desdemona*, he insisted it was important that Africa no longer be "ventriloquized" by Shakespeare, or even by Morrison, for that matter. He proposed the collaboration with Traoré, a native of Mali, because the project "required a voice of an African woman to speak as an African woman and to sing as an African woman."

(258)

In *Othello*, the very name Barbary would have recalled exotic, savage, and sexualized foreign difference, and Desdemona's allusion to her at the critical moment when she is herself accused of sexual misdeeds suggests a transgressive association between the two women. In *Desdemona*, Barbary, who leaves no doubt about her black identity, complicates the more conspicuous binaries of *Othello*, for here she is associated with both Desdemona and Othello. Barbary and Desdemona both find comfort in the arts of storytelling and music; they both appreciate the sensual pleasures of the outdoors; and they both die because of ill-fated love. But Barbary is also identified with Othello: her race, her origins, her captivating narratives, and her reverence for the natural world all signal their kinship.

Through this fuller characterization of Barbary, Morrison reminds us that Othello would not have been Desdemona's first encounter with a person of color, nor were his infamous and seductive tales the first such stories she heard. In both *Othello* and *Desdemona*, storytelling is Othello's means of wooing, but in Morrison's version, the tales Barbary tells to Desdemona as a young girl—fantastic narratives "of other lives, other countries/ places where gods speak in thundering silence"—are what stimulate further interest in Othello's adventures. In *Desdemona*, another critical correspondence between Barbary and Othello occurs when Desdemona first meets Othello. At the time, Desdemona is mourning Barbary's recent death: forsaken by her lover, "her spacious heart drained and sere, Barbary died" (20). Complicating Desdemona's grief is her determination to learn from Barbary's experience and "search more carefully for the truth of a lover before committing my own fidelity" (20). When she is introduced to Othello, she immediately thinks of Barbary: "I saw a glint of brass in his eyes identical to the light in Barbary's eyes" (23). There is a disconcerting suggestion that for Desdemona, all people of color are similar and that the loss of one black person can be so quickly filled by another.

If Desdemona is forced to reckon with how social status unbalanced her relationship with Emilia, she must also confront her racial naiveté. In the problematic posture of alleged "color blindness" she tells Sa'ran that racial differences were irrelevant to her: "Think. I wed a Moor. I fled my home to be with him. I defied my father, all my family to wed him. I joined him on the battlefield" (46). Sa'ran refuses Desdemona's justification and proffered kinship and elaborates on her role as servant: "I have no rank in your world. I do what I am told." But Desdemona counters that she too suffered restraints: "I had no more control over my life than you had. My prison was unlike yours but it was prison still." Desdemona's next question is even more revealing: "Was I ever cruel to you? Ever?" to which Sa'ran replies, "No. You never hurt or abused me" (48). But Sa'ran's silence about the possibility of cruelty is conspicuous and does not entirely fill the gap that remains between the two women.

Sa'ran acknowledges that her deepest suffering was caused by the lover who betrayed her, an experience Desdemona understands: while social status and race separate them, they share common ground as women who died because of the men they loved. Desdemona seems to invoke her own death when she asks Sa'ran: "Remember the song/ You sang every day until you wasted away/ and embraced death without fight or protest?" Sa'ran then sings the iconic "willow song" from *Othello*, but follows with a more triumphant revision, concluding, "What bliss to know I will never die again." Desdemona rejoins, replacing Sa'ran's individual pronoun with a plural: "We will never die again" (48–49), though it is not clear whether Sa'ran agrees that their separate experiences are unified. Morrison's purpose is not to rewrite the women's past experiences and differences but to transcend them in the afterlife: now, they both refuse to represent victimized women. Ayanna Thompson points out that in performance, the staging choices suggest that "the gulf between Sa'ran and Desdemona seems almost insurmountable" *(Desdemona* 503), but the text is more ambiguous about the possibility of reciprocal understanding.

Desdemona's conversation with Othello is also marked by a painstaking progression towards mutual revelation and acceptance. They begin by acknowledging what numerous readers and critics of *Othello* have cited as a source of their tragic outcome: Desdemona and Othello fell in love with idealized versions of each other. Morrison elaborates on this reading with Othello's complaint to Desdemona: "You never loved me. You fancied the idea of me, the exotic foreigner who kills for the State, who will die for the State" (50). While Shakespeare's Othello takes pride in Desdemona's appreciation of his storytelling, Morrison's Othello criticizes Desdemona for her blind attraction to his preposterous narratives that were "a useful myth, a fairy's tale cut to suit a princess' hunger for real life" (51).

As with the other characters, Morrison allows Othello a fuller backstory, rendering a more complex character that becomes both more and less sympathetic. Just as Morrison's more substantial characterization of Desdemona is informed by an account of her girlhood, Morrison's Othello offers a detailed description of his boyhood. His mother died when he was young and he was raised by a woman whose affinity for music and the natural world recalls Barbary:

> As an orphan child a root woman adopted me as her son and sheltered me from slavers. I trailed her in forests and over sere as she searched for medicinal plants ... She worshipped the natural world and encouraged me to rehearse songs to divine its power.
>
> *(31)*

Though not a pastoral idyll, this upbringing in a maternal and nurturing outdoor world ends when he is captured by Syrians and becomes a child soldier. His immersion into a violent military milieu challenges Shakespeare's representation of Othello as noble warrior and great general. Morrison's Othello offers a frank explanation of his early training "where food was regular and clothing respectable" and where he turned his "childish anger" into military accomplishments: "I was happy, breathless, and hungry for more violent encounters" (31). Othello tells Desdemona stories of his far-flung travels during wartime, including an account of powerful Amazon women that Desdemona finds inspiring, and some of these tales are even more lyrical and outlandish than their counterparts in Shakespeare's play. But he also adds "tales of horror and strange," of a soldier's world in which drugs were routine and "rape was perfunctory." He then confesses the most disturbing experience of all: once, "aroused by bloodletting" in combat, he and Iago came upon two elderly women hiding in a stable and they raped them repeatedly. This horrific act, witnessed by a young boy, created a bond between the two men, "an exchange of secrecy" (38).

Shakespeare's works frequently highlight a tension between homosocial friendships and heterosexual romance and marriage; same-sex friendship is often portrayed as pre-sexual and innocent, almost prelapsarian, while relationships between men and women are corrupted by the specter of sexuality. While this distinction is prominent in many plays, it should not obscure the homoerotic elements of many other same-sex relationships, nor should it idealize same-sex friendships as inherently more noble or valuable. Nonetheless, in both *Othello* and *Desdemona*, heterosexual and same-sex relationships are positioned against each other, and while there is no spotless relationship in either work, female community is distinguished from "brotherhood." In *Desdemona*, the female characters have difficult confrontations that eventually develop into conversation and affirmative community, but the homosocial bonding among the male characters is only destructive.

Particularly in a war zone, male alliances result from shared atrocities, a propensity for cruelty and toxic masculinity that often carries over into the civilian world. In taking on the project of *Desdemona*, Morrison explained that one of her goals was to eliminate Iago's overwhelming presence so that other characters could reclaim the narrative—but while Iago is not given a role in her text, she does not erase him entirely, as his catastrophic impact is still evident. While Shakespeare's Othello seems entirely deceived by Iago, Morrison's Desdemona insists that Othello must have known that Iago was lying about her alleged infidelity, yet still chose to believe him because of the power of "brotherhood." As Desdemona describes the "bright, tight, camaraderie" between men, she positions it explicitly against their relationships with women:

> The wide, wild celebrity men find with each other cannot compete with the narrow comfort of a wife. Romance is always overshadowed by brawn. The language of love is trivial compared to the hidden language of men that lies underneath the secret language they speak in public.
>
> *(37)*

Othello does not contradict Desdemona's accusations but admits the obscenity of his behavior in violating so many women, and asks for her forgiveness.

Morrison's reunion of Desdemona and Othello in the afterlife is not romantic and joyous, but tentative and sober; Peter Erickson argues even further that "In contrast to the female encounters, Desdemona's meeting with Othello ultimately seems unresolved, suspended, beside the point" (7). Desdemona tells Othello that she cannot forgive the violence he committed against her—and other women—but that she can still love the flawed man: "Honest love does not cringe" (39). For his part, Othello regrets his behavior and realizes that "we should have had such honest talk, not fantasy" when they married. They apologize to each other, though Othello says "apology is a pale word for what I am called upon to recognize" (54). At the end of her work, Morrison directs Desdemona and Othello to a vision that is larger than their individual relationship. What they can now possess is "the possibility of wisdom" and the potential of helping create a world in which "human peace" can be imagined and created:

> If it's a question
> of working together
> on the task,
> I would be happy to take part.
> Whether we are from the same place or not.
> Whether we are from the same culture or not.
> Should we celebrate this moment?
> It would fill me with joy.
>
> *(56)*

Desdemona culminates by celebrating the possibility of a community that can negotiate gender, racial, and social differences, of a world that offers hope and redemption. In the hands of a less accomplished writer, these concluding passages could threaten to be overly sentimental, even saccharine. Given Morrison's gift for lyricism, her conclusion is instead a profound alternative to the tragic destruction of *Othello*. It is almost axiomatic in Shakespearean studies that the male-centered tragedies privilege the individual while the female-centered comedies celebrate community. Morrison's *Desdemona* does not transform *Othello* into a life-affirming Shakespearean comedy, but it does redirect the spotlight from the individual to the "greater good."

As discussed earlier, Gérard Genette's theory of adaption describes character revaluation as one of many possible strategies for literary revision (343–350). Following Genette's intertextual taxonomy, Morrison's revisionary project imbues Desdemona with greater significance in the "value system" than she had in *Othello*. Through the incorporation of Desdemona's girlhood experiences that reveal her nascent sense of autonomy, her confrontations and conversations within the parameters of female community, and the challenge to her myopic assumptions about race, Morrison empowers Desdemona to reconstruct her sense of self and her problematic relationships with the other characters. But Morrison's project extends beyond giving Desdemona herself a more complex role to amplifying her relationships with the other women in *Othello*; she also refocuses the dispositions of the marginal characters in *Othello*—especially Barbary. In creating a space that undermines male dominance and asserts female autonomy, Morrison does not ignore the urgency of confronting our racial divisions as well, for as Desdemona concludes, "We will be judged by how well we love" (56).

References

Andrea, Bernadette. "Assimilation or Dissimulation?: Leo Africanus's Geographical History of Africa and the Parable of Amphibia." *ARIEL: A Review of International English Literature* 32. 3 (2001): 7–29.

Bartels, Emily. "Othello on Trial." In *Othello: New Casebooks*, ed. Lena Cowen Orlin. Basingstoke: Palgrave Macmillan, 2004.

Boose, Lynda. "'Let it Be Hid': The Pornographic Aesthetic of Othello." In *Othello: Contemporary Critical Essays*, ed. Lena Cowen Orlin. New York: Palgrave Macmillan, 2004: 22–48.

Enterline, Lynn. "Eloquent Barbarians: *Othello* and the Critical Potential of Passionate Character." In *Othello: The State of Play*, ed. Lena Cowen Orlin. London: Bloomsbury, 2014: 149–176.

Erickson, Peter. "'Late Has No Meaning Here': Imagining a Second Chance in Toni Morrison's Desdemona." *Borrowers and Lenders: A Journal of Shakespeare and Appropriation* 8. 1 (2013): 1–13.

Genette, Gérard. *Palimpsests: Literature in the Second Degree*. Trans. Channa Newman. Lincoln: U of Nebraska Press, 1997.

Gruber, Elizabeth. "Erotic Politics Reconsidered: Desdemona's Challenge to Othello." *Borrowers and Lenders* 3. 2 (2008): 1–16.

Guarracino, Serena. "Africa as Voices and Vibes: Musical Roots in Toni Morrison's Margaret Garner and Desdemona." *Research in African Literatures* 46. 4 (2015): 56–71.

Hall, Kim, ed. *Othello: Texts and Contexts*. New York: Bedford St. Martins, 2007.

Harris, Bernard. "A Portrait of a Moor." In *Shakespeare and Race*, eds. Catherine Belsey and Stanley Wells. Cambridge: Cambridge UP, 2000: 23–36.

Heng, Geraldine. *The Invention of Race in the European Middle Ages*. Cambridge: Cambridge UP, 2018.

Iyengar, Sujata. "Woman-Crafted Shakespeares: Appropriation, Intermediality, and Womanist Aesthetics." In *A Feminist Companion to Shakespeare*, 2nd ed., ed. Dympna Callaghan. Hoboken: Wiley Blackwell, 2016: 507–519.

James, Heather. "Dido's Ear: Tragedy and the Politics of Response." *Shakespeare Quarterly* 52. 3 (2001): 360–382.

Kitts, Lenore. "The Sound of Change: A Musical Transit Through the Wounded Modernity of Desdemona." In *Toni Morrison: Memory and Meaning*, eds. Adrienne Lanier Seward and Justin Talley. Jackson: U Press of Mississippi, 2014: 255–268.

Lanier, Douglas. "Drowning the Book: Prospero's Books and the Textual Shakespeare." In *Shakespeare, Theory, and Performance*, ed. James Bulman. New York: Routledge, 1995: 189–212.

Macdonald, Joyce. "Black Ram, White Women: Shakespeare, Race, and Women." In *A Feminist Companion to Shakespeare*, 2nd ed., ed. Dympna Callaghan. Hoboken: Wiley Blackwell, 2016: 206–225.

Marcus, Leah. "Constructions of Race and Gender in the Two Texts of Othello." In *Rethinking Feminism in Early Modern Studies: Gender, Race, and Sexuality*, eds. Ania Loomba and Melissa Sanchez. New York: Routledge, 2016: 113–134.

Matz, Robert. "Slander, Renaissance Discourses of Sodomy, and Othello." *ELH* 66. 2 (1999): 261–276.

Mendelson, Sara and Patricia Crawford. *Women in Early Modern England*. Oxford: Oxford UP, 1998.

Morrison, Toni and Rokia Traoré. *Desdemona*. London: Oberon Books, 2012.

Neill, Michael. "Othello's Black Handkerchief: Response to Ian Smith." *Shakespeare Quarterly* 64. 1 (2013): 26–31.

Novy, Marianne. *Shakespeare and Feminist Theory*. New York: Bloomsbury Arden, 2017.

Pechter, Edward. *Othello and Interpretative Traditions*. Iowa City: U of Iowa Press, 2012.

Roark, Chris. "'My Mother's Fussing Soliloquies': Toni Morrison's Bluest Eye and Shakespeare." *Borrowers and Lenders: A Journal of Shakespeare and Appropriation* 7. 2 (2013): 1–29.

Rose, Mary Beth. "Where are the Mothers in Shakespeare?" *Shakespeare Quarterly* 42. 3 (1991): 291–314.

Sanchez, Melissa. *Shakespeare and Queer Theory*. New York: Bloomsbury Arden, 2020.

Sellars, Peter. *"Foreword" to Desdemona, Toni Morrison*. London: Oberon Books, 2012.

Shakespeare, William. *Othello: Texts and Contexts*, ed. Kim F. Hall. New York: Bedford St. Martin's, 2006.

Smith, Ian. "We Are Othello: Speaking of Race in Early Modern Studies." *Shakespeare Quarterly* 67. 1 (2016): 104–124.

Thompson, Ayanna. "Desdemona: Toni Morrison's Response to Othello." In *A Feminist Companion to Shakespeare*, 2nd ed., ed. Dympna Callaghan. Hoboken: Wiley Blackwell, 2016: 494–506.

Thompson, Ayanna, ed. *The Cambridge Companion to Shakespeare and Race*. Cambridge: Cambridge UP: 2021.

UC Berkeley Events. "Desdemona Panel Discussion: Dialogues Across Histories, Continents, Cultures." Youtube: https://www.youtube.com/watch?v=79K_hMW102g&ab_channel= UCBerkeleyEvents. 04–11–2011.

Vaughan, Virginia M. *Othello: A Contextual History*. Cambridge: Cambridge UP, 1997.

Walther, Malin LaVon. *Toni Morrison's Cross-Cultural Performances: Differences in Women's Re-Visions of Shakespeare*. Urbana: U of Illinois Press, 1993: 137–149.

Whalen, Denise A. "Unpinning Desdemona." *Shakespeare Quarterly* 58. 4 (2007): 487–508.

Zhiri, Oumelbanine. "Leo Africanus and the Limits of Translation." In *Travel and Translation in the Early Modern Period*, ed. Carmine diBiase. Amsterdam: Rodopi, 2006: 175–186.

2

ELIZABETH NUNEZ'S *PROSPERO'S DAUGHTER* AND WILLIAM SHAKESPEARE'S *THE TEMPEST*

The Tempest is undoubtedly the play in the Shakespeare canon alongside *Othello* that has engendered the most vigorous discussions about racial oppression and othering. Like *Othello, The Tempest* portrays the intersection of racism with class and gender inequality, but with a particular emphasis on colonial appropriation. Elizabeth Nunez, a Trinidadian-American author of nine novels and a memoir, boldly tackles these issues in *Prospero's Daughter* (2006), an explicit exposure of patriarchal and political entitlement and ecological desecration. Nunez's creative and scholarly work is grounded in her familiarity with the dynamic history of the Caribbean where she grew up as well as the complex influence of Shakespeare on her literary development. In *Prospero's Daughter*, Nunez resituates the fraught racial and social conflicts of *The Tempest* to Trinidad as it neared independence from Britain in 1962, but as the novel's title suggests, she is also reorienting her story away from the play's problematic hero towards the next generation.

Shakespeare's plays have all been approached through a rich array of critical and creative lenses, but in recent decades *The Tempest* has been a particular site of interpretive reversal. For centuries *The Tempest*, believed by many to be Shakespeare's last play, was seen as his theatrical farewell as he renounced the "rough magic" of his creative powers and then shuffled off to comfortable retirement in Stratford. While this legend does not stand up against the evidence that Shakespeare continued to co-author several works after *The Tempest* and maintained professional ties in London until his death, the play does have a valedictory air and invites some parallels between Shakespeare the successful playwright and Prospero the powerful impresario. However, since the mid-twentieth century a rich body of post-colonial criticism and creative work has impelled re-evaluations of Prospero, interrogating his patriarchal authority over Miranda, his tyranny over Caliban and Ariel, and his imperial exploitation of an island for his own purposes. While *The Tempest* has been one of Shakespeare's most frequently performed and adapted plays since its first appearance in 1611,

DOI: 10.4324/9781003166580-3

the outpouring of literary appropriations and analyses that specifically target the play's political implications has profoundly influenced how contemporary audiences view the play.

Responding to anti-government uprisings he witnessed in Madagascar, the French psychoanalyst Octavio Mannoni explored the trauma caused by oppressive political forces in *Prospero and Caliban: The Psychology of Colonization* (1956). This work prompted contesting responses, most notably from Cuban poet Roberto Fernandez Retamar and Martinique philosopher Frantz Fanon who countered Mannoni's theory of the oppressed man's "dependency complex" by positing Caliban instead as a symbol of resistance. A number of Caribbean writers followed with adaptations of the play inspired by their own experiences as subjects of the British Empire. In George Lamming's collection of essays, *The Pleasures of Exile* (1960), and his novel, *Water With Berries* (1971), the Barbadian writer identifies with Caliban to explore the precarious position of the colonized subject; the Martinique writer Aimé Césaire's play, *Une tempête* (1969), is a scathing indictment of Prospero's imperialism and racism and now a touchstone in post-colonial curricula; in Barbadian poet Edward Kamau Brathwaite's poetic trilogy, *The Arrivants*, his Caliban figure celebrates ancestral African rituals and embodies cultural and political rebellion; Jamaican writer Nalo Hopkinson's short story, "Shift" (2002), recounts the journey of Caliban and Ariel in a contemporary world where identity is still determined by racialized categories. These works by Caribbean authors mostly preceded the spate of similar interpretations of the play by Anglo-American critics that emerged in the last quarter of the twentieth century, and Shakespearean scholarship was late in acknowledging the previous work by writers of color. Even as some scholars still insist that *The Tempest*'s connections to imperial expansion have been exaggerated, it is now commonplace to view European colonialism as central to the play and its afterlives.

Prospero's Daughter joins this tradition with its emphasis on the tension between a moribund empire and its subjects who are struggling to emerge from centuries of colonial domination. Nunez's adaptation quickly dispels any notion that Prospero is a beneficent genius and an ultimately forgiving and moral sage. Her Prospero counterpart represents the British Empire at its most rapacious: his unequivocal authoritarianism is manifest in his control over his daughter, the island residents he exploits, and his fanatic manipulation of the island's ecology—driven by his belief in the superiority of all things British. Nunez depicts these acts as crimes against humanity and crimes against the environment. Finally, she rewrites one of the most unsettling aspects of *The Tempest* in which Prospero's daughter, Miranda, and Caliban, the islander he has enslaved, are set against each other; instead, Nunez imagines them as allies who unite to resist the misogyny and racism that Prospero represents. *Prospero's Daughter* talks back to *The Tempest* by replacing an entrenched male-centered nationalism with a new generation that promises to work towards gender and social equity and a respectful environmental ethos.

The Tempest and *Prospero's Daughter:* Brief synopses

For the purposes of adaptive comparison, it is necessary to provide brief synopses of Shakespeare's *The Tempest*, first performed in 1611, and Nunez's *Prospero's Daughter*, published in 2006.

In *The Tempest*, Prospero, the Duke of Milan and an aspiring magician, is deposed by his conniving brother Antonio with the help of Alonso, the King of Naples, and Alonso's brother Sebastian. Prospero and his three-year-old daughter Miranda are put to sea, but his kind councillor Gonzalo gives him a small library of his books on magic. They land on an island already inhabited by Caliban and the androgynous spirit Ariel; before her death, Caliban's mother, the witch Sycorax, had imprisoned Ariel in a pine tree because he did not follow her orders. Prospero frees Ariel from Sycorax's spell and then consigns him to servitude; at first he befriends Caliban, but when he allegedly tries to rape Miranda, Prospero enslaves him.

Twelve years later, happenstance and Prospero's magic bring his enemies nearby. They are returning to Italy from northern Africa, where Alonso's daughter Claribel has been married to the King of Tunis, and Prospero and Ariel conjure a tempest that causes them to shipwreck on the island. His rivals Antonio, Alonso, and Sebastian; his one-time helper Gonzalo; Ferdinand, son of Alonso and prince of Naples; and two crewmates, Trinculo and Stephano, all find their way to shore but are unsure of each other's fate. Prospero's vengeful machinations ensue: he contrives internal divisions and psychological torments for his former enemies and he implicates Caliban in a murder conspiracy with Trinculo and Stephano. But in the end Prospero's revenge partially gives way as he absolves his usurpers, sets Ariel free, pronounces ownership of Caliban, and most importantly, renounces his magic and reclaims his dukedom. Prospero can afford this pivot to forgiveness for his European enemies because he achieved his ultimate plan: in bringing about the promised union between Miranda and Ferdinand, heir to the kingdom of Naples, he has ensured his own dynastic legacy.

In *Prospero's Daughter* the Prospero counterpart, Peter Gardner, is an eccentric doctor in England who flees to a small island in Trinidad in the early 1960s with his three-year-old daughter, Virginia. Gardner, the name adopted as a protective alias, was involved in dangerous practices with experimental medicines and the cloning of body parts, which led to a patient's death. He comes to the island Chacachacare as a fugitive, but he is also eager to continue his extreme experiments intended to improve human and non-human nature. Gardner quickly takes over the home owned by the orphaned teenager Carlos Codrington, the Caliban figure, left to him when his mother died; he then declares himself master over Carlos and the house servant Ariana, the Ariel counterpart, as well as Virginia. Gardner regularly sexually abuses Ariana but he also occasionally assaults his daughter, with the weak justification that he limits his behavior with Virginia to oral sex to protect her virginity. Although Carlos, whose father was a poet, is already literate, Gardner takes over his education as part of his "civilizing project." Gardner's agenda is to maintain the influence of the British Empire, imposing his notions of English supremacy on humans as well as on the local landscape.

Motivated by greed and to avoid further incestuous desire for his daughter, Gardner tries to marry Virginia to a wealthy American, but he learns that she and Carlos have fallen in love. Outraged at this impropriety, Gardner tortures Carlos and falsely accuses him of attempted rape. A British officer is ordered to investigate but Ariana, Carlos, and Virginia convince him that Gardner is lying and they expose his other crimes as well. Gardner commits suicide, Ariana is liberated, and Virginia and Carlos marry, their quest for independence paralleled by the larger Trinidadian resistance to the Empire.

The Tempest: Colonialism and control

"Providence divine" delivered Prospero and Miranda to the island that has been their sanctuary for twelve years. The island is life-saving but confining, as much by Prospero's tyrannical measures as by its geographical isolation and constraints. Since they arrived on the island when Miranda was only three years old, it is the only home she can recall and Prospero her only caretaker. Although Prospero assures Miranda, "I have done nothing but in care of thee" his treatment of her, particularly on display when he finally explains their history, is an exercise in authoritative control. In his long-winded exposition of their backstory, Prospero allows Miranda only a few questions and repeatedly admonishes her to be more attentive: "Dost thou attend me?," "Thou attend'st not!," "Dost thou hear?" (1.2. 77–105). Later, when Ferdinand and Miranda meet, Prospero again attempts to direct her actions, even though her immediate attraction to the young prince fits within his intended design of match-making their politically advantageous union. Ferdinand too is smitten, but Prospero, like the harshest of fairy tale fathers, decides the suitor must "obey" and prove his love for the princess through hard labor: "I'll manacle thy neck and feet together." When Miranda protests this severe trial, Prospero is furious: "Hang not on my garments! … One word more/ Shall make me chide thee, if not hate thee" (1.2. 477–480). Prospero's severe scolding reminds us that the narrow parameters of Miranda's life are not just spatial but psychological.

In defending his raising of Miranda, Prospero invokes his parental rights but also his role as her teacher. By his own account and others' validation, Prospero is, above all else, a scholar, even though becoming so "rapt in secret studies" led to his usurpation and banishment. He claims that once his "library was dukedom large enough" and is still immersed in intellectual pursuits, though after several years on the island he appears interested in returning to political power. But Prospero has expanded his scholarly reach from his own private studies to his teaching where he seems equally confident in his expertise, boasting to Miranda how "I, thy school-master, made thee more profit/ Than other princess' can, that have more time/ For vainer hours and tutors not so careful" (1.2. 172–175).

What, then, has been the effect of Miranda's homeschooling? In general, females in the Renaissance had less access to education, but there were still a number of progressive parents and guardians who invested in learned daughters, so the issue is not *that* Miranda has been educated but *how*. Has Prospero's teaching empowered her to be more autonomous or has it indoctrinated her to be an obedient deputy for the status quo? As Jessica Slights reminds us, for centuries Miranda was viewed as one of Shakespeare's more passive heroines, "an unwitting object of exchange in a matrix of colonial and nuptial economies ... [or] an archetype of pliant womanliness," but Slights counters that Miranda consistently challenges Prospero, thinks for herself, and makes her own decisions (360). Deanne Williams also argues that Miranda "complicates the narrative of the salvific 'cherubim' that Prospero wants to tell about her, and produces instead a sense of confidence that this pragmatic and realistic girl will be no one's victim when she returns to the mainland" (116). This view of the free-thinking Miranda is, however, further complicated by her extreme reprimand to the "abhorrèd slave" Caliban:

> I pitied thee,
> Took pains to make thee speak, taught thee each hour
> One thing or other. When thou didst not, savage,
> Know thine own meaning, but wouldst gabble like
> A thing most brutish, I endowed they purposes
> With words that made them known. But thy vile race,
> Though thou didst learn, had that in't which good natures
> Could not abide to be with; therefore wast thou
> Deservedly confined unto this rock
> Which hast deserved more than a prison.
>
> *(1.2. 358–366)*

Stephen Orgel has demonstrated how a history of textual and performance emendations considered this speech too severe and unladylike for Miranda and reassigned it to Prospero in a "persistent tendency to simplify and flatten" her character (17). But if the passage is properly reattributed to Miranda and demonstrates that she is nobody's fool, its references to Caliban's brutishness and savagery also show that

> to the extent that it reveals Miranda as Prospero's able pupil, perfectly parroting her father's colonialist ideology of racial difference, the speech may just as well, then, be from Prospero's mouth ... Miranda presents herself ... as schoolmaster, slave-owner, and prison-guard.
>
> *(Williams 109)*

Miranda creates a problem for contemporary audiences, perhaps as does Portia in *The Merchant of Venice*: we want a learned heroine as long as she is not a mouthpiece for an oppressive government. Miranda has also become a thorn in critical interpretations because the reason she is scolding Caliban is not for failing at his homework but for attempting to "violate her honor." If indeed Caliban tried to rape Miranda, our sympathy is then withdrawn from one victimized character for another. Melissa Sanchez argues that Caliban's "objectification of Miranda repeatedly casts doubt on his ability to rule any more moderately than Prospero, for he, like Prospero, dismisses her right to consent to the use of her body, the ultimate form of personal property." Sanchez adds that both men "behave equally tyrannically, and the similarity of these two contestants for the island and its lone female inhabitant bespeaks the difficulty of finding a single point of political or moral identification in the play" (64). Sanchez and other critics read Miranda's forward scolding of Caliban not as her channeling of Prospero but as her resistance to all men who would "sexually subjugate her"—her father and Ferdinand included.

While Miranda is a consensual party in her romance with Ferdinand, she also steps out of the boundaries of prescribed acquiescence; whether her boldness in their wooing comes from her own naiveté about conventional gender expectations or Prospero's tutelage, Miranda is assertive in their brief courtship. Such confidence is further evident in the final scene where she plays chess with Ferdinand:

MIRANDA: Sweet lord, you play me false.
FERDINAND: No, my dearest love
    I would not for the world.
MIRANDA: Yes, for a score of kingdoms you should wrangle,
    And I would call it fair play.

(5.1. 171–174)

These lines, so often overlooked amidst her wide-eyed "O brave new world!" exclamation, reveal Miranda's political savvy. Miranda appears to have absorbed some practical training from Prospero and may well realize that her father is using her as a pawn in this arranged marriage to support his return to government. She is not afraid to call out her beloved for cheating at chess, but more importantly she understands that just such intrigue may be called for in their future as king and queen. Gina Bloom argues that Shakespeare's use of chess—a game early modern audiences would have recognized as one of skillful maneuvering—to symbolize the union of Miranda and Ferdinand "opens up a critique of official state narratives of dynastic marriage" (420–421). As Orgel observes, Miranda and Ferdinand's marriage is not just a promise of heterosexual romance and reproduction, it is also a measure that prevents Antonio from succeeding him. If Miranda is married to Alonso's son, and Miranda is the heir to the dukedom, "Milan through marriage becomes part of the kingdom of Naples, not the other way around. Prospero recoups his throne from his brother only to deliver it over, upon his death, to the King of Naples once again." Miranda then becomes "a means of preserving his authority, not of relinquishing it" (63). Whether Miranda has become a canny young woman attuned to the precarious game of politics and her role in dynastic continuity or a passive agent serving her father's grand schemes continues to be a subject of debate. What is undeniable, however, is Prospero's certainty that she is his property to control.

Patriarchal and political dominance intersect in Prospero's treatment of Miranda, but Prospero's more egregious abuse of authority is his dealing with Caliban. At first their relationship is cooperative and mutually beneficial, if purely transactional. Prospero tells Miranda that they must tolerate Caliban because "He does make our fire/ Fetch in our wood, and serves in offices/ That profit us" (1.2. 314–316). Caliban also taught Prospero about the resources on the island necessary for survival and admitted that Prospero shared his own knowledge in return: "When thou cam'st first, Thou ... wouldst give me/ Water with berries in't, and teach me how/ To name the bigger light, and how the less/ That burn by day and night. And then I loved thee" (1.2. 335–339). In exchange for natural lore Prospero taught Caliban his language, though both the motivation and outcome of that transfer of knowledge are called into question with Caliban's outburst: "You taught me language, and my profit on't/ Is I know how to curse" (1.2. 366–367). Stephen Greenblatt's foundational essay, "Learning to Curse", points out that this clash between the alleged linguistic superiority of an educated Prospero and a presumed "mute and demonic" islander represents prevailing attitudes Europeans held towards unfamiliar—and in their view uncivilized—people. Colonizers adamantly disavowed the ability of indigenous people to possess their own literacy and culture, even though they were assumed capable of learning the colonizers' own language. Caliban "would gabble like a thing most brutish" so Prospero made it his mission to train him. As Tom Lindsay demonstrates, that training was not only linguistic: *The Tempest* is also "a drama about the working of Prospero's household and schoolroom, his 'cell.' Caliban entered that 'cell' as an apolitical subject committed to a non-hierarchical and egalitarian worldview, and he changed profoundly as a result of his experiences there" (400). That change resulted from coercion into "docility and deference," in contrast to the training for political rule that Miranda received. Caliban also absorbed an understanding of the insidious potential of knowledge. The lesson that has most impressed Caliban is that the one with access to learning can use it for purposes of dominance rather than altruism or communal advancement; when Caliban allies with Stephano and Trinculo he advises them that to overpower Prospero they must first "possess his books, for without them/ He's but a sot, as I am, nor hath not/ One spirit to command. They all do hate him/ As rootedly as I. Burn but his books ..." (3.2. 86–90).

Prospero's ostensibly benevolent teaching is predicated on his racist assumption of Caliban's innate inferiority: even though Prospero deemed Caliban as "savage" and "brutish," he hopes that his civilizing measures will overcome Caliban's supposed natural deficiencies. How we are meant to understand Caliban's otherness is the subject of extensive critical scholarship: Caliban has been variously claimed as African, Afro-Caribbean, Irish, and indigenous American, and in performances he has been depicted in a range of hybrid animal/human or monstrous guises (Lupton, Vaughan and Vaughan). Common to these multiple possibilities is the claim that the play's representation of Caliban—Prospero's "thing of darkness," Stephano's "savage(s) and men of Ind(ia)"—is racialized even if Shakespeare's description is racially indeterminate. Edward Kamau Brathwaite, Jerry Brotton, Paul Brown, Dympna Callaghan, Kim Hall, George Lamming, Ania Loomba, and Martin Orkin are but a few of the scholars who have made significant contributions to the discussion of Caliban's racial profile, as well as to the play's geographical cruxes. But while individual audiences, critics, and directors may lean heavily towards one identification over another, it is generally understood that Caliban can "occupy multiple sites of difference" (Hall 151) and that the play can accommodate various articulations of otherness. Most scholars agree that the play ultimately establishes Prospero and Caliban in a relationship that rests on Manichean binaries—light/dark, master/servant, civilized/savage, educated/illiterate, usurper/usurped—that are then repeatedly complicated and destabilized.

If Caliban's otherness is racialized but unspecified, geographic precision is also elusive. *The Tempest* names several actual but contradictory points on the map: Caliban's mother Sycorax is from Algiers and the entourage from Italy is traveling back from nearby Tunis, both of which suggest northern African associations. But the play also alludes to expansion in the Americas with Stephano's comment about "dead Indians" being kidnapped for display in England and references to English colonist William Strachey's letter about the Virginia Company's shipwreck near the Bermuda islands in 1609. In spite of Shakespeare's occasional carelessness in matters of geography, these seemingly inconsistent markers can coalesce to encompass the various ways Shakespeare's contemporary and future audiences could understand the strangeness of unfamiliar worlds.

Much of Prospero's antipathy to Caliban is a result of a presence beyond Caliban's control: the specter of his dead mother Sycorax. For a character who is not even present during the play and who is shrouded in mystery, Sycorax exercises considerable influence over how Prospero, Caliban, and Ariel understand their positions on the island. What little we know about her presumably comes to Prospero via Ariel and Caliban, though he seems compelled to repeat back to them the darkest parts of her backstory:

> This damned witch Sycorax,
> For mischiefs manifold and sorceries terrible
> To enter human bearing, from Algiers,
> Thou know'st, was banished. For one thing she did
> They would not take her life ...
> This blue-eyed hag was hither brought with child
> And here was left by sailors.
>
> *(1.2. 263–270)*

This mediated information calls the reliability of Prospero's narration into question, but if his account is accurate, we know that Sycorax was seen as a witch with powers magical and sinister enough that they were punishable by death. "For one thing she did," however, she was exiled instead of killed. The nature of her act is not named, but the immediate reference to her being "with child" suggests that pregnancy was both her crime and her means of avoiding death. It is possible that Sycorax deliberately became pregnant to postpone or escape execution, a strategy known as "pleading pregnancy" used by some female convicts in early modern England, though some of them may have already been pregnant or have been the victims of rape (Levin 25–26).

The ambiguity surrounding Sycorax's reproductive history is matched by the multiple gendered and racialized ways Prospero describes her as a threat. If her arrival on the island was marked by her sexual transgression, the child she delivered is also described in aberrant terms: "the son that she did litter here/ A freckled whelp, hag-born—not honored with a human shape" (1.2. 283–285). But if Sycorax's deviant sexuality produces Caliban's assumed monstrosity, her status as an agèd hag is also frequently invoked. In language right out of the discourse of early modern witchcraft, Prospero refers to Sycorax as old, deformed, grotesque: "The foul witch Sycorax, who with age and envy/ Was grown into a hoop" (1.2. 258–259). Though her span on the island is not stated, if Caliban was born there and is now a young man, Sycorax would have arrived as a younger woman who aged during their time on the island—and Prospero finds both states of womanhood vile.

Sycorax's female monstrosity is related to her racial descriptors, which, like Caliban's, are somewhat nebulous, though we are told that she is from Algiers. Rachana Sachdev describes the overwhelmingly negative portrait Englanders had of Algeria due to disputes over piracy and trade; she argues that "Sycorax's ugly and deformed body can be seen as the quintessential representative of the moral and religious corruption associated with the land, and provides visual contrast between the 'civil' Europeans and the 'barbaric' Algerians" (238). But added to Sycorax's north African affiliation is Prospero's reference to her as "blue-eyed," a description that complicates conventional notions of African physiognomy and racial stereotypes. Leah Marcus explains how vexing the "blue-eyed hag" has been to decades of textual scholars: some editors insist that the First Folio mistakenly printed "blew-eyed" instead of "blear-eyed," others maintain that the reference is to bluish eyelid coloration from pregnancy, while others have advanced a "black and blue" face in keeping with her assumed ugliness. Any of these alternative explanations is possible, but as Marcus points out, most editors and critics have rejected any possibility that blue eyes can mean just that; instead, they gloss the phrase "in a way that cancels out its potential for disrupting the self/other binary that has characterized most readings of the play" (6). Like her blue eyes, Sycorax's worship of Setebos, an Amerindian god, also precludes clear racial identity and geographic origin (Gillies 197).

Indeed, as much as Prospero's worldview is based on strict gendered and racialized categories, these circumscribed identities and boundaries repeatedly prove slippery. For example, Prospero positions himself in clear contrast with Sycorax, but the similarities between the two are striking: both are exiled on the island over which they then claimed sovereignty, both are single parents of one child, both use imprisoning tactics to maintain power, and both employ magical arts. While Sycorax's sorcery is often seen as a darker version of magic than that which Prospero exercises, there is certainly nothing benign in Prospero's manipulation of Caliban, Miranda, and Ariel, and later the Italian entourage. And as much as Prospero contrasts the legitimate conception of Miranda ("thy mother was a piece of virtue") with Sycorax's alleged criminal coupling with the devil, the fact that both Miranda's mother and Caliban's father are erased from the stage draws further similarities between Prospero and his nemesis.

Beyond reinforcing his own hierarchical worldview, why does Prospero need to so urgently denounce Sycorax who, long dead, poses no tangible threat? Because Prospero, who sees himself as a benevolent ruler in contrast to the malevolent Sycorax, seeks to justify his theft of Caliban's home. Caliban reminds Prospero,

"This island's mine, by Sycorax my mother,/ Which thou tak'st from me" and he curses him, in the name of his mother, for his authoritarian takeover:

> All the charms
> Of Sycorax, toads, beetles, bats, light on you!
> For I am all the subjects that you have,
> Which first was mine own king; and here you sty me
> In this hard rock, whiles you do keep from me
> The rest o'th'island.
>
> *(1.2. 342–347)*

Like all effective tyrants, Prospero reverses the blame and insists that it was Caliban's attempted violation of Miranda that forced him to be punitive: "I have used thee,/ Filth as thou art, with humane care, and lodged thee/ In mine own cell, till thou didst seek to violate/ The honor of my child" (1.2. 348–351). Not only does Prospero question Sycorax's claim to the island, but in his vengeful mind, Caliban attempted to steal his property—Miranda—so he is justified in taking Caliban's property, equating a body of land with the body of his daughter. Caliban does not deny his attempted attack on Miranda: "Would't had been done!/ Thou didst prevent me; I had peopled else/ This isle with Calibans," a response that strikes at Prospero's worst fears of interracial mixing. Not only was Prospero repulsed by Sycorax's possible intercultural identity and delivery of Caliban, but the play also reveals an anxiety about interracial coupling in its references to the union between Dido, an African queen, and Aeneas, founder of Rome, as well as the marriage of Alonso's daughter Claribel to the King of Tunis. Kim Hall demonstrates that the fear of miscegenation was ubiquitous in early modern literature and culture—a fear also at the center of *Othello*—and argues,

> Caliban's threat "to people the isle" with his offspring clearly suggests that he would control the island by creating a new "mixed" race and rebuts Prospero on his own terms. Territorial claims are backed here by a need of patriarchal control over women.
>
> *(143)*

While it is easy enough to find fault with Prospero's dehumanizing handling of Caliban, it is difficult to justify Caliban's assault on Miranda, since his advances appear unsolicited and unwanted. Some critics have suggested that given Prospero's unreliability as an objective narrator, perhaps the event never occurred, but both Miranda and Caliban corroborate the charge. These wishful attempts to erase the act can promote the binary view that underscores so many readings of the play: if Prospero is cruel and abusive, Caliban is therefore a guiltless and sympathetic victim. But as we have seen, the play repeatedly challenges clear oppositional paradigms. As Jessica Slights claims,

Understanding Caliban as a moral agent, which entails acknowledging that he
is wrong to try to rape Miranda, does not logically (and certainly not ethically)
require either that we justify his enslavement or that we deny Miranda the
right to freedom from violence.

(375)

Nonetheless, without rationalizing Caliban's behavior, we can put it next to the
parallel dynastic goals that permeate the play. What Slights refers to as Caliban's
"obsession with lineage" and "fixation with dynasty" (372) is even more evident in
Ferdinand's greeting upon first seeing Miranda: "O, if a virgin,/ And your affection
not gone forth, I'll make you/ The queen of Naples (1.2. 450–452). While Ferdinand is represented as the desirable and proper suitor to Miranda in contrast to
Caliban's savage lawlessness, many critics have noted their similarities. Not only do
they share dynastic ambitions, but when Prospero cautions Ferdinand against violating Miranda's "virgin knot," Ferdinand's protestations that his honor "shall never
melt … into lust," suggest that his own repressed fantasies of rape or even pre-
marital sex are only checked by the fear of delegitimizing their royal union and
progeny (Kunat 310). Caliban's desire for Miranda is non-consensual and, thus,
inexcusable, but it cannot be divorced from the way Prospero and Ferdinand also
view her as primarily a vessel of reproduction.

Caliban continues to be represented as an indeterminate object capable of both
rebellion and subservience. Prospero repeatedly reminds Caliban of his status as
"slave"; he only releases him from his cell to perform hard labor; and he tracks and
enforces his behavior with "pinches" and "lashes"—"euphemisms of state torture, not
benign comforts from fairy literature" (Doty 245). Caliban has so internalized his
abject status that when he meets Stephano and Trinculo, he first imagines replacing
one state of submissiveness with another: "I'll kiss thy foot. I'll swear myself thy subject." Caliban seems to find comfort that he "has a new master," but he also begins
singing about his "Freedom, highday, freedom," and plotting rebellion against Prospero. Stephano and Trinculo also find it difficult to pinpoint Caliban, referring to him
both in such otherworldly terms as "devil," "mooncalf," "monster," and "spirit," and
yet likening him to more earthly analogues, something between "a man or a fish" or a
"dead Indian." That Caliban obdurately remains both amorphous and the categorical
"other" is epitomized in Prospero's infamous claiming of Caliban in the play's finale,
"This thing of darkness, I acknowledge mine." Caliban is still the racialized "dark"
other but he is also a dehumanized and vaguely defined "thing"—recalling the word
used for Sycorax's crime as "one thing she did"—and thus, exactly how Caliban will
be incorporated into Prospero's future cultural and political frameworks remains
uncertain.

Finally, we cannot separate Prospero's command over Caliban and Miranda from
his larger appropriation of the island and the natural world. Ecocritical approaches to
Shakespeare, and in literary studies in general, have emerged in the last few decades
with a particular urgency aimed at interrogating the exploitative encounters between
the human and non-human worlds, a subject explored more fully in our discussion

of *Station Eleven* (Chapter 6). The largely outdoor location of *The Tempest* as a small island surrounded by powerful seas has made the play especially open to environmental analyses, and scholars have examined the climactic disturbance of the opening storm, the reiteration of animal metaphors, and the preoccupation with transmutation. Particularly notable is Gabriel Egan's reading of the play in terms of arboreal imagery and forest devastation. Egan argues that "Prospero's main activity since his arrival on the island has been its deforestation" and that early modern audiences would have understood the obsession with the "axeing of trees" to be a sign of colonization (155–156). The colonial endeavor in Ireland was especially known to involve the clearing of vast forests to harvest wood for building and to appropriate lands for agriculture and profit. Since Prospero showed no signs that the gathering of wood was to build a ship preparatory to departure, his clear-cutting activity seemed directed towards inhabiting and reshaping the island to serve his exploitative purposes.

Prospero's appropriation of the land, as Simon Estok and others have shown, is inseparable from his simultaneous appropriation of Caliban: "Part of the problem for Caliban is that he is part of the exotica that defines the landscape of the imperialist gaze. The play is a showcase of exotica … a wild land ready for taking and taming … It is also a space whose Otherness, difference, exoticism, and promise of wealth make it very fertile ground for the seeds of colonialist ambitions and fantasy" with which Caliban is associated (104). While the island is filled with the wondrous attractions that Caliban lyrically praises, the natural world is also depicted as dangerous and unruly, and Prospero aims to control it as much as he does its inhabitants.

In our focus on Prospero's dominance over Miranda and Caliban and the island they occupy, little attention has been given to the spirit Ariel, Prospero's third subject, for Ariel is largely the focus of the next chapter. But in keeping with our examination of Prospero's abusive authority, the power he wields over Ariel must also be acknowledged. Sycorax had imprisoned the spirit in a pine for refusing "to act her earthy and abhorred commands," and Prospero repeatedly reminds Ariel that "it was mine art … that let thee out" (1.2. 275–293). But in spite of Ariel's indebtedness, Prospero's ability to manipulate Ariel is limited, for like Sycorax, he needs the spirit to execute his own "commands." Prospero and Ariel negotiated a finite term of service and Ariel repeatedly reminds Prospero that his obeisance is conditioned on his eventual freedom.

Ariel does attain his freedom in the final scene, but it is a finale that rests on uncertain resolutions. Prospero seems ever in charge as he brings the various constituents together and forces their confessions or cooperation. Gonzalo weeps, Alonso apologizes for assisting with Prospero's former overthrow and offers restitution, and Sebastian and Antonio are silenced by Prospero's threat that he will reveal the conspiracy they were planning against Alonso if they resume their old tricks. Prospero's drowning of his books, his return to political life, and the security provided by Miranda's marriage have been seen as providing a peaceful and satisfying closure to a play that was poised to end more tragically. But as many critics have pointed out, Prospero's ability to so quickly quell political dissent is not assured (Brown 48; Barker and Hulme 203–204). Ariel is thrilled with his liberty and takes off without a backward glance, Caliban apologizes but there is no guarantee that he will remain obedient, and Miranda has done her part in falling in love with Ferdinand but seems cannily aware of how she is being used. Prospero's success in reclaiming his former state is not a given, for the coercive tactics he employed on the island may not transfer to a "brave new world."

Prospero's Daughter: Colonialism and freedom

Prospero's Daughter begins with this acknowledgement: "My gratitude to Shakespeare for attributing some of his most lyrical lines to Caliban." In numerous interviews, Elizabeth Nunez has discussed her longstanding engagement with Shakespeare in her scholarly and creative writing. In her memoir, *Not For Everyday Use*, she claims, "Shakespeare never ceases to teach me about our human condition, our triumphs and our flaws" and, on the more practical level of craft, she credits his work for providing models of characterization, literary language, and narrative pacing (122). Nunez explains that in the British influence on her education in Trinidad and in her immediate family, Shakespeare was omnipresent: her father often quoted lines from the plays and her grandmother hosted a literary salon where the plays were a topic of conversation alongside the works of Caribbean artists. In addition to *Prospero's Daughter*, Nunez's other work is layered with references to Shakespeare and in 2016 she published a second full-length adaptation, *Even in Paradise*, a novel based on *King Lear* and also set in the Caribbean.

Nunez's recognition of Shakespeare's influence should not, however, be read as unconditional reverence. Like all of the authors in this study, her appreciation for his work does not preclude revision and talking back in light of contemporary political and social imperatives—especially *The Tempest*, which she acknowledges as the one play that most "stirs up controversy among Caribbean writers, if not outright anger ... For many, this play epitomizes the evils of colonialism." She then cites George Lamming and Aimé Césaire as influential works that preceded hers, as well as a short story, "The Parrot and Descartes," by Guyanese writer Pauline Melville (Nunez Goodreads).

But if Nunez's retelling of *The Tempest* firmly situates itself in the company of male-authored post-colonial adaptations, her novel is also a departure. In her discussion of Caribbean adaptations of *The Tempest*, Ania Loomba suggests that prominent male writers, including Césaire and Lamming, do "not consider a female anti-colonial subject and her possible interactions with the play; indeed *The Tempest* is notoriously difficult to appropriate from a feminist perspective" (164). However, while it is true that *The Tempest* is the only one of Shakespeare's works that lists just one female in its cast of characters, many scholars and writers are not willing to cede to claims of a male-centered play. In *The Tempest*, numerous other women are invoked if not visible—not only Claribel and Sycorax, but Miranda's mother; Prospero and Antonio's mother; Dido, Queen of Carthage; and the goddesses of the wedding masque.

Nonetheless, several scholars have addressed the neglect of the female perspective in *The Tempest* and its offspring. Jyotsna Singh also discusses Césaire and Lamming as exemplifying a tendency among anti-colonial appropriations to simply reverse the roles of oppressor and oppressed that still ignore the role of women and do "little to question the inevitability of hierarchical structures." Singh argues that "what these writers do not acknowledge is that their focus on Caliban ... often posits a utopia in which women are marginalized or missing" (209). Irene Lara also argues that the emphasis on the Prospero–Caliban dyad in post-colonial readings and adaptations has minimized and even erased women, particularly Sycorax: "From a colonial and patriarchal perspective, the dark, markedly feminine, spirituality of Sycorax within and outside one's self engenders too much fear and, thus, loathing" (94).

However, in her study, *Tempests After Shakespeare*, Chantal Zabus highlights the various creative works by women—what she calls "Caribbean increments to Miranda's story"—that instead "downplay the place of men" and redirect narrative attention to the female characters (127). These include the novels *Annie John* (1983) by Antiguan-American author Jamaica Kincaid and *No Telephone to Heaven* (1987) by Jamaican-American author Michelle Cliff, as well as Marina Warner's *Indigo* (1992); Warner is British but her work repositions Ariel and Sycorax at the novel's center and insists that the British Empire reckon with its damaging presence in the Caribbean.

An even more explicit adaptation of *The Tempest*, *Prospero's Daughter* follows these works by women writers in ascribing greater value to the female roles, particularly Virginia, the Miranda figure, but also Ariel whose counterpart in the novel, Ariana, is a young Caribbean woman, and the ghost of Sycorax, Sylvia. Nunez fully confronts the power dynamic between Prospero and Caliban while centering the women as agents of cooperation and change. Second, *Prospero's Daughter* focuses on the overlap between masculine control of female sexuality and an entitled exploitation of the natural world; in her emphasis on the environmental damage wrought by the colonialist mindset, Nunez brings to the forefront currents in *The Tempest* that have not been fully considered in previous adaptations. Finally, Nunez disrupts the fatalistic framework of the oppressor and oppressed with alternative trajectories for Virginia, Carlos, and Ariana, and an evolving mindset for John Mumsford, the British officer charged with investigating Gardner's accusations of rape. Nunez's challenge to the binary paradigms that have dominated discourse around the play and its afterlives is evident in the novel's structure: while it is largely chronological, it comprises three chapters from different perspectives, allowing Carlos and Virginia to offer their versions to counter Gardner's hegemonic narrative.

The protagonist, Dr. Peter Gardner, is not a total caricature of evil, but he elicits scant sympathy. He and his brother Paul grew up as fierce rivals for their parents' love and later, both doctors, they competed for professional acclaim. Their father had been left a quadriplegic from combat in World War 2 and Peter vowed to "grow new arms and legs for him in the laboratory," but his radical medical research becomes increasingly obsessive amidst his egotistical and careless ambitions. His beloved wife was seen as a humanizing influence but when she died three years after giving birth to their daughter he "was his old self again … he became, in all his human interactions, cold and distant" (86). After his clandestine use of experimental medicines led to a patient's death and threatened criminal investigations, Paul helped him find refuge on Chacachacare, eager to rid himself of his brother and the related scandal and take control of his inheritance. Peter's ill treatment from Paul and the loss of his wife garner some pity, but once he arrives in Trinidad his cruel practices and extreme nationalism are fully unleashed.

On the island Gardner learns of the home inhabited by the teenaged Carlos Codrington, the housekeeper Luciana, and her daughter Ariana. Carlos' innocent father was violently killed by drug dealers and his mother Sylvia died of grief soon after, leaving her young son in the care of Luciana with sufficient money and her home for their support. But Luciana is dying of cancer when Gardner arrives years later, so he promises to provide her medical care and make improvements on the property wrecked by recent storms in exchange for room and board. Once Luciana dies, he assumes ownership of the house and the money left to Carlos and his authoritarianism quickly manifests in his treatment of Virginia, Ariana, Carlos, and the surrounding property. In a throwback to the height of the British Empire, he refurnishes the house in Victorian décor entirely unsuited for the climate and he attacks the natural landscape, all in the name of promoting what he insists are superior British ways.

Gardner's paternal control over Virginia parallels Prospero's over Miranda, but it is portrayed even more blatantly in his strict surveillance, his abusive teaching, and his arrangement of her marriage without her consent. He confines her to her room most of the time, only allowing her brief walks when he accompanies her; Virginia grows up to love Chacachacare, but she has never been allowed to leave their small island. Gardner boasts that he does not send his "English rose" to school because he is such a superb teacher and because lascivious school boys could endanger her virtue. In fact, Gardner is the real threat in both areas: during their lessons Gardner is a harsh taskmaster so Carlos secretly helps Virginia overcome her fear and teaches her to read. When Virginia turned twelve, her father "announced that Virginia had learned all that was necessary for a woman to learn. Anything more would make her unmarketable" (183). Perhaps it is not surprising that Gardner fails as Virginia's tutor since he views her worth as transaction in strictly monetary and proprietary terms. Even worse, it is Gardner, not adolescent boys, who endangers her chastity: Gardner sexually abuses her but refrains from intercourse so as to preserve the virginity that he so values. But by the novel's end, Virginia is not the passive daughter he desires: if Miranda's seeming compliance in *The Tempest* belied a stronger, more confident young woman, so too Virginia's quiet reserve contains a strong, ethical refusal to accept her father's control over her body, her mind, and her future.

Resistance eventually comes as well from Ariana, the house servant. Perhaps even more than Miranda and Caliban, *The Tempest*'s Ariel has defied strict categorization—an airy spirit with human characteristics, a servant in bondage but partially liberated, and, as Kirilka Stavreva points out, "central to Ariel's character, of course, is its elusive gender." Prospero refers once to Ariel with the male pronoun but other references signal female stereotypes: "dainty," "delicate," "my chick." Since "a gender of some sort must be assigned to Ariel," Stavreva explains, this ambiguity poses "productive challenges to actors and directors," and it also offers various possibilities for writers adapting the play (104). Nunez's choice to represent Ariel as a teenaged girl who recently lost her mother heightens her fragility and vulnerability. When John Mumsford, the British functionary on the island called upon to investigate Gardener's accusations of rape first sees her, he thinks: "*Ethereal.* That was the word he was searching for, yet it was a word that was inconsonant with her deep brown skin, her black wavy hair ... but not with her slight frame, her small bones ..." (41). But Nunez also portrays her racial identity as inconclusive and troubling to Mumsford who frets over whether she is Indian or African, finally deciding that she was "doogla ... the name the native people gave to such mixtures" (41). After her mother Luciana dies, Gardner coerces Ariana into sexual servitude; he justifies his daily violations as a means of protecting him from his incestuous desire for Virginia but entirely dismisses the trauma he is inflicting upon Ariana. Gardner is also an exacting household master, assigning all of the domestic chores to Ariana and insisting that she cook only British food. Gardner learned that when Ariana was a young girl she had taken some diamond earrings from Carlos's mother, and he threatens to report this childhood transgression to the police if she does not comply with his every wish. Ariana is outwardly obedient but her hatred for Gardner finally prompts her to report his behavior to the authorities and defend Carlos when he is wrongly accused.

Gardner does not attempt to hide his cruel treatment of Carlos, an islander whose assumed inferiority is deemed even more outrageous because his mixed background defies Gardner's strict racial taxonomies: Carlos's father was Afro-Caribbean and his "white" mother, Sylvia Codrington, was British. At first, Inspector Mumsford echoes Gardner's revulsion over racial mixing; when he hears the hybrid name of the accused, Mumsford complains, "Charles Codrington would have made perfect English sense; Carlos Rodriguez would have been logical. But Carlos Codrington?" (12). Mumsford finds everything about the island repellent—the food, the weather, the flora and fauna, the relaxed lifestyle—and is eager to return to England: "He for one, would not be sad to see independence come. Let them have the whole damn place, damn insects and all, damn miserable, stifling weather, damn mixing of bloods. Bloody impurities" (15). Mumsford reluctantly acknowledges that many of the Amerindian and African islanders contain the "European blood" of their conquerors and he finds this appalling.

Dr. Gardner embodies an even more extreme version of Mumsford's racial paranoia. When Mumsford arrives to investigate the alleged rape, Gardner is obsessed with complaining about Carlos's mother Sylvia, even though she died several years before Gardner and Virginia came to Chacachacare. Gardner tells Mumsford that Sylvia, a spoiled, rich, white woman who grew up in Algiers, where her British parents owned a profitable rug business, ran away from home with her money and jewels. She went on a cruise and ended up on the island where, Gardner insists, she was sexually promiscuous with multiple black men: "She screwed them all on the island" and "birthed a misshapen bastard … because of his father's black blood" (54). Carlos's more reliable account contradicts Gardner's. Sylvia left because her parents thought Sylvia's love of Algiers and the local culture and people inappropriate, and when she nearly drowned in a swimming accident while on the cruise, it was Carlos's father, a fisherman, who saved her. They fell in love and built their home on Chacachacare where Carlos was born and where they lived happily until the tragic murder of Carlos's father. What most infuriates Gardner, who has fabricated his own version of Sylvia's backstory, is that she chose to control her own emotional and sexual life with a man of color: "a slut he called her, for lying down with a black man" (116). After Luciana dies, one of Gardner's first acts is to force Carlos to witness a ritualistic burning of Sylvia's bed, a transparently symbolic gesture intended to indict her sexual autonomy and eradicate her presence as he declares "Nothing in here belongs to her now. All is mine. I am lord of it all" (117).

Thus, just as Prospero's vilification of Sycorax is transferred to Caliban, Gardner's hatred of Carlos originates with his outrage over what he sees as Sylvia's sins: he is shocked that she would "want to change the nature of her own child … giving him African blood" (160). Carlos is the living embodiment of Sylvia's crime of miscegenation: "Carlos has freckles and the skin color of a colored man but … the facial features of many an Englishman … broad brow, thin lips, a wide, substantial chin, blue eyes undoubtedly inherited by his mother" (64). Carlos's mixed racial identity so offends Gardner that he forces him to do hard physical labor to confirm his lower role in their social hierarchy. When he discovers that Carlos is literate and that he has been teaching Virginia to read, he is embarrassed and furious that his assumptions about the young boy have been disproven. But Gardner soon turns the occasion into another opportunity for appropriation, viewing Carlos as yet another subject for his experimentation. Gardner vows to teach him to read and speak like an Englishman and he takes credit for Carlos's learning.

Carlos tells us otherwise. His literacy came from his parents—his father was a poet and his mother was an enthusiastic reader and owner of a beloved collection of books. Carlos was reading and writing his own poetry before Gardner arrived on the island. But Gardner is invested in believing that Carlos's lack of intelligence is a gap only he can correct. He begins tutoring Carlos and his lectures begin with a defense of the British Empire, as Gardner tells Carlos about

> the right of his people, their manifest destiny, to rule the world … he jabbed at spots on the map: India, China, Africa, the lands of the Turks and the Arabs, islands and continents spread apart by the great seas and oceans. His people had brought civilization everywhere, he said. "Without us, these places you see would have nothing."
>
> *(162)*

Carlos recognizes the colonialist and racist ideology that informs all of Gardner's lessons:

The European colonists had set the rules. They had discovered that they could use gradations of skin color to replicate a class system ... Gardner believed in the absurd notion of race, the classification of Homo sapiens based on skin color, hair texture, bone structure. He believed my father's black skin determined his nature, "his race," and so made him a different kind of man, a subcategory of Homo sapiens.

(160)

When Carlos proves to be a quick and eager learner, Gardner congratulates himself on his ability to impart knowledge to a "wild, savage creature" and occasionally praises his student, even as he remains the strict master. Carlos comes to love the rigorous lessons Gardner gives him in astronomy, biology, chemistry, music, and Shakespeare, even as he knew the education "was British, it was European," for Gardner is entirely dismissive of any history or advances to civilization of "Africa ... or the Amerindians who originally populated the islands" (159–160). As Elizabeth Rivlin points out,

> Nunez resists the stultifying effects of a traditional colonial education featuring Shakespeare but recuperates its value for colonized subjects. Crucially, though Carlos eventually rejects Peter Gardner, he does not reject colonial education as a cornerstone of his identity. In his expressions of appreciation, Carlos serves as a mouthpiece for Nunez, who has said, "I love classical music. I love John Keats. I love Shakespeare. I love it all."
>
> *(23)*

But if Carlos admits his gratitude for what he has learned, especially his love of British literature, he is also a poet in his own right, paralleling Caliban's singular lyricism. From Samuel Coleridge on, many critics have noted that Caliban's language is among the most evocative in all of Shakespeare, a seeming incongruence with his alleged savagery and yet more evidence of the play's complication of categorical assumptions. In his study of Caliban's various representations, Bill Ashcroft suggests that Caliban's facility with language may serve another purpose as well; he asks why it is "that Caliban is given some of the most beautiful lines of the play? Could it be that the radical difference of Caliban and Prospero is seated in a kind of sameness, the similarity of their engagement with language?" Ashcroft compares Prospero and Caliban's similarly eloquent utterances and their invocation of magic and curses, and suggests that Caliban's language "may be a premonition of his transformative agency in the future" (31). Certainly, Carlos is successful when he has the opportunity to use his language to defend himself and convince Mumsford of the truth about Gardner's behavior, and he will continue to use his poetic gifts in the future.

Gardner's brutal treatment of Carlos is inseparable from his abuse of Carlos's home and property. Before Gardner installs air conditioning in his portion of the house and renovates it with British interior decoration, he attacks the landscape. The deforestation prominent in *The Tempest* is enacted even more brazenly here when Gardner decides to chop down all of the nearby trees. Gardner paid a fisherman to help him, and as Carlos explains,

> When they were done, not a single one of the trees my father had planted was left standing: not the coconut tree, the breadfruit tree, the chataigne tree, or the avocado tree, and not one of the fruit trees, neither the plum, orange, grapefruit, sapodilla, soursop nor the two mango trees that were in our yard.
>
> *(111)*

Gardner argues that the destruction is necessary because the native plants and trees do not provide food, they breed disease, and they are aesthetically intrusive and unpleasant. These false claims contrast with Carlos's love of his outdoor world, inherited from his father who always reminded "us that the island where we lived belonged first to the flora and fauna we found here" (113). But Gardner insists that "only primitive man accepts life the way Nature has presented it to him ... civilized man uses his brain to make his world better" (149). Like his approach to humans, Gardner views the non-human world as subject to his control, so after destroying the local plants, Gardner sets out to raise his own, creating an artificially watered lawn in a surreal plasticized green, and growing a variety of garish "flowers that won't wilt in the sun, plants that will live forever" (150). The irony is that the very "cross-breeding" that Gardner objects to so strenuously in human relationships is precisely what he is propagating in horticulture. Gardner seems unaware of this contradiction when he tells Mumsford that Carlos was particularly skilled at helping him with his prize orchids: "He learned quickly about crossbreeding, cross-pollination. He was a bastard ... a crossbreed himself" (57).

Given Gardner's violation of the land, his sexual abuse of his daughter and of Ariana, and his emotional and physical abuse of Carlos, it is hypocritical that he falsely accuses Carlos of rape. The degree to which rape is considered a crime on the island depends on the victim and the perpetrator: Mumsford refers to it as a "soft crime" unless the victim is a white woman, and then it was "the nightmare of any red-blooded Englishman who had brought wife, daughters, sisters to these dark colonies" because it was unthinkable that "the purity of an English woman, that her unblemished flower, had been desecrated by a black man" (7). But the only sexual predator is Gardner himself, as we learn from Carlos, Virginia, and Ariana.

Carlos recounts Gardner's increasing callousness towards him and Ariana, then the emotional abuse inflicted on Virginia. By the time they are teenagers, the friendship between Virginia and Carlos has deepened into a trusting love; they acknowledge the external impediments to their relationship but are determined to face them honestly: "Their dialogue always pushes through the recognition and resolution of their ethnic differences to achieve spiritual and ethical choices in their relationship" (Creque-Harris 31). When Gardner decides to arrange Virginia's marriage to a wealthy American, Carlos confesses to Gardner his own love for her and their intention to marry. Carlos tries to persuade Gardner by turning his practice of cross-pollination back on him, but Gardner insists, "There can be no improvement of the white race from a marriage with the black race." *The Tempest* is one of the many works Gardner and Carlos have read together, familiar enough that Carlos refers to Gardner as Prospero, so when he screams, "You filthy bastard. You vile savage, you born devil ... I will kill you. I will kill you if you even try," Carlos bursts out, "Thou didst prevent me; I had peopled else/ This isle with Calibans" (216). Gardner is so furious that he drugs Carlos, tortures him, and pens him in a cage under the hot sun. He then calls the authorities to take Carlos to jail and sends Virginia to the chaperonage of another British woman until her marriage can be safely arranged. When Inspector Mumsford arrives to investigate he expects to side with Gardner, but he is dismayed at how Carlos has been treated. His doubts about Gardner are heightened when he suspects his sexual relationship with Ariana, who then comes forward to testify to Gardner's abusive behavior and his lies about Carlos and Virginia. Mumsford takes Carlos to a monastery instead of jail until he can gather further corroboration from Virginia.

Virginia's story in the final section of the novel, much of which comprises her interview with Mumsford, complements the narratives of Ariana and Carlos and reiterates Gardner's abuse of all three of them. She explains that throughout her entire life Gardner has psychologically manipulated her. He has lied about their past lives, he convinces her she is unworthy of education, he belittles the Caribbean and its people, and he repeatedly insists on England's greatness:

> But these stories never took root in my imagination. No matter how often he tried to convince me I belonged to the world he described of castles and manor houses, or lords and ladies—*civilized gentry*—a world ... that had conquered continents, I felt removed from it, distant, a stranger, an alien to the people and places he said were mine.
>
> *(244)*

Virginia loves Chacachacare and its people, especially Carlos. She not only confirms Carlos's innocence, but in spite of Mumsford's disbelief, she proudly acknowledges her love for him.

Together, Mumsford, Virginia, and Carlos return to confront Gardner and ask him to recant his fabricated charge of rape. When they arrive at their home, Gardner is not there but Carlos suspects that he is at the lighthouse where he has been practicing his scientific experiments during tempestuous weather. When they find him, Gardner is furious at their accusations and "stunned that the inspector had sided with a brown man against him." He and Carlos fight. Virginia intervenes, and Gardner asks Virginia for forgiveness, but she says he must first admit his crimes. Gardner refuses to apologize to Virginia or Carlos or confess to Inspector Mumsford that the rape did not occur, and when he senses that he is no longer in control, he suddenly hurls himself off the cliff in a dramatic suicidal performance.

Virginia is left to reckon with her ambiguous feelings for her father: she still felt a daughter's devotion, but she also comes to understand that "He had no remorse for what he had done to Carlos or what he had done to Ariana," and later she is told that he fled England years ago not to protect her, but himself: "After I learned this, nothing was left in my heart for my father, neither pity or sorrow nor anger" (304–305). Carlos and Virginia marry; he renovates a boat and builds a business ferrying tourists around the islands, and in his spare time he writes poetry, like his father. The house returns to Carlos; he and Virginia replant the native fruit trees and restore the carvings on the walls from his parents' original design. As the novel closes, Virginia is several months pregnant with their child and she finally confesses to him her last secret, of her father's sexual abuse, and he responds with compassionate understanding. Their personal liberation is mirrored by changes in the larger political landscape: "Independence was on the horizon, politics in the favor of people born here. Englishmen were returning home. By the following year they would lose another colony" (306).

Years later when Virginia reflects on her father's oppressive ideology and behavior, it is not *The Tempest* that she thinks of, but *Othello*, the play in which Shakespeare dared to tell a "story about a white woman in love with a Moor." Carlos had told her about Queen Elizabeth I's expulsion of "Negroes and blackamoors" from England and Virginia suspects that this edict was not about the claim that Englanders were losing their jobs to immigrants, but because of "the fear of too many English men and women marrying Africans." But Virginia is optimistic that progress is possible, citing her marriage to Carlos, Ariana's courageous revelations to the police about Gardner and her decision to become a police officer herself, and finally Inspector Mumsford, who begins to question his colonial assumptions and admits, perhaps grudgingly, that "it's a new world" (308).

As we have discussed, the divisiveness between Caliban and Miranda in *The Tempest* has long troubled audiences and scholars, who want to sympathize with both characters suffering Prospero's iron rule but cannot justify sexual assault. Lorie Leininger was among the first to point out, in her influential essay, "The Miranda Trap," that we should not blame Caliban or Miranda, but rather Prospero—as written by Shakespeare—who "needs Miranda as sexual bait" and then needs to protect her from the threat that confirms Caliban's place in his hierarchical worldview. Miranda is needed as "a pawn to counterbalance Caliban's lust." Pitting subordinates against each other is a common strategy for tyrants, so Leininger concludes her essay with Miranda "springing the 'Miranda-trap,' being forced into unwitting collusion with domination." She imagines Miranda announcing, "I need to join forces with Caliban—to join forces with all those who are exploited or oppressed—to stand by Caliban and say, 'As we from crimes would pardon'd be/ Let's work to set each other free'" (294). In *Prospero's Daughter*, Nunez frees Virginia—and Carlos and Ariana—from the Miranda trap, imagining the death of one of Shakespeare's most familiar and powerful dramatic heroes so that others can flourish. As Brian Richardson argues,

> Justice is done, and all its principals are thriving ... in its very refusal of tragedy or nonresolution, it is performing significant ideological work ... Nunez, one may argue, has performed just this feat: not only rewriting *The Tempest* from a postcolonial perspective, but rewriting and undoing the racism and horror of

miscegenation that had grounded and legitimized the colonial enterprise in the modern era.

Richardson concludes that "the happy resolution she provides is a powerful act of ideological defiance" (254).

But the final word should go to Elizabeth Nunez herself, who has explained the legacy of Shakespeare and British colonialism that informed this novel:

> I have written scholarly articles about Shakespeare's *The Tempest*, but it was only in writing the novel *Prospero's Daughter*, following fictive characters through plot lines their thoughts and actions dictated, that I released all the negative associations that I had been taught to make between Caliban and a person like me from a former British colony who was expected to be grateful for the systems of law, education, and government the British had established.
>
> *(*Truth in Fiction *502)*

In *Prospero's Daughter*, Nunez not only frees Miranda, Ariel, and especially Caliban from their entrapment, but she frees herself to talk back to Shakespeare and his participation in centuries of British colonialism.

References

Ashcroft, Bill. *Caliban's Voice: The Transformation of English in Post-Colonial Literatures*. New York: Routledge, 2009.

Barker, Francis and Peter Hulme. "'Nymphs and Reapers Heavily Vanish': The Discursive Contexts of *The Tempest*." *Alternative Shakespeares*, ed. John Drakakis. New York: Methuen, 1985: 191–205.

Bloom, Gina. "Time to Cheat: Chess and *The Tempest's* Performative History of Dynastic Marriage." In *The Oxford Handbook of Shakespeare and Embodiment: Gender, Sexuality, and Race*, ed. Valerie Traub. Oxford: Oxford UP, 2016: 419–434.

Brown, Paul. "'This Thing of Darkness I Acknowledge Mine': The Tempest and the discourse of colonialism. " In *Political Shakespeare: New Essays in Cultural Materialism*, eds. Jonathan Dollimore and Alan Sinfield. Manchester: Manchester UP, 1985: 48–71.

Creque-Harris, Leah. "Charting Territories of Love in the Works of Elizabeth Nunez." *Africology: The Journal of Pan African Studies* 10. 8 (2017): 25–40.

Doty, Jeffrey S. "Experiences of Authority in *The Tempest*." In *Shakespeare and Politics of Commoners*, ed. Chris Fitter. Oxford: Oxford UP, 2017: 236–252.

Egan, Gabriel. *Green Shakespeare: From EcoPolitics to Ecocriticism*. New York: Routledge, 2006.

Estok, Simon C. *Ecocriticism and Shakespeare: Reading Ecophobia*. New York: Palgrave Macmillan, 2011.

Gillies, John. "The Figure of the New World in *The Tempest*." In *The Tempest and its Travels*, eds. Peter Hulme and William Sherman. Philadelphia: U of Penn Press, 2000: 180–201.

Greenblatt, Stephen. *Learning to Curse: Essays in Early Modern Culture*. New York: Routledge, 2016.

Hall, Kim. *Things of Darkness: Economies of Race and Gender in Early Modern England*. Ithaca: Cornell UP, 1995.

Kunat, John. "'Play me False': Rape, Race, and Conquest in *The Tempest.*" *Shakespeare Quarterly* 65. 3 (2014): 307–327.

Lara, Irene. "Beyond Caliban's Curses: The Decolonial Feminist Literacy of Sycorax." *Journal of International Women's Studies* 9. 1 (2007): 80–98.

Leininger, Lorie Jerrell. "The Miranda Trap: Sexism and Racism in Shakespeare's Tempest." In *The Women's Part: Feminist Criticism of Shakespeare*, eds. Carolyn Lenz, Gayle Greene, and Carol Thomas Neely. Champaign: U of Illinois Press, 1980: 285–294.

Levin, Carole. "'Murder Not Then the Fruit Within My Womb': Shakespeare's Joan, Foxe's Guernsey Martyr, and Women Pleading Pregnancy in English History and Culture." In *Shakespeare's Foreign Worlds: National and Transnational Identities in the Elizabethan Age*, eds. Carole Levin and John Watkins. Ithaca: Cornell UP, 2009: 25–50.

Lindsay, Tom. "'Which First Was Mine Own King': Caliban and the Politics of Service and Education in The Tempest." *Studies in Philology* 113. 2 (2016): 397–423.

Loomba, Ania. *Shakespeare, Race, and Colonialism*. Oxford: Oxford UP, 2002.

Lupton, Julia Reinhard. "Creature Caliban." *Shakespeare Quarterly* 51. 1 (2000): 1–23.

Marcus, Leah. *Unediting the Renaissance: Shakespeare, Marlowe, Milton*. New York: Routledge, 1996.

Nunez, Elizabeth. *Prospero's Daughter*. New York: Ballantine Books, 2006.

Nunez, Elizabeth. *Not For Everyday Use*. New York: Akashic Books, 2014.

Nunez, Elizabeth. "Truth in Fiction, Untruths in Memoir." *Callaloo* 37. 3 (2014): 499–504.

Nunez, Elizabeth. *Even in Paradise*. New York: Akashic Books, 2016.

Nunez, Elizabeth. Goodreads interview. https://www.goodreads.com/author/show/62867. Elizabeth_Nunez. 01–04–2014.

Orgel, Stephen, ed. *The Tempest*. Oxford. Oxford UP, 1987.

Richardson, Brian. "Negotiating Closure in Victory and Postcolonial Rewritings of *The Tempest.*" *Conradiana* 48. 2/3 (2016): 245–256.

Rivlin, Elizabeth. "Shakespeare for Use and Pleasure: Elizabeth Nunez's and Terry McMillan's Middlebrow Fiction." *Journal of American Studies* 54. 1 (2020): 19–26.

Sachdev, Rachana. "Sycorax in Algiers: Cultural Politics and Gynecology in Early Modern England." In *A Feminist Companion to Shakespeare*, 2nd ed., ed. Dympna Callaghan. New York: Wiley-Blackwell, 2016: 226–243.

Sanchez, Melissa. "Seduction and Service in *The Tempest.*" *Studies in Philology* 105. 1 (2008): 50–82.

Singh, Jyotsna. "Caliban Versus Miranda: Race and Gender Conflicts in Postcolonial Rewritings of The Tempest." In *Feminist Readings of Early Modern Culture: Emerging Subjects*, eds. Valerie Traub, M. Lindsay Kaplan and Dympna Callaghan. Cambridge: Cambridge UP, 1996: 191–210.

Slights, Jessica. "Rape and the Romanticization of Shakespeare's Miranda." *SEL: Studies in English Literature 1500–1900* 41:2 (2001): 357–379.

Stavreva, Kirilka. "Ariel's Groans, or Performing Protean Gender on the Bulgarian Post-Communist Stage." *Shakespeare Survey* 71 (2018): 103–112.

Vaughan, Alden and Virginia Vaughan. *Shakespeare's Caliban: A Cultural History*. Cambridge: Cambridge UP, 1993.

Williams, Deanne. *Shakespeare and the Performance of Girlhood*. New York: Palgrave Macmillan, 2014.

Zabus, Chantal. *Tempests after Shakespeare*, 2nd ed. New York: Palgrave Macmillan, 2002.

3

MARGARET ATWOOD'S *HAG-SEED* AND WILLIAM SHAKESPEARE'S *THE TEMPEST*

When the Hogarth Press asked Canadian author Margaret Atwood to adapt one of Shakespeare's plays, she was ready with *The Tempest*, her "first choice, by miles" for its spotlight on the uses and abuses of creative power and magic. That Atwood would embrace the challenge of reimagining an iconic work is not surprising, for her long career is marked by innovation and intertextual experimentation. Atwood, one of the world's most powerful and prolific writers, has produced more than fifty books, including children's stories, critical essays, graphic novels, historical novels, poetry, short stories, speculative fiction, and even a novel for the "100 Year Future Library" time capsule project that will not be revealed until 2114.

Atwood's fiction frequently reconfigures prior works, including classical mythology and Homeric epics, fairy tales, and historical documents. One direct adaptation, *The Penelopiad*, published as part of the Canongate Myth Series, recounts *The Odyssey* from the perspective of Penelope and the female slaves Odysseus slaughters. Atwood's challenges to canonical works—what Sharon Wilson refers to as her "textual assassinations" (xii–xiii)—combine irreverence and homage. Many of Atwood's own novels have been adapted for theatre, television, and film, including *Alias Grace, The Robber Bride*, and *Surfacing*. *The Handmaid's Tale*, perhaps Atwood's most famous novel, has been transformed into an opera and also expanded into a well-received series on Hulu. Cleverly perpetuating the adaptive process, Atwood in turn incorporated elements of the television show into her long-awaited sequel, *The Testaments*. Like Shakespeare, Atwood is on both ends of the borrowing cycle.

Shakespeare appears in multiple guises in Atwood's work: in allusions to *A Midsummer Night's Dream, Cymbeline, Hamlet, Macbeth*, and other plays threading throughout her writing; in the interfacing between *King Lear* and her novel *The Cat's Eye*; and in "Gertrude Talks Back" from *Good Bones*, a collection of short stories that gives voice to various marginalized female characters. *Hag-Seed* is Atwood's first full-

DOI: 10.4324/9781003166580-4

length adaptation of a Shakespeare play, though she has written previously about Prospero—"the granddaddy of all"—in a critical essay comparing the writer's craft to a magician's transformative arts (*Negotiating* 114).

Since its initial performance, *The Tempest* has been one of Shakespeare's most frequently adapted plays, but as discussed in the previous chapter, the last century has seen a particular outpouring of retellings. In addition to the many post-colonial revisions the play has inspired, numerous fictional appropriations have taken other directions: Iris Murdoch's *The Sea, The Sea* (1978), winner of the Booker Prize, recounts the extreme narcissism of a retired Prospero-like playwright; Rachel Ingalls's satirical novella *Mrs. Caliban* (1983) portrays a love affair between a dissatisfied housewife and an amphibious Caliban figure; Jane Rogers's *The Island* (1999) is a dark parable inspired by the play's island setting and complex family relationships; and fantasy author Jacqueline Carey's *Miranda and Caliban* (2017) explores the doomed love between the eponymous characters. Filmmakers have been especially drawn to *The Tempest* for its incorporation of supernatural elements and its representation of political conflict and power. *Forbidden Planet* (1956), a foundational work in science fiction cinema, emphasizes the play's themes of exploration and hubris; Derek Jarman's controversial *The Tempest* (1976) infuses a historical setting with a contemporary queer sensibility; Peter Greenaway's avant-garde *Prospero's Books* (1991) is a phantasmagoric, visually spectacular rendering of Prospero's magical world; and Julie Taymor's *The Tempest* (2010) subverts the gender politics of the play with Helen Mirren playing the lead role as Prospera. *The Tempest* has also been the source of a range of musical interpretations from opera and symphonic works to pop culture musicals.

In spite of the title's evocation of Caliban, Atwood's *Hag-Seed* is largely focused on Prospero's trajectory, although in a different context from *Prospero's Daughter*. This novel explores the tensions between professional obsessions and personal and social responsibilities; it also celebrates spectacle and theatre—especially Shakespeare—as a collaborative rather than an egotistical enterprise. Ousted from his job as theatre director, Felix, the Prospero counterpart, teaches in a prison and stages a performance of *The Tempest* with the inmates, hoping to seek revenge on his enemies and repent for his failures as a father. In situating her story in a correctional facility, Atwood, known for her political activism, draws on the recent successes of secure-setting literacy programs, collectively referred to as "Prison Shakespeare" or "Shakespeare Behind Bars," and concretizes the play's tropes of captivity and incarceration. *Hag-Seed* balances humor and playful associations with a serious consideration of the source text's troubling issues—and, like *Prospero's Daughter*, talks back to Shakespeare by offering alternative outcomes.

The Tempest and *Hag-Seed*: Synopses

For the purposes of adaptive comparison, it is necessary to provide brief synopses of Shakespeare's *The Tempest*, first performed in 1611, and Atwood's *Hag-Seed*, published in 2016.

Prospero, magician, scholar, and the Duke of Milan, is usurped by his ambitious brother Antonio with the help of Alonso, the King of Naples, and his brother Sebastian. Prospero and Miranda, his three-year-old daughter, are sent to their probable death in a small boat, but his kind friend Gonzalo ensures he has some supplies and his books on magic. They land on an island, where the native Caliban and the spirit Ariel live; before her death, Caliban's mother, the witch Sycorax, imprisoned Ariel in a pine tree for failing to do her bidding. Prospero frees Ariel from Sycorax's spell and persuades him to fulfill a year of service; he also befriends Caliban, but when he allegedly tries to rape Miranda, Prospero punishes and imprisons him.

When the "auspicious star" of fate or magic brings Prospero's seafaring enemies nearby twelve years later, he and Ariel stir up a storm that wrecks their ship, but many of the passengers find their way to the island. Antonio, Alonso, and Sebastian; his kindly old councillor Gonzalo; Ferdinand, son of Alonso and prince of Naples; and two crewmates, Stephano and Trinculo, all arrive on shore safe but confused. Prospero's schemes get underway with Ariel's assistance: under his direction, Ferdinand and Miranda fall in love, Caliban joins with Stephano and Trinculo in a feeble assassination plot, and Antonio and Sebastian begin to argue and conspire against Alonso. After tormenting all of them, Prospero relinquishes his further plans for revenge and forgives his former enemies, takes responsibility for Caliban, blesses the dynastic promise of the marriage of Miranda and Ferdinand, sets Ariel free, and most importantly, renounces his magic and returns to Milan.

Hag-Seed generally adheres to the character and plot outlines of *The Tempest*. The novel's Prospero, Felix, is artistic director of a Canadian theatre festival but is driven out by his partner Tony (Antonio), the operational manager. While Felix creates increasingly boundary-pushing productions, Tony worries about the commercial draw of these experimental shows and he convinces his allies, Sal (Alonso) and Sebert (Sebastian), to fire Felix so he can take over his position. Lonnie, the Gonzalo figure, is not in favor of the firing, but his weak objections are ineffective. Compounding Felix's problems, his wife dies in childbirth and then his daughter Miranda dies of meningitis when she is three. Overwhelmed with grief at the loss of his wife and daughter, as well as his job, Felix becomes a recluse. But after several years he begins teaching in a local prison where he immerses himself in staging *The Tempest* with his students. Felix's regret that he may have been a neglectful parent to Miranda haunts him and he often imagines her presence; he hopes that his production of the play will resolve his guilt over her death. When a fortuitous event brings his enemies, Tony, Sal, and Sebert—now powerful politicians who oversee the funding of cultural programming—to the prison to review his literacy program, Felix has an additional motivation for staging the play: revenge. Felix and the inmates collaborate in a dark, interactive tour-de-force that guarantees the continuation of Shakespeare in the prison, allows Miranda and Felix liberation from the past, and achieves justice and restitution for some of the characters, especially the Ariel counterpart.

Atwood acknowledges the post-colonial readings of *The Tempest*, but her focus is the debate over Prospero as creative genius versus Prospero as the maniacal and vengeful despot as it plays out within a theatrical setting. In *Hag-Seed* Prospero is depicted more as a tragicomic hero trapped between conflicting imperatives: he imprisons others even as he himself is imprisoned; he derives power from diligent study and creative execution as well as manipulation and oppression; he obsesses over revenge and moralizes over forgiveness.

The Tempest: Collaboration and control

Good fortune brought Prospero and Miranda safely to the island where they have managed to survive for twelve years, but life there is extremely limited by its geographical boundaries, as well as Prospero's severe rule. The play is saturated with imagery of captivity, enclosure, and imprisonment, along with corollary references to freedom and liberty. The effects are felt by virtually everyone: Miranda, Caliban, Ariel, the ship-wrecked party, and even Prospero himself, who begs his audience to set him free at the end of the play.

Prospero describes the dwelling where he and Miranda live as their "cell," suggestive of both ascetic sanctuary and, for later readers, penal containment. Caliban's confinement is even more extreme, as he complains to Prospero: "For I am all the subjects that you have,/ Which first was mine own king, and here you sty me/ In this hard rock, whiles you do keep from me/ The rest o'th'island" (1.2. 341–344). Prospero repeatedly reminds Caliban of his status as "slave" and only releases him from his "hard rock" to force him into hard labor. It is not surprising that when Caliban meets Stephano and Trinculo he fantasizes about release from captivity and sings "freedom, high-day! High-day, freedom! Freedom, high-day, freedom!" (2.2. 178). Even the smitten Ferdinand describes his condition in prison imagery; when he first stumbles ashore and sees Miranda, he proclaims that his grief over his father's assumed death would be manageable "Might I but through my prison once a day/ Behold this maid. All corners else o' th'earth/ Let liberty make use of; space enough/ Have I in such a prison" (1.2. 494–497).

Ariel was released from his imprisonment by Prospero, but his freedom is still conditioned on the terms of their agreement. When Ariel dares to remind his "great master, grand sir" that they negotiated a deal of finite service—"Let me remember thee what thou hast promised/ Which is not yet performed me ... my liberty"—Prospero is enraged (1.2. 243–246). He tells Ariel, as he apparently does once a month, that he already freed him after he was imprisoned by Caliban's mother, the witch Sycorax, "into a cloven pine, within which rift/ Imprisoned thou didst painfully remain/ A dozen years ... It was mine art,/ When I arrived and heard thee, that made gape/ The pine and let thee out" (1.2. 275–294).

Prospero's threat to re-imprison Ariel certainly does not signal a more compassionate liberator: "If thou more murmur'st, I will rend an oak/ And peg thee in his knotty entrails till/ Thou hast howled away twelve winters" (1.2. 293–296).

So Ariel is not free either; he has been paroled and still needs to satisfy the terms of his release. In the exchange that follows, Prospero continues to berate and threaten: the primary "vehicle of his rule of terror," as Kirilka Stavreva makes clear, is his malevolent speech, "the language magic" he uses "to whip into the shape he desires the imagination and experience of others" (74). Ariel makes one last effort to defend himself: "I have done thee worthy service/ Told thee no lies, made thee no mistakings, served/ Without grudge or grumblings" (1.2. 246–249), but faced with Prospero's fury, Ariel shifts to compliant mono-syllabic answers. Jeffrey Doty's careful reading of this scene demonstrates how Prospero executes his dominance over Ariel rhetorically and concludes that

> Prospero's intent is not to persuade Ariel that he is in error but to arraign him for insubordination. There is hardly a passage in Shakespeare that suggests so powerfully "the hidden injuries of class" than Ariel's forced acknowledgement of his master's version of history.
>
> *(243)*

If Prospero is the island's self-appointed prison warden, he is also its self-appointed schoolmaster, presumably a more humane position of authority. Prospero is, above all else, a scholar, even though his obsession with his "secret studies" led to his political downfall. He claims that once his "library was dukedom large enough" and he is still immersed in his studies, even if the purpose of his scholarly work is not entirely clear. But Prospero also boasts of his expertise as a teacher and insists that the homeschooling he has given Miranda is far superior to the education that any other young princesses would have received. As we have discussed in the previous chapter, the effect of Prospero's pedagogy on his daughter is ambiguous: does his teaching make Miranda a free-thinking, intellectually curious young woman or a mere echo of his own ideological beliefs? Furthermore, we see little enactment of Prospero's actual teaching; other than the long exposition scene at the play's beginning when Prospero explains— or in contemporary parlance "mansplains"—their backstory, productive interactions with Miranda are remarkably absent in the play. Even though Prospero tells Miranda, "I have done nothing but in care of thee," the encounters we witness between them are few, and even then, Prospero is more the authoritarian than the loving father. When Prospero insists on presenting a masque as a wedding gift to the young couple, he speaks only to Ferdinand and refers to Miranda as an "acquisition" and his precious "gift" to bestow (4.1. 8–12). In the final scene, when Miranda first sees the ship-wrecked group of men, she famously proclaims, "How beauteous mankind is! O brave new world/ That has such people in 't!" and Prospero replies simply, "'Tis new to thee" (5.1. 182–183). This exclamation has been seen as a lovely expression of Miranda's youthful optimism and wonder, but as her tutor over the past twelve years, Prospero might have given her more serious instruction about the human race.

Prospero's teaching of Caliban is more transactional. At first Prospero's exchange of knowledge with Caliban was mutual, for Caliban taught Prospero about the resources on the island and Prospero shared information in return. Caliban laments to Prospero that

When thou cam'st first, Thou ... wouldst give me

Water with berries in't, and teach me how
To name the bigger light, and how the less
That burn by day and night. And then I loved thee
And showed thee all the qualities of the isle,
The fresh springs, brine pits, barren place and fertile.
(1.2. 335–339)

Caliban offered local knowledge useful for their survival, and Prospero responded with lessons in his own, presumably superior, language. But after Caliban's alleged assault on Miranda, Prospero appointed himself Caliban's master rather than his schoolmaster.

With Ariel, Prospero's pedagogy intersects with his third role—after jailer and teacher—as magical impresario. Prospero uses his punitive charms to torture Caliban and his manipulative hypnotism to sedate Miranda, but the exercise of his magic with Ariel is more extensive and co-dependent, though their complex relationship is often overshadowed by Prospero's treatment of Caliban and Miranda. Many post-colonial interpretations argue that Prospero's use of magical power mirrors strategies of political exploitation; others argue that Prospero wields his illusory arts like a director in the early modern theatre. These readings need not be incompatible as they both involve patterns of authority and compliance, but in Prospero's relationship with Ariel, there is something especially relevant in the theatrical model, which can be both hierarchical and collaborative. Daniel Vitkus advances a reading of *The Tempest* as a play about the power of theatre "to influence and control minds and about the conditions of labor that made the cultural production of theatre possible … Ariel's desire for freedom is analogous to a boy actor's desire to complete his years of bond-servitude and be freed" (415–417). At the same time, early modern theatre depended on willing cooperation, as the work needed to execute the play "must be undertaken by a group of cooperative and mutually dependent agents … the playhouse owner, the sharers, the players, the stage-prompter, the other playhouse employees … the spectators, all of whom come together to make drama happen" (415–417). Douglas Bruster also sees an analogy between Prospero and Ariel and the older and younger actors in early modern theatre, and notes the importance of mentorship: "the relations between Prospero and his industrious servant are deeply analogous to the relations among mature players and boy actors in the early modern playhouse … It matters to Prospero that his spirit is a particularly good actor" (265).

As we have seen, Ariel acknowledges his status of "bond-servitude" and he appeases Prospero by addressing him accordingly: "All hail, great master," "ay, sir," "no, sir," "my potent master," and "I will be correspondent to command." And because Prospero needs Ariel to execute his master-plot against his enemies from start to finish, his commands are many: Ariel is ordered to conjure the tempest, separate the principal ship's passengers into groups, deliver them safely to land, bedevil their conversations, expose their various assassination plots, and invade their consciences. Ariel, it appears, is doing most of the work while his master gives directions, but Prospero is not just delegating out of laziness; he needs his "spirit" to perform the roles he does not have the power to play himself. Any redemption in the play eventually comes from

Prospero's admission that he depends on Ariel, that reciprocity rather than control should define their partnership.

Although Ariel wants his freedom, he also takes pride in what he brings to the project. Andrew Gurr also reads the play in the context of early modern labor relations, but he argues that as an apprentice or indentured servant, Ariel

> shows no special enthusiasm for the magic trade he is agent and servant in ... Considering how close the verbal links to London social conditions are, neither of these two servants in the play works at all straightforwardly in the role of student and learner to Prospero. His power is his magic, and Ariel does not try to learn it.
>
> *(202)*

However, while Ariel's resistance to his servitude is evident, that does not mean he is not interested in his work; furthermore, it is not clear how much of that magical trade he needs to learn from Prospero and how much he is already capable of himself. When Prospero asks if Ariel produced the initial storm as ordered, Ariel delivers a proud and lively report of his work:

> I boarded the King's ship. Now on the beak
> Now in the waits, the deck, in every cabin
> I flamed amazement. Sometimes I'd divide
> And burn in many places; on the topmast,
> The yards, and bowsprit would I flame distinctly
> Then meet and join.
>
> *(1.2. 196–201)*

Ariel's creative energy is in full display as he describes his whirlwind movements and improvisations: anyone who can boast "I flamed amazement," does not entirely hate his job. If Caliban's character as savage barbarian is complicated by the fact that he speaks some of the most lyrical lines in the play, then notions of Ariel as recalcitrant apprentice are equally complicated by his exuberant reports of his doings. Ariel may resent his employer but not the work itself.

If Ariel already has his own expertise to draw on, he still absorbs some lessons from his mentor, as cruel as they might be. Stephen Orgel emphasizes the psychological motivation in Prospero's grandiose vision and sees the magical authority he exercises as a form of power exerted over children: "his daughter Miranda, the bad child Caliban, the obedient but impatient Ariel, the adolescent Ferdinand, the wicked younger brother Antonio." Orgel argues that while the play presents Prospero as Renaissance scientist, "what the play's action presents is not experiments and empiric studies but a fantasy about controlling people's minds" (*Representations* 12). If Prospero takes pleasure in psychological manipulation, then Ariel, who can do more with his magic besides dazzling pyrotechnics, emulates his master's tactics. Ariel puts Alonso and Gonzalo to sleep to expose Sebastian and Antonio's murder conspiracy and then awakens them just in time; he produces a sumptuous feast for the starving men and then whisks it away; he creates bickering divisiveness between Stephano and Trinculo with his invisible taunts; he tantalizes them with rich garments to confound their plans to assassinate Prospero. When he teases the Alonso contingent with a magical feast and then appears as a harpy to lecture them, he speaks as Prospero's surrogate:

> You fools! I and my fellows
> Are ministers of Fate ... But remember—
> For that's my business to you—that you three
> From Milan did supplant good Prospero,
> Exposed unto the sea, which hath requite it,
> Him and his innocent child; for which foul deed
> The powers, delaying, not forgetting, have
> Incensed the seas and shores, yea, all the creatures
> Against your peace.
>
> *(3.3. 60–75)*

Ariel then makes the men believe that because of their treachery, Alonso's son is dead and they are exiled on this desolate island with nothing but their grief and guilt; he ends his sermon with a flourish and disappears, along with the lavish banquet. Prospero is pleased with Ariel's performance: "Bravely the figure of this harpy hast thou/ Perform'd, my Ariel; a grace it had, devouring./ Of my instruction hast thou nothing bated/ In what thou hadst to say ..." (3.3. 83–86). Douglas Bruster claims that at this moment "Prospero sounds exactly like an older actor, one who has spent a life in the theater, praising a boy actor" (265). However, in order to earn that praise Ariel has been forced to "descend from his original, rarefied condition ... Ariel is dragged down from his airy paradise into the terrestrial theater of human affairs" (Cohen 75). Just as Caliban and Miranda absorbed some of Prospero's more calculating lessons, so did Ariel, who has proven as adept at mind games as his master.

But Ariel's collusion with callous human affairs has its limits. Joshua Cohen reminds us that as a spirit, especially one who is intrinsically musical and responsible for the "pleasing airs" on the island, Ariel "exists along a continuum between heaven and earth. Thus he becomes, for Prospero, an emissary of higher worlds and a source of supernal knowledge and power" (76). As that connection to a higher power, Ariel becomes Prospero's instrument of forgiveness in what is arguably the turning point of the play. After all of the parties have been thoroughly tormented and traumatized, Ariel reports that he has followed Prospero's charge and they are now "confined together ... all prisoners," filled with "sorrow and dismay," and "cannot budge till your release." But now, no longer acting on a command from Prospero, Ariel gently urges Prospero to relent:

ARIEL: Your charm so strongly work 'em
　　　That if you now beheld them your affections
　　　Would become tender.
PROSPERO: Does thou think so, spirit?

ARIEL: Mine would, sir, were I human.
PROSPERO: And mine shall.

(5.1. 17–20)

Prospero then decides that, after all, he cannot allow a spirit to be more compassionate than a human and agrees that though he is still furious about his enemies' wrongdoing, he will listen to his "noble reason" and decide that "The rarer action is/ In virtue than in vengeance. They being penitent/ The sole drift of my purpose doth extend/ Not a frown further" (5.1. 27–28). Now that Prospero claims to redirect his project from revenge to rehabilitation, he accepts Ariel's suggestion and sends him to release the men and promises to restore "their senses."

Prospero gathers everyone together for the finale that he has painstakingly assembled out of so many moving parts. Caliban repents, Alonso admits his wrongdoing and offers a peaceful alliance, and Sebastian and Antonio are held in check with Prospero's aside that he will reveal their conspiracy plans against Alonso if they further misbehave. Miranda has fortunately agreed to the love match with Ferdinand, next in line as the King of Naples, a canny move on Prospero's part. As Orgel observes, Miranda and Ferdinand's marriage is not just the promise of heterosexual romance and reproduction, it is a measure that prevents Antonio from succeeding him. If Miranda is married to Alonso's son, she becomes heir to the dukedom and "Milan through marriage becomes part of the kingdom of Naples, not the other way around. Prospero recoups his throne from his brother only to deliver it over, upon his death, to the King of Naples once again." Miranda thus becomes a "means of preserving his authority, not of relinquishing it" (*Tempest* 54). All of this resolution is brought about through a combination of cooperation and coercion: Prospero is still the puppet-master.

But Prospero understands that he can no longer sustain this manner of control. Sarah Beckwith argues that when Ariel earlier told Prospero that the prisoners "cannot budge until your release," the syntactical ambiguity of "your release" also implies that Prospero's own release needs to be achieved as well. If Ariel's moral suasion motivates Prospero to replace vengeance with virtue, it also convinces Prospero to relinquish the magical arts that have both empowered and imprisoned him.

Prospero finally acknowledges that the very obsessions that cost him his job and years of exile may have allowed him to re-enact his authority over the island, but they did not hone his skills as a benevolent ruler or as a compassionate being. His supernaturally inflected execution of power will not transfer to human and humane governance. As Beckwith argues, maintaining his magic would prevent him from being fully vulnerable: "release for Prospero will involve learning to accept his humanity, becoming kind, inhabiting his kind… [it] is a play about the task and difficulty of 'becoming human'" (165). Prospero also realizes that the best practices in political rule, as in theatrical performance, involve collaboration rather than control—in Italy, he cannot delegate tasks to invisible spirits but will need to work with other humans as fallible as he is: "Now my charms are all o'erthrown/ And what strength I have's mine own" (Epilogue 1–2). Prospero concludes the play by granting Ariel's liberty and then requesting his audience to grant him his own: "As you from crimes would pardoned be/ Let your indulgence set me free" (Epilogue 19–20). To what extent Prospero fully recognizes that the self-indulgence and vanity of his talent can also be used for moral and communal purposes remains to be seen.

Hag-Seed: Let your indulgence set me free

What happens when one of Shakespeare's most powerful protagonists is taken down from his grand pinnacle and turned into a disgruntled ex-theatre director, now unemployed with bad teeth and no dental insurance? In *Hag-Seed*, gone are any concerns about Prospero presiding imperially over an island of lesser subjects. Instead, Atwood's hero, Felix Phillips, adopts the alias "Mr. Duke" when he loses his job and moves by himself to a secluded shanty outfitted with jerry-rigged electricity and a latrine. He dwells, not among perfumed air and enchanted melodies, but amidst dead car batteries and a dwindling savings account, his worries entirely quotidian and realistic. Douglas Lanier observed that the Shakespeare adaptations commissioned by the Hogarth series have adopted a principle of literary realism:

> Elements of magic or intrusions of the divine are naturalized ... this impulse to naturalize the metaphysical or magical speaks ... not so much to a rationalist sensibility than to an avoidance of the marks of fantasy writing and with it the taint of genre fiction.
>
> *(235)*

Fantasy writing and genre fiction, however, have not been off-putting to Atwood, who has experimented with multiple genres and has recently been immersed in several speculative fiction projects. As Coral Howells points out, Atwood has embraced popular forms during her career with great enthusiasm and in *In Other Worlds: SF and the Human Imagination* (2011) and elsewhere she has fiercely defended the value of genre fiction (298). But Lanier is correct that in this case Atwood situates *Hag-Seed* in the territory of literary realism. Atwood herself calls attention to her choice:

> How exactly did Prospero and Miranda bathe themselves when on the island? Felix ponders this question while gingerly soaping himself under the arms. Did they have a tub? Unlikely ... It's an omission in much literature of the theatre, Felix decides: nobody bathes or even thinks about it, nobody eats, nobody defecates. Except in Beckett.
>
> *(Hag-Seed 121)*

Atwood's first strategy, then, is not just realistic but iconoclastic: bring Shakespearean romance out of the enchanted clouds and down to earth and knock Prospero, with his supposed parallels to the bard himself, from his majestic pedestal. Atwood also teases us that she will not be mired in scholarly debates:

> So many contradictions to Prospero! Entitled aristocrat, modest hermit? Wise old mage, revengeful old poop? Irritable and reasonable, kindly and caring? Sadistic,

forgiving? … They cheated for centuries when presenting this play. They cut speeches, edited sentences, trying to confine Prospero within their calculated perimeters. Trying to make him one thing or the other.

(184)

This protest is tongue-in-cheek, for Atwood is clearly familiar with the critical conversation surrounding the play, even if she wears that knowledge lightly. But for all of her humor and knowing winks, Atwood fully engages with the fundamental issues *The Tempest* raises. In *Hag-Seed* the protagonist's journey is towards a more honest understanding of his relationships with his daughter, the students and prisoners he influences, and his former enemies. He comes to a gradual realization about the place that art—and Shakespeare in particular—should occupy in his life and the larger world. Felix's engagement with Shakespeare is obsessive but, ultimately, enables him to reconcile his personal and professional responsibilities. Atwood talks back to Shakespeare the icon not to diminish his work but to defend our appropriation of it for moral and social ends.

In an adaptation that otherwise respects the plotlines of its source text, Atwood makes a noticeable change from the very beginning: in *Hag-Seed*, Miranda's mother dies in childbirth and then Miranda dies at the age of three of meningitis—her death is not Felix's fault but perhaps it could have been prevented had he not been so preoccupied with his work and sought medical care for her sooner. In *The Tempest*, Prospero's immersion in his art costs him his job, but here it also costs him his daughter. Even though there are other female characters in *The Tempest*—Sycorax, Dido, Claribel, Miranda's mother—who are conspicuous by their absence, Miranda is the only female character physically present in the play. Atwood at first appears to be making an already male-centered text even more so by removing its one female character, which may seem surprising given her strong affiliation with feminist literature. But Atwood's association with feminist writing has never been simplistic or predictable.

The complex relationship between Atwood's fiction and her feminism has been explored by a number of scholars, including Madeleine Davies, Reingard Nischick, and Fiona Tolan. Even though much of Atwood's literary production coincided with the evolution of second-wave feminism, her enormous range makes it nearly impossible to make any generalizations about her work. Furthermore, Atwood has repeatedly resisted reductive labels or categorization of her fiction or her philosophy as simply "feminist." However, as Fiona Tolan points out, these denials do not "preclude a feminist examination of her writing … Her work is never presumed to be a sole influence or a direct precipitant of feminist development, but it is identified as a salient and intelligent component of a general cultural discourse" (2). Within the enormity of Atwood's production, some works are more preoccupied with questions of gender than others, and those concerns invariably intersect with other power dynamics. In *Hag-Seed*, the loss of Miranda reveals how Felix's inadequate but patriarchal parenting overlaps with his professional narcissism.

Though Miranda dies at the age of three, she nonetheless has a haunting presence in *Hag-Seed*, first as an imaginary conscience and later as an actress he persuades to play her in his prison production. Shortly after she died, Felix, then still a theatre director, had planned an extravagant version of *The Tempest*, casting himself as Prospero that would allow a kind of "reincarnation" for Miranda. When he is fired and goes into self-imposed exile, he grieves for Miranda but also for his lost opportunity to stage the most cutting-edge production of his theatrical career. For the next decade he shapes the tragic circumstances of his own life around the contours of Shakespeare's play, imagining himself as a single-parent Prospero homeschooling his daughter, reading her fairy tales, and teaching her chess as she grows a few years older. In his imaginary resurrection of Miranda, Felix is a doting but controlling father, not allowing her to reach adolescence:

> If she'd lived, she would have been at the awkward teenager stage: making dismissive comments, rolling her eyes at him, dying her hair, tattooing her arms. Hanging out in bars, or worse. He's heard the stories. But none of that has happened. She remains simple, she remains innocent. She's such a comfort.
>
> *(62)*

Even as he convinces himself that he is making up for neglectful parenting with his hallucinatory role-playing with Miranda, he still refuses to allow her own autonomy and growth.

But when he begins to think he can actually hear Miranda speaking to him, Felix recognizes that he has become an eccentric recluse, so he takes a teaching job at a nearby correctional facility offered to him by his "auspicious star" Estelle, a local patron of arts programs. In the first few years he and his students put on various Shakespeare plays, but when he learns from Estelle, soon his friend and would-be love interest, that his enemies are coming to view one of their productions, he returns to his vision of *The Tempest*. Now his thoughts of Miranda recede as there is more motivating him than reincarnating her on the stage and educating the inmates—he finally has his opportunity for revenge.

Newly energized, Prospero contacts "his other Miranda," Anne-Marie, the actress he had hired to the play the part years ago. Anne-Marie was a champion gymnast as a teenager; now she's older, forcing Felix to accept aging as part of the human experience. Anne-Marie counters Felix's vision of Miranda as a sweet naif with her own interpretation of how Miranda should be performed:

> First off, she's a strong girl. She hasn't been tied up in corsets and stuffed into glass slippers and such at court. She's a tomboy; she's been clambering all over that island since she was three … She's got some muscles too—look at the way she was heaving those logs around so Ferdinand didn't have to.
>
> *(260–261)*

Anne-Marie admires Felix's directorial talents so she agrees to take on the role, but she insists on participating on her own terms. Atwood allows no chance that we will see this Miranda as an archetype of pliant womanliness: Anne-Marie is brash, confident, and physically fit, she wins the confidence of the inmates with her no-nonsense approach, and she schools Felix on how to treat women with respect.

If Atwood rewrites the script for Felix's view of Miranda, her reconfiguration of his role as teacher and director in the prison is even more explicit. Atwood explains that one of her first steps after she agreed to adapt *The Tempest* was to start

> counting up the prisons and imprisonments in the book. There are a lot of them. In fact, every one of the characters is constrained at some point in the play ... so I decided to set my novel in a prison.
>
> *(Guardian)*

She then acknowledges the long tradition of prison literature that informed her setting in the Fletcher Correctional Facility, the fictionalized name perhaps a nod to Shakespeare's fellow playwright, John Fletcher.

The discourse surrounding "Prison Shakespeare" has become its own subspecialty in Shakespearean studies, as the educational and recreational application of his work in incarceration has an extensive history. Simon Mayo's recent *Mad Blood Stirring* (2019) novelizes actual events during the War of 1812 when a group of all-black American prisoners staged a production of *Romeo and Juliet* in the imposing British prison Dartmoor. Amy Scott-Douglass reports evidence of Shakespeare performances in American prisons "as far back as the Civil War" (4). In the 1970s, one of the best-known examples is the *Robben Island Bible*, an edition of Shakespeare's collected works owned by a political prisoner on South Africa's Robben Island. The book was secretly circulated among the prisoners and thirty-four of them—including Nelson Mandela—signed their names next to their favorite passages (Schalkwyk iv).

However, it was in the 1980s that the "Prison Shakespeare" phenomenon began in earnest. Rob Pensalfini notes the important work begun in England by Cicely Berry of the Royal Shakespeare Company:

> Berry's already established status as a leading professional theatre practitioner meant that when she went into a prison to do a workshop, she was crossing several cultural boundaries: the boundary between the high culture of the RSC and the pessimal status of the prison, and the line between professional performance and applied theatre.
>
> *(15)*

In the U.S., the pioneering work of Curt Tofteland has had a profound influence on the proliferation of similar programs; his experience with inmates at a correctional facility in Kentucky was publicized in the 2005 documentary *Shakespeare Behind Bars* by director Hank Rogerson. Tofteland's work, alongside several other similar efforts, continues to evolve and Prison Shakespeare programs are now in place all over the world. Many of these successful experiences have been recounted in works including Amy Scott-Douglass' journalistic *Shakespeare Inside: The Bard*

Behind Bars (2007) and Laura Bates' memoir, *Shakespeare Saved My Life* (2013), which Atwood credits as part of her research.

If Prison Shakespeare initially emerged as a series of independent experiments and pilot programs, it has now developed into an impressive network with shared practices. This does not mean that the projects are homogenous or that the field is uncontested. Proponents of Prison Shakespeare defend the educational objectives that result in improved literacy as well as the increased confidence and social skills among the inmates who participate, benefits that help them endure incarceration and provide transferrable skills should they be released. Some of these ambitious results are demonstrable and measurable, while others are anecdotal. The therapeutic advantages that enable the rehabilitation are also touted, as are other lofty claims: Scott-Douglass explains that many see

> Shakespeare as a spiritual force …. Indeed, many *inmates* themselves consider Shakespeare to be a moralizing force, and not just any moralizing force, but the best and sometimes the only option after other methods, including religion and institutional surveillance, have failed.
>
> *(4)*

Given such ambitious outcomes it is inevitable that skeptics urge a more circumspect analysis of these programs. Criminologists, educators, and psychologists have questioned the logistical and security challenges of teaching theatre in prison and the potential trauma of inmates re-enacting the violent roles that Shakespeare's plays can demand. Among Shakespeare scholars there are concerns of essentializing Shakespeare and of perpetuating the bardolatry that already persists in the "outside" community. Ramona Wray points to the dangers of the excessive praise that surrounds Prison Shakespeare discourse—the talk of epiphanies, humanizing effects, and redemptive timelessness: "This results in a universalizing discourse about Shakespeare that would not be acceptable in other critical situations …" (343). Ayanna Thompson argues further that even with the best of intentions for a transformative educational experience, it appears "as if these programs merely inculcate the prisoners with a sense that morality and redemption stem from white, Western authors and their white, Western texts" (125).

Atwood situates Felix right in the midst of this conversation, but at first he is too driven and self-important to let it distract him. He scorns the naysayers who think the prisoners are not emotionally or intellectually capable of handling Shakespeare:

> Felix stays away from these people—the other teachers, the rights advocate, the shrinks and chaplains. He doesn't want to hear their theories. He also doesn't want to get tangled up in their judgment of him and what he's doing … so he keeps his mouth shut while being bombarded with sanctimonious twaddle.
>
> *(79)*

On the other hand, he is fairly cautious about making inflated claims: "the performances were a little rough, maybe, but they were heartfelt" (58). Felix's relationship to his prisoners is also less authoritarian than Prospero's: he is their teacher and director, not their prison warden—in fact, he is more of an ally, smuggling in cigarettes and snacks for them and advocating for small privileges. Still, at first, he sees himself as morally and professionally superior:

> When he was back in his hovel full-time, he reverted to despondency. After a stellar career like his, what a descent—doing Shakespeare in the clink with a bunch of thieves, drug dealers, embezzlers, man-slaughterers, fraudsters, con men. Was that how he would end his days, petering out in a backwater?
>
> *(59)*

Felix's journey, as much as Prospero's, is about becoming more humble, which means taking pride in his students' work for their sake, not just his own gratification and the perpetuation of his own personal and artistic agenda. After some initial obstacles, his Shakespeare classes become popular and literacy scores rise by fifteen percent. Felix is invigorated by this success and embraces his new mission: "He was back in the theatre, but in a new way, a way he'd never anticipated in his earlier life" (54). His humanizing transformation is interrupted, however, when he has the opportunity to stage *The Tempest* and exact his self-serving revenge on his enemies—"Suddenly revenge is so close he can actually taste it"—but he is quickly reminded that he cannot execute his plan without the help of the inmates. So begins the gradual process of finding the middle ground between directorial control and collaboration. He tells his students: "I'm the director. That means I'm in charge of the overall production, and the final say is mine. But we work as a team" (85). Felix's plan is that the actors will perform and videotape the play to be shown on closed-circuit television to the staff and inmates, as they do every year, but this time they will simultaneously produce a separate interactive version in the classroom area for their private audience—his enemies—aimed to disorient them and expose their wrongdoing.

Before Felix can hatch his intricate revenge plot, he first needs the inmates to produce their "official" version of *The Tempest* that will be broadcast to the prison at large. As absorbed as Felix is with his own dramatic visions, he also urges his actors to produce quality theatre, not just for their emotional gratification but for their own artistic pride. Ramona Wray points out that in Prison Shakespeare programs,

> The notion that an adaptation by prisoners might have a purchase beyond the therapeutic has generally been neglected ... the genre is invariably approached by way of a drama therapy model ... First, these investigations are circumscribed by a general reluctance to engage with the characteristics of the final product. Instead, what is demonstrated is a journey of personal development.
>
> *(341)*

Felix, however, is determined that his actors will produce a play that is "actually good," even as he is learning to be more flexible about the process and the product. He begins with casting, using the discussions of each character as teachable moments, but he also allows the students to lobby for their preferred roles. He anticipated that his first challenge would be the role of Miranda. In her research on the Shakespeare Prison Project at the Racine Correctional Institution, Jenna Dreier observes that the casting of women's roles in prison programs for men is one of the most difficult ethical questions that arises:

> Within the hypermasculine context of men's prisons, facilitators traverse an ethical minefield when it comes to casting the women's roles in an institutional space in which performing femininity invites physical violence, and yet where creating positive representations of women is of paramount importance for disrupting the violent misogyny demanded by that hypermasculine environment.
>
> *(1)*

Felix is prepared for this problem: "He's faced the gender issue in the other plays, but those female characters had been grown women and either ciphers or downright nasty, and thus much easier to accept" (88). Expecting the men's reluctance to play the part of a young girl, he already cast Anne-Marie, though his desire to have the Miranda of his choosing was as important as his concern over his students' discomfort.

Ariel is also a hard sell because none of the men want to play an effeminate character—until Felix convinces them of his central importance:

> Where would the play be without the tasks Ariel carries out for Prospero? Without the thunder and lightning? Without, in fact, the tempest? … he acts behind the scenes—nobody but Prospero knows that it's Ariel making the thunder and singing the songs and creating the illusions. If he were here with us now, he'd be called the special effects guy.
>
> *(106)*

Suddenly everyone wants to be Ariel, but Felix is able to cast his first choice, a young man who goes by the nickname 8Handz, and was convicted for hacking, identity theft, and impersonation: Felix needs his technological expertise to pull off the clandestine version of the play.

Most of the men want to play Caliban because they identify with his oppression: "We *get* him." At first Felix struggles to allow their various interpretations of Caliban, especially when their enthusiastic defenses are directly related to their condemnation of Prospero, but he finally concedes their point: "Okay, you don't like Prospero … and there are some reasons why you shouldn't" (123). Philip Smith argues that Felix's self-absorbed identification with Prospero and the prisoners' competition over who should play Caliban suggest that Atwood is criticizing "the compulsion to find our own values and affirmation of our own self-perception in Shakespeare." Smith claims that the aspiring Calibans find

> that Shakespeare's snarling subaltern not only reflects their own lives, but does so with such exactness as to exclude other readings ... Felix and his prisoner/ actors find in Shakespeare confirmation of their own values and self-perceptions even as, for the reader, the problems of such readings, and the strain of such interpretive practice, are obvious.
>
> *(36)*

I would argue, however, that while Felix's obsessive appropriation of *The Tempest* and his view of himself as Prospero at the beginning of the novel is clearly a sign of his self-delusion, it does not follow that Atwood is critical of *all* attempts to find "self-perception in Shakespeare" or that she and her readers are as troubled by the prisoners' readings of Caliban as Smith maintains. Indeed, the entire trajectory of Felix's evolution towards a more collaborative spirit is grounded in an understanding that the interaction between Shakespeare and his interlocutors should be flexible, generous, and personally meaningful.

The next critical step in that process occurs when Felix invites the actors to rewrite parts of the play that they think are too inaccessible for a modern audience. This concession is one of the most contested aspects of many Prison Shakespeare programs: some practitioners insist on study and performances of pure, unadulterated Shakespeare, while others allow for varying degrees of colloquial transcription and invention. Underlying this argument is the larger academic debate over Shakespeare's plays as stable and inviolable texts versus unstable and adaptable material. In her analysis of Prison Shakespeare and various other reform programs, Ayanna Thompson explores this divide and ultimately praises the more open and innovative missions of programs such as Will Power to Youth (WPY) that

> value appropriation, adaptation, and revision ... at-risk youth who participate in WPY are enabled to bring their own voices, narratives, and civic concerns to bear on equal footing with Shakespeare and Shakespeare's texts. This is not dumbed-down Shakespeare; it is a critical engagement that encourages dialogue, debate, and critique.
>
> *(141–142)*

At first Felix fiercely insists on Shakespearean language: even in the classroom, students are only allowed to use insults in their conversations directly culled from *The Tempest*. But as rehearsals proceed, he gradually learns to yield control—he encourages teamwork and agrees that they can rewrite lyrics to the songs. The actors embrace this creative license enthusiastically, though it takes Felix a little longer to adjust. With Anne-Marie's encouragement and guidance, the men first rewrite Prospero's long exposition scene with Miranda, daring to voice what even die-hard Shakespeareans might be thinking: the scene can be somewhat "long and boring."

The group reassigns the narrative to Antonio, who transforms the information as a rap "flashback number." Felix is both annoyed and impressed: "He's cutting me out, thinks Felix. Elbowing me aside … But isn't this what he's asked them to do? Rethink? Reframe? … Scene-stealer! But he tamps down on that emotion: it's their show, he scolds himself" (159–163). Felix is forced to admit that his former theatrical goals—"To create the lushest, most beautiful, the most beautiful, the most awe-inspiring, the most inventive, the most numinous theatrical experiences ever"—were perhaps self-centered (12). So, the reframing continues as the inmates preserve some of Shakespeare's language and mix in their own lyrics and musical numbers. Caliban adds a set piece with his backup band, The Hag-Seeds. Anne-Marie senses how much Felix is struggling with giving up ownership of the production and teasingly asks him "Are we crapping up your play?" to which Felix replies, "'It's not my play … it's our play.' Does he believe this? Yes. No. Not really. Yes" (181).

Felix's gradual acknowledgment of a theatrical process that encourages revision proceeds in tandem with the ongoing execution of the revenge version of the play that will be shown only to the small audience of his enemies: both versions depend on a high degree of collaboration. The inmates' cooperation is ensured when Felix decides to tell them that the visitors intend to cut program funding, so their Prison Shakespeare classes depend on the successful execution of Felix's plan. When the group arrives for their VIP visit, he will secure them in the private viewing space; unbeknownst to the prison wardens or the visitors, they will be participating in a "performance art" experience while the rest of the prison watches the standard videotaped play in their separate locations. The interactive version of *The Tempest* involves costumed goblins, eerie sound effects and music, food and drink doctored with street drugs, pretended kidnapping, and eventually a confrontation with Felix—all intended to frighten Tony, Sal, and Sebert into admission of their past wrongdoings and offers of restitution. The complex plot requires meticulous planning as the inmates rehearse their various roles as spirits and security pager pickpockets. Felix relies heavily on 8Handz, his Ariel, to set up the sound and surveillance system and to help procure the psychedelics from sellers outside the prison. Felix and 8Handz work well together but, like their counterparts in *The Tempest*, their relationship can be testy. Felix becomes exasperated when the inmates occasionally joke:

> They goof around behind his back, they have their own disparaging names for him and for Prospero too—that's normal—but 8Handz has to remember who he's supposed to be. Granted, Ariel has a lot of tasks to keep track of—he's Prospero's secret sharer …
>
> (157)

8Handz and all of the inmates work hard and, before the live performance, Felix gives the actors an inspiring speech:

We'll never be more ready ... these are the politicos who want to destroy our Fletcher Correctional Players ... they don't care about your education, they want you to stay ignorant. They aren't interested in the life of the imagination, and they have failed to grasp the redemptive power of art.

(285)

In spite of several inmates' worry that the plan is too dangerous and they will be punished by the prison officials, they are finally convinced by Felix's argument and his "vengeance" proceeds flawlessly. In a production every bit as carefully planned as Prospero's engineering of the plot in *The Tempest*, Felix and his company contain the "politicos" in a locked room where they believe they will be viewing the standard production of *The Tempest*. They are first served "refreshments"—drug-infused drinks and enhanced grapes—and then, amidst a planned blackout, the inmates confiscate their phones and pagers and confine the confused group in separate cells. Sal's son, Freddie, the Ferdinand counterpart, is put in a cell with Miranda where the two promptly fall into lovelust through the discovery of their mutual passion for the theatre. The Sal–Tony–Sebert–Lonnie cohort ends up in a cell, and while the sedated Lonnie and Sal—terrified that his son Freddie has been shot by prisoners—fall asleep, Tony and Sebert conspire to rig an upcoming election, kill Sal and Lonnie right there, and blame it on the prisoners. Meanwhile, 8Handz has wired each of the cells so he can record all of the conversations and events that transpire.

But as Felix is congratulating himself for his artistic and retaliatory success, his Ariel, 8Handz, urges him to pull back: "You sure you maybe didn't overdo it? With the grapes? This is, like, over the top ... I know they're assholes and they're trying to snuff our Players, but this is too sick even for me ... It's beyond a bad trip, they're scared shitless .... Don't you feel sorry for them?" Felix, who depends on and respects 8Handz, at first insists, "they had it coming," but then agrees, "You're right, that's enough vengeance. Not a frown further. Time to reel them in." Eventually Felix turns on the lights before any further damage occurs, reveals his identity, and assures them this has all been a work of performance art. The revenge plot achieves the intended effect of thoroughly disconcerting the men and Felix has the taped evidence he needs of Tony and Sebert's continued treachery: "It's much better than I could have hoped for" (235–238).

Shuli Barzilai explains that revenge, in the form of character motivation and plot construction, is a recurrent narrative component of Atwood's fiction and often interfaces with her interest in Shakespeare's depictions of revenge. Furthermore, revenge is

neither divorced nor precluded from justice ... sometimes revenge is justice. Particularly where access to socially sanctioned mechanisms of justice is denied ... revenge may be doubly "authorized": both vindicated as a response to otherwise unanswerable injury and valued for the inventive opportunities it affords the author. Getting even generates good stories ...

(317)

Although Barzilai is discussing Atwood's short fiction, her argument aptly characterizes the use Atwood makes of Felix's revenge, for his aim is retribution and Atwood's aim is the generative process of artistic expression: it makes for a good story.

More importantly, as Barzilai suggests, "sometimes revenge is justice." Felix reveals himself to his former enemies and pronounces the sentence:

> Sal, you're the Justice Minister, so I want some justice. First, I demand my old job back ... you'll tell the world that the Fletcher Correctional Players presented a very creative piece of interactive theatre ... Tony will announce a guarantee of five more years of funding ... After that, Tony will resign and Sebert will back out of the leadership race.
>
> *(240–241)*

Felix quietly quells any protests from Tony and Sebert by informing them that their conspiratorial murder plan in the cell was recorded and will be revealed should they not abide by his conditions. Sal is so relieved to find his son still alive that he approves of Freddie's decision to pursue a career in theatre instead of law. Felix also procures early parole for 8Handz.

In *The Tempest*, Prospero's pursuit of revenge was ultimately tempered with forgiveness; after all, Prospero achieved the ends he desired so he could afford to emphasize justice rather than pure retaliation. In *Hag-Seed* we see more fully how the development from retribution to restitution affects Felix, as well as his former enemies, so he can also be freed from the stranglehold of his authoritarian manner and theatrical obsessions. Like Prospero, Felix must cede control over his prisoner subjects and his single-minded view of what Shakespeare means. He realizes that theatre, just as in the early modern period, cannot be a single endeavor; the production of any play requires many hands—or 8Handz—working together. In this sense, as Thompson points out, "Authenticity and authority, then, do not reside in the text or the fantasy of the author, but in the individuals who must work long and hard to communicate, cooperate, and collaborate" (142). For contemporary productions of Shakespeare, there is a second form of collaboration possible: interaction with the Shakespearean text that allows for creative rewriting.

Felix's acceptance of his actors' revisions of *The Tempest* leads to his final assignment: to imagine their characters' afterlives and share their reports at their last class and cast party. Ariel announces that he intends to fight climate change:

> He's really happy to be doing that kind of work because he wants to help ... he just didn't like being told what to do all the time, he wanted a project of his own, and he's got more soul and feelings than Prospero used to think he had.
>
> *(254)*

In the interests of "sticking to life the way it is, no sugarcoating," Team Antonio presents a violent scenario in which Antonio murders everyone and rapes Miranda, but Anne-Marie quickly offers a counter-version in which Miranda, who spent her years on the island getting physically fit from hauling logs, teaching herself magic from Prospero's library, and allying with Ariel, vanquishes Antonio and Sebastian and saves the "good guys" (264). Team Caliban has decided that he will continue his career with his band, The Hag-Seeds, and announces that they are currently writing a musical that they hope Felix will eventually direct: "He's absurdly pleased by the offer, though of course this will never happen. Or will it? It's possible. You never know" (279).

There is an entrenched divide between local Shakespeareans and universal Shakespeareans, between those who remind us of Shakespeare's specificity and historicity and those who make broad, essentialist claims about Shakespeare's perennial value. These camps need not be mutually exclusive, and nowhere is that more evident than in Prison Shakespeare programs and the experiences Margaret Atwood fictionalizes in Hag-Seed. The opportunity to study and perform "authentic" Shakespeare—if we define that, as many practitioners do, by the plays as they appear in the First Folio—can offer enormous benefit for any population, marginalized or not. But it can be equally valuable to give up the cultural idolatry and protective ownership of "Shakespeare" and recognize that the Shakespearean text, never stable in the first place, should be open to revision from a varied audience.

In an essay on the relationship between the artist and his "moral and social responsibility," Margaret Atwood asks if artistic talent confers any particular privilege or burden:

> Does it exempt you from the duties and responsibilities expected of others? ... Are you to be a detached observer, pursuing your art for its own sake, and having arcane kinds of fun ... and if you do this to the exclusion of other people and their needs, will you become your own sin-soaked gargoyle?
>
> (Negotiating 106)

Atwood's closing metaphor clearly suggests that the artist—poet, playwright, theatrical director—has a certain moral obligation beyond the confines of their own artistic and self-absorbed concerns, and that is certainly Felix's evolution in Hag-Seed.

Atwood does not, however, overstate or romanticize Felix's transformative impact. Upon regaining his job as festival director, he turns around and appoints Freddie as assistant director and Anne-Marie as choreographer, anointing the next generation of theatrical artists:

> They're working beautifully together, those two. It's as if they were made for each other, like a pair of ice-dance champions. Watching them as they pore over the costume sketches and solemnly discuss their aesthetics ... Felix finds himself choking up, as if at a wedding: that strange mixture of nostalgia for the past mixed with joy for the future; the joy of others.
>
> (288–289)

Felix agrees to accompany Estelle on an ocean cruise and give theatre lectures, as long as he can bring 8Handz, whose parole he obtained, as his well-paid assistant. But Felix—and Atwood—have not altered the basic fact that the rest of his students will remain in prison.

Yu Jin Ko writes about attending one of Curt Tofteland's productions of *Macbeth* at the Luther Luckett Correctional Institution. When Ko realized that he couldn't just invite one of the actors to join them afterwards for dinner, he was reminded of the harsh reality of prison confinement. Ko acknowledges the crimes the prisoners committed and the suffering of their victims,

> But after watching the inmates perform and talk, it was difficult to avoid thinking of what a colossal and tragic waste of human potential it was for these men to be locked up for so many years. It was then, however, that maybe the most obvious point behind the Shakespeare Behind Bars program hit home: even inside, the men have to keep living, sometimes with no hope of parole or release. In the end, Shakespeare Behind Bars offers one way to give that life the moral dignity of a purpose.
>
> *(Ko)*

This genuine and circumspect recognition reflects Atwood's re-creation of Prospero and *The Tempest* in the twenty-first century, and her larger understanding of the uses to which we put Shakespeare. In the end, Prospero arrives at the recognition himself:

> It comes over him in a wave: he's been wrong about his *Tempest*, wrong for twelve years. The endgame of his obsession wasn't to bring his Miranda back to life …What has he been thinking—keeping her tethered to him all this time? Forcing him to do his bidding? How selfish he has been!
>
> *(291)*

And so, Prospero closes by addressing the ghost of Miranda with the words he said to Ariel: "To the elements be free." A novel primarily about literal and metaphorical imprisonment ends with some measure of freedom, albeit limited: Felix is free of his anger and self-pity, he is free from using Shakespeare to support his obsessions, and he is free to share Shakespeare in a way that can give other lives, still imprisoned, the moral dignity of a purpose.

References

Atwood, Margaret. "Temptation: Prospero, the Wizard of Oz, Mephisto & Co." In *Negotiating with the Dead*. Cambridge: Cambridge UP, 2002: 91–122.

Atwood, Margaret. "A Perfect Storm: Margaret Atwood on Rewriting The Tempest." *The Guardian*. September 24, 2016.

Atwood, Margaret. *Hag-Seed*. New York: Hogarth Publishing, 2016.

Barzilai, Shuli. "How Far Would You Go? Trajectories of Revenge in Margaret Atwood's Short Fiction." *Contemporary Women's Writing* 11. 3 (2017): 316–335.

Bates, Laura. *Shakespeare Saved My Life*. Naperville: Sourcebooks, Inc., 2013.

Beckwith, Sarah. *Shakespeare and the Grammar of Forgiveness*. Ithaca: Cornell University Press, 2013.

Bruster, Douglas. "Local Tempest: Shakespeare and the Work of the Early Modern Playhouse." In *The Tempest: Critical Essays*, ed. Patrick Murphy. New York: Routledge, 2001: 257–275.

Cohen, Joshua. "The Music of The Tempest." *Raritan: A Quarterly Review* 33. 1 (2013): 70–82.

Doty, Jeffrey S. "Experiences of Authority in The Tempest." In *Shakespeare and Politics of Commoners*, ed. Chris Fitter. Oxford: Oxford UP, 2017: 236–252.

Dreier, Jenna. "From Apprentice to Master: Casting Men to Play Shakespeare's Women in Prison." *Humanities* 8. 3 (2019).

Gurr, Andrew. "Industrious Ariel and Idle Caliban." In *Travel and Drama in Shakespeare's Time*, eds. Jean-Pierre Maquerlot and Michèle Willems. Cambridge: Cambridge UP, 1996: 193–208.

Howells, Coral. "True Trash: Genre Fiction." *Contemporary Women's Writing* 11. 3 (2017): 297–315.

Ko, Yu Jin. "Macbeth Behind Bars." *Borrowers and Lenders: The Journal of Shakespeare and Appropriation* 8. 2 (2013).

Lanier, Douglas. "The Hogarth Shakespeare Series: Redeeming Shakespeare's Literariness." In *Shakespeare and Millennial Fiction*, ed. Andrew James Hartley. Cambridge: Cambridge UP, 2018: 230–250.

Mayo, Simon. *Mad Blood Stirring*. New York: Pegasus Books, 2019.

Orgel, Stephen. "Prospero's Wife." *Representations* 8 (1984): 1–13.

Orgel, Stephen, ed. *The Tempest*. Oxford: Oxford UP, 1987.

Pensalfini, Rob. *Prison Shakespeare: For These Deep Shames and Grave Indignities*. New York: Palgrave Macmillan, 2015.

Rogerson, Hank, dir. *Shakespeare Behind Bars: A Documentary*. Philomath Films, 2005.

Schalkwyk, David. *Hamlet's Dreams: The Robben Island Shakespeare*. London: Bloomsbury Academic, 2013.

Scott-Douglass, Amy. *Shakespeare Inside: The Bard Behind Bars*. London: Continuum, 2007.

Smith, Philip. "Margaret Atwood's Tempests: Critiques of Shakespearean Essentialism in *Bodily Harm* and *Hag-Seed*." *Margaret Atwood Studies* 11 (2017): 29–40.

Stavreva, Kirilka. "'We are Such Stuff': Absolute Feminine Power vs. Cinematic Mythmaking in Julie Taymor's Tempest (2010)." In *Queens Matter in Early Modern Studies*, ed. Anna Riehl Bertolet. New York: Palgrave Macmillan, 2017: 67–80.

Thompson, Ayanna. "Reform: Redefining Authenticity in Shakespeare Reform Programs." In *Passing Strange: Shakespeare, Race, and Contemporary America*. Oxford: Oxford UP, 2013: 119–144.

Tolan, Fiona. *Margaret Atwood: Feminism and Fiction*. Amsterdam: Rodopi, 2007.

Vitkus, Daniel. "'Meaner Ministers': Mastery, Bondage, and Theatrical Labor in The Tempest." In *A Companion to Shakespeare's Works*, Volume IV, eds. Richard Dutton and Jean E. Howard. New York: Blackwell Publishing, 2003: 408–426.

Wilson, Sharon Rose. *Margaret Atwood's Textual Assassinations*. Columbus: Ohio State UP, 2003.

Wray, Ramona. "The Morals of Macbeth and Peace as Process: Adapting Shakespeare in Northern Ireland's Maximum Security Prison." *Shakespeare Quarterly* 62. 3 (2011): 340–363.

4

JEANETTE WINTERSON'S *THE GAP OF TIME* AND WILLIAM SHAKESPEARE'S *THE WINTER'S TALE*

To the vexed and varied terminology of literary adaptations and appropriations—interfaces, intertextualities, iterations, remakes, retellings, revisions—Jeanette Winterson adds "cover" to the mix. Winterson calls her 2015 novel, *The Gap of Time*, "the cover version" of Shakespeare's "original," *The Winter's Tale*. Calling the novel a cover, the popular term for one artist's rendition of another's song, signals its currency and contemporaneity as well as the centrality of music to the narrative.

When Hogarth Press invited Winterson, one of Britain's most renowned contemporary authors, to join the Shakespeare Project, she immediately signed on for *The Winter's Tale*, calling the play a central and talismanic text in her life. Near the end of *The Gap of Time*, she explains, "I wrote this cover version because the play has been a private text for me for more than thirty years … It's a play about a foundling. And I am" (268). In the novel, Winterson explores the motif of child abandonment and the attendant potential for recovery, forgiveness, and redemption. And, as in many of her works, she conveys the fraught relationship between homoerotic desire and emotional attachment, and the troubled intersection between complex sexual identity and selfhood.

That Winterson would eventually produce an adaptation of Shakespeare seems inevitable. In her memoir, *Why Be Happy When You Could Be Normal?*, Winterson explained that in working class Manchester where she grew up, Shakespeare was a familiar cultural presence and his work became as foundational to her own writing as mythology, fairy tales, or the Bible. Winterson's oeuvre is also deeply grounded in intertextual and adaptive practice; historical, literary, religious, and scientific allusions permeate her work. Two novels, *Oranges Are Not the Only Fruit* (1985) and *Sexing the Cherry* (1989), appropriate traditional fairy tale tropes and *Weight* (2005) updates the myth of Atlas and Hercules. In 2011 she wrote "Godblog," a play based on the Book of Genesis, for Sixty Six Books, a project which commissioned works to mark the 400th anniversary of the King James Version of the Bible. In 2012 she responded to

DOI: 10.4324/9781003166580-5

another 400th anniversary with *The Daylight Gate*, a novelization of the Pendle Hill witch trials of 1612. Most recently her novel *Frankissstein: A Love Story* (2019), a response to Mary Shelley's *Frankenstein*, addresses our fears and fascination with artificial intelligence, gender fluidity, and transhumanism. Winterson herself described the creative impulse that draws her to rework previous texts:

> My work is full of Cover Versions. I like to take stories we think we know and record them differently. In the re-telling comes a new emphasis or bias, and the new arrangement of the key elements demands that fresh material be injected into the existing text.
>
> *(Weight xiv)*

Although *The Winter's Tale* is popular on stage, it has been subject to relatively few adaptations into other media compared to many of Shakespeare's other plays. In 2014, the Royal Ballet of London performed a ballet based on the play by choreographer Christopher Wheeldon, and in 2017, Ryan Wigglesworth adapted it for the English National Opera. In fiction, E. K. Johnston published a well-received young adult novel in 2016, *Exit, Pursued by a Bear*. Winterson's inventive retelling is a rich addition to the body of contemporary homages and challenges to Shakespeare.

In *The Gap of Time*, Winterson's most conspicuous "injection of fresh material" into *The Winter's Tale* is the bold exposure of the play's simmering sexual tensions and anxieties. Second, the novel explores the trope of lost children, their suffering, and their survival. Without diminishing the gravitas and social critique that these subjects demand, Winterson, like Margaret Atwood, infuses her novel with her characteristic humor and an element of play. In so doing, Winterson acknowledges the early modern preoccupations and the spirit of Shakespeare's source while creating a work that reflects contemporary issues and concerns.

The Winter's Tale and *The Gap of Time*: Brief synopses

For the purposes of adaptive comparison, it is necessary to provide brief synopses of Shakespeare's *The Winter's Tale*, first performed in 1611, and Winterson's *The Gap of Time*, published in 2015.

Shakespeare's play begins with Polixenes, King of Bohemia, concluding a nine-month visit to his close friend Leontes, King of Sicilia. Leontes urges him to stay longer, and when Polixenes refuses, he asks his queen, Hermione, to persuade their guest. When Polixenes agrees at Hermione's urging, Leontes suddenly becomes jealous and wrongly suspects his friend of committing adultery with Hermione and of fathering the child she is about to deliver. Leontes orders his servant Camillo to kill Polixenes, but Camillo instead warns Polixenes and the two of them escape to Bohemia. Leontes sends Hermione to prison where she gives birth to a baby girl, Perdita; he denies paternity and orders his servant Antigonus to abandon the infant in the wild, but he is killed by a bear in the process. Hermione is put on trial for treason, and though she is exonerated by the Oracle, she falls dead when she hears that their young son, Mamillius, has died. The first half of the play concludes with Antigonus' wife Paulina, a loyal and honest lady-in-waiting, forcing Leontes to repent his folly and the loss of his entire family.

The second half of the play focuses on Perdita, found in Polixenes' kingdom of Bohemia by a Shepherd and his son who raise her as their own. Now, sixteen years later, Perdita is a young woman in love with Florizel, Polixenes' son and heir who is eager to marry her in spite of her presumed low birth. Polixenes discovers his son's plan and orders Florizel to abandon Perdita, but instead they flee to Sicilia, with Polixenes close behind. Perdita's identity as Leontes' long-lost daughter is revealed, the couple's union is blessed, and a stone statue of Hermione that Paulina commissioned comes alive. Hermione is reunited with Perdita, the daughter she lost at birth, and Leontes and Polixenes reconcile.

Winterson's contemporary updating follows the plot structure closely. Leontes, now Leo, is a brash, aggressive hedge fund manager in London when the city is recovering from the 2008 financial crisis. Polixenes' counterpart is Xeno, an artistic video game designer and Leo's teenage friend and former lover. Leo is convinced that Xeno is having an affair with his pregnant wife MiMi, a singer he met in Paris. In a jealous rage, Leo tries to run over Xeno in a parking garage, rapes MiMi, and isolates himself with their young son, Milo. After MiMi gives birth to a daughter, Perdita, Leo pays his gardener Tony to take the infant to Xeno in New Bohemia, a fictionalized New Orleans. Disasters accumulate when Milo is killed in an accident, MiMi has a nervous breakdown and retires to Paris, Tony is murdered, and Perdita abandoned. Leo is left with Pauline, his personal assistant and moral compass, helping him repent the devastation he has caused.

After a sixteen-year gap of time, the novel turns to Perdita who was found in New Bohemia and raised by an African-American piano bar owner, Shep, and his son Clo. Perdita is now a young woman in love with Zel, Xeno's son. While Perdita loves her adoptive family, Zel is angry at his father for his parental failures and has taken refuge with a local used car dealer, Autolycus. Xeno, whose successful career was marred by alcoholism and reclusiveness, reveals Perdita's identity, and they all return to London. The play concludes with everyone attending a concert held in a building Leo's company is about to tear down, and the guest singer, who has just emerged from seclusion, is MiMi.

The Winter's Tale, part one: Innocence and temptations or love, sex, and power

Many of Shakespeare's plays are about the use and abuse of royal power and the intrusion of political tyranny into the private sphere; a monarch's family members can be as vulnerable to his fury as any of his subjects. The entire trajectory of *The Winter's Tale* hinges on King Leontes' abrupt and seemingly inexplicable suspicions, and the ways in which he takes advantage of his power to execute his rage. Although *The Winter's Tale* is often seen as a more reparative answer to *Othello*, it is driven by similarly destructive jealousies and conflicts between same-sex bonds and heterosexual marriage. Even if the outcomes are not as fatal, the play's conclusion offers no assurance that these tensions have been resolved, nor can the trauma that the characters have endured be entirely erased by the conciliatory finale.

Very early in the play, Leontes convinces himself that Hermione has committed adultery with Polixenes and the ensuing destruction originates in this green-eyed monster of sexual anxiety. The scholarly discourse over the cause of Leontes' behavior has been vigorous: some locate his jealousy in a repressed homoerotic attachment to his boyhood friend and a resistance to aging; others in a mistrust of the female body and a broader, essentializing misogyny; and yet others in the motif of the love triangle that Shakespeare addresses in other works as well, most notably in *The Merchant of Venice, Twelfth Night*, and the *Sonnets*.

In keeping with the larger trends in literary and cultural studies of the past few decades, scholars have engaged in productive analyses and lively debates about early modern sexualities. Following upon Michel Foucault's monumentally influential, if contested, *History of Sexuality* of the late 1970s, a wave of feminist criticism and a dynamic body of queer theory emerged, energized by social and political movements. In early modern studies, feminist and queer theory focused on circumscribed constructions of masculinity and femininity and representations of same-sex relationships, and argued that contemporary distinctions between homosexuality and heterosexuality did not always map on to earlier centuries. Early modern drama is an especially fruitful site for such inquiry precisely because gender and sexuality were such significant factors in the male-dominated world of early modern transvestite theatre and because Shakespeare's preoccupation with the construction of sexual identity is evident throughout his work.

The aim of the often-overlapping approaches of feminist, gender, and queer theory is not meant to prove, as Valerie Traub points out, that "Shakespeare was sympathetic to the plight of women, or to berate him for being misogynous, or to prove that he was homosexual" but to help us understand the many ways in which "Shakespeare responded imaginatively to sex, gender, and sexuality as crucial determinants of human identity and political power" (129). Acknowledging that sexual behaviors and identities were understood differently in the early modern period does not prevent us from exploring their presence in Shakespeare's work, even as we must contextualize them within historical, literary, and social frameworks. Describing Leontes as a jealous heterosexual, frustrated homosexual, or confused bisexual may be ahistorical and reductive, but the sexual anxieties that propel and dominate this play are nonetheless undeniable.

Once Polixenes agrees to prolong his time in Sicilia, Hermione asks him about the two kings' childhood bond: "Come, I'll question you/ Of my lord's tricks and yours when you were boys./ You were pretty lordlings then?" (1.2. 61–62). While it seems curious that this subject has not come up earlier during Polixenes' long stay, his description of their boyhood friendship at this point provides some explanation for Leontes' explosion of jealousy: "We were, fair Queen/ Two lads that thought there was no more behind/ But such a day tomorrow as today,/ And to be boy eternal (1.2. 62–65). Polixenes' nostalgia is rooted in a wishful conflation of time; past, present, and future merge in an atemporal idyll, a queering of time. Individual identity is collapsed as well: when Hermione then presses him to admit that Leontes was "the verier wag" of the two, Polixenes instead insists upon their sameness, their indistinguishable selves.

> We were as twinned lambs that did frisk i'th'sun
> And bleat the one at th'other. What we changed
> Was innocence for innocence; we knew not
> The doctrine of ill-doing, nor dreamed
> That any did. Had we pursued that life,
> And our weak spirits ne'er been higher reared
> With stronger blood, we should have answered heaven
> Boldly "Not guilty," the imposition cleared
> Hereditary ours.
>
> *(1.2. 66–74)*

Marjorie Garber's argument about the "coming of age" process in Shakespeare's plays describes a separation, usually from a childhood friend of the same sex, to an adult relationship normatively defined by marriage. The "common Shakespearean paradigm for the condition of childhood is that of twins and twinned experience" in which two same-sex friends "appear to themselves and others as interchangeable, undifferentiated in character, feature, or affection," while the next stage, heterosexual marriage, is defined by otherness and difference (31). Victoria Sparey argues that historical evidence challenges Garber's paradigm as anachronistic, "directing attention to apparently immediate transitions between ages rather than developments within ages themselves ... Changes were significant but they were not immediate" (450). But whether this shift was gradual or sudden, the conflict that Garber and others have pointed out between homosocial friendships—both male and female—and heterosexual courtship and marriage is a common theme in early modern literature.

Polixenes' "twinned lambs" metaphor illustrates this model of identical pairing and halcyon innocence associated with childhood; its rupture comes in the form of sexual knowledge and experience with women, as evident in Hermione's interruption: "By this we gather/ you have tripped since." Polixenes confirms her suggestion that when they both fell out of their state of innocence—"tripped"—it was because of the specter of heterosexual marriage:

> O my most sacred lady,
> Temptations have since been born to's, for
> In those unfledged days was my wife a girl;
> Your precious self had not then crossed the eyes
> Of my young playfellow.
>
> *(1.2. 76–80)*

However, the sexual innocence of youthful, same-sex relationships should not be overstated, for there are often homoerotic overtones in Shakespeare's evocations of childhood friendship. In *As You Like It*, Celia reminds Rosalind that "We still have slept together,/ Rose at an instant, learned, played, eat together'/ And whereso'er we went, like Juno's swans,/ Still we went coupled and inseparable" (1.3. 72–75). In *A Midsummer Night's Dream*, Helena reminds Hermia that they "grew together,/ Like to a double cherry ... Two lovely berries molded on one stem," and even more suggestive is Emilia's description of her childhood friend, Flavina, in *The Two Noble Kinsmen*: "The flower that I would pluck/ And put between my breasts—O then but beginning/ To swell about the blossom—she would long/ Till she had such another, and commit it/ To the like innocent cradle ..." (1.3. 66–71).

Polixenes and Leontes, two lambs frisking and bleating in the sun, fit within a pattern of what Stephen Guy-Bray calls "total homosocial solidarity." Guy-Bray, however, claims even more homoerotic import in Polixenes' pastoral account:

> it has usually been assumed that he is describing a pre-sexual existence [but] ... there is nothing in the passage itself to rule out sexuality. Polixenes does not say that he and Leontes never did anything that might be considered wrong, but merely that they did not know the "doctrine of ill-doing."
>
> *(203)*

Guy-Bray argues that it is entirely plausible that Polixenes was suggesting that what adulthood brought them was not their first sexual experience, but the *knowledge* that their youthful sexual activity would have been considered "ill-doing." Indeed, when Hermione goes on to question Polixenes about possible previous sexual experiences, she does not specify whether the encounters were with men or women:

> Grace to boot!
> Of this make no conclusion, lest you say
> Your queen and I are devils. Yet go on,
> Th'offenses we have made you do we'll answer,
> If you first sinned with us, and that with us
> You did continue fault, and that you slipped not
> With any but us.
>
> *(1.2. 80–87)*

The absence of gender specificity in "with any" leaves open the possibility for prior sexual experience or more recent infidelities with either men or women.

Regardless of the exact sexual nature of the friendship between Leontes and Polixenes, it is portrayed as a sanctuary from the exigencies of passing time. Same-sex friendship here represents a state that is idyllic precisely because its opposite signals the next stage of maturity and aging. Polixenes' memory of an Edenic childhood evokes a wistful state of youth as much as any specific experience, and his description triggers a similar nostalgia in Leontes, manifest in his encounter with his young son Mamillius:

"Looking on the lines/ Of my boy's face, methoughts I did recoil/ Twenty-three years, and saw myself unbreeched …" (1.2. 153–155). Several critics have noted that Leontes' resistance to leaving his youth behind propels his rage as much as his insecure sexual identity. Kathryn Bond Stockton argues,

> I am not suggesting that Leontes is a "gay" child. But Leontes's childhood wish to arrest the clock on his love with Polixenes to live inside that state, to curl up in it, adumbrates a pattern that would emerge as "gay" child suspensions centuries later.
>
> *(425)*

Leontes' desire to revert to an earlier time is determined as much by temporal resistance as by sexual ambivalence.

Still, Leontes' romanticizing of the past is matched by his aversion to any threats posed by female interference. Even though Leontes asked Hermione to help him persuade Polixenes to stay in Sicilia, her very intervention is the catalyst for his furious reaction. As Stephen Orgel argues,

> Critics for two hundred years have declared Leontes' paranoid jealousy inexplicable, but within the context of that dream of what it means to be a child, Leontes' behavior is not only understandable, it is in a way inevitable … Leontes' paranoid jealousy; the translation of the inseparable friend into the dangerous rival, and of the chaste wife into a whore … is the consequence of women entering the world of male friendship.
>
> *(Impersonations 16–17)*

Leontes is not only resisting the intrusion of women into the male sphere, he is retreating from his role as husband and father in the heteronormative family dynamic of marriage.

Mario DiGangi also argues that disdain for marriage was not unusual and reflected a widespread fear that "male identity could be undermined by sexual intimacy with women." For many men in early modern England,

> relations with women were considered paradoxically both necessary to and threatening to the accomplishment of adult masculine identity. On the one hand, manhood was associated with becoming a husband and father. On the other hand, the period's dominant gender ideologies assumed the moral and intellectual inferiority of women, and typically portrayed sexual passion for women as emasculating.
>
> *(199–200)*

Thus, the bonds that men shared with each other were often considered preferable to their relationships with women.

At the same time, Leontes' resistance to heterosexuality is due to more than any presumed superiority of homosocial bonds: it is a mistrust and even loathing of the female presence, evident in his denunciations of Hermione, Paulina, and women in general. Leontes' essentializing misogyny is also reflected by many of the other male characters who otherwise profess to defend their queen, their wives, and their daughters. In the past several decades, a substantial body of feminist criticism by scholars including Janet Adelman, Peter Erickson, Gail Kerns Paster, and Susan Snyder has illuminated the cultural, historical, and psychological underpinnings of the profound ambivalence towards women that permeates this play.

Leontes' sexual anxiety is also channeled into a perverse obsession with imagining the adulterous acts committed by Hermione and Polixenes. In her analysis of Shakespeare's other great play driven by jealousy, Lynda Boose described what she calls the "pornographic aesthetic" of *Othello*: "Pornography in its literary manifestation is ... not only authored by a male but subscribed by a culture which deprecates the feminine and invests the masculine with sexual desire accompanied by fear, guilt and loathing of female sexuality" (28). Iago manipulates Othello's need for "ocular proof" into a pornographic voyeurism to produce evidence of Desdemona's wrongdoing. Imagining heterosexual infidelity, however, not only reveals the enactment of female sexuality, but male activity as well. Leontes's description to Camillo of the infidelity of his wife and best friend is notable for its frenzied account of their supposed behavior:

> Is whispering nothing?
> Is leaning cheek to cheek? Is meeting noses?
> Kissing with inside lip? Stopping the career
> Of laughter with a sigh—a note infallible
> Of breaking honesty? Horsing foot on foot?
> Skulking in corners? ... Is this nothing?
> Why, then the world and all that's in't is nothing,
> The covering sky is nothing, Bohemia nothing,
> My wife is nothing, nor nothing have these nothings,
> If this be nothing.
>
> *(1.2. 283–294)*

The reiteration of "nothing" here does double work: it results in a universalizing nihilism that reflects Leontes' despair and it also emphasizes the colloquial association of female genitalia as nothing, or "no thing." But if Leontes' fantasies implicate Hermione, they also include Polixenes, as he imagines both "Bohemia" and "my wife" as equally complicit "nothings."

How then does Leontes' sixteen years of penance resolve his sexual anxieties, mistrust of women, and divided allegiances? Perhaps Leontes' blessing of Perdita's marriage to Polixenes' son Florizel reflects his reconciliation with his friend while his joy at Hermione's resurrection suggests that he has embraced his expected normative role as husband. But the extent to which these individual outcomes can co-exist harmoniously is not entirely clear. The miraculous animation of Hermione's statue has become an iconic piece of stagecraft and Leontes' wondrous response to it may signal that his transformation is as complete as hers, although that spectacle should not diminish his reunion with Polixenes. As one gentleman describes the event to another,

> Then you have lost a sight which was to be seen, cannot be spoken of. There might you have beheld one joy crown another, so and in such manner that it seemed Sorrow wept to take leave of them, for their joy waded in tears. There was casting up of eyes, holding up of hands ... our King ... then asks Bohemia forgiveness ...
>
> *(5.2. 31–38)*

It is a moving account of their reconciliation, and it recalls the tribute to their friendship that opened the play.

Nonetheless, for dramatic effect Shakespeare chose to stage just one reunion, so in keeping with the romance genre's emphasis on heterosexual union and the promise of dynastic continuity, he shows Leontes' reunion with Hermione rather than with Polixenes. Still, while many have seen *The Winter's Tale* as a triumph of female correctiveness, reciprocity, and the promise of renegotiating homosocial and heterosexual alliances, the silences in the final scene are conspicuous. Hermione speaks to Perdita but not Leontes, though her words to him earlier when she was falsely accused still resonate: "How this will grieve you,/ When you shall come to clearer knowledge, that/ You thus have published me! Gentle my lord,/ You scarce can right me thoroughly then to say/ You did mistake" (2.1. 97–101). Her trauma and his abusive behavior are not easily forgotten. As Stephen Greenblatt says,

> New life may lie on the other side of years lost to tyranny, but this life will not be the same as it once was ... [the play] allows itself the dream of a second chance. The event that makes this renewal possible ... is one of the playwright's most daring and implausible fantasies: the tyrant's full, unfeigned, utterly sincere repentance. Imagining this inner transformation is almost as difficult as imagining a statue coming to life.
>
> *(Tyrant 136)*

The Winter's Tale concludes with the potential for overcoming tensions between the play's many binaries—youth and age, male and female, friendship and marriage, power and justice, penance and forgiveness—but possibility is not promise.

The Gap of Time, part one: Innocence and temptations or love, sex, and power

Winterson was first drawn to "covering" *The Winter's Tale* because of the orphan motif, but in terms of adaptive practices, the most overt change she makes is in the portrayal of the sexual and romantic relationships. Whether the connection between Leontes and Polixenes in *The Winter's Tale* is homosocial, homoerotic, or homosexual continues to be debated, but in *The Gap of Time*, Winterson explicitly portrays the friendship between Leo and Xeno during their teenage boarding school years as sexual. As Julie Sanders points out, adaptation can "be an amplificatory procedure engaged in addition, expansion, accretion, interpolation ..." (18–19). It could be argued that in "amplifying" this episode, Winterson is not re-writing Leo and Xeno's experiences as much as she is making visible what the play represses. However, the novel offers more than a graphic exposure of their adolescent relationship; as in many of her works, Winterson is challenging restrictive notions of sexual identities and exploring their complex emotional consequences.

Winterson is widely admired for her inventive adaptations of canonical texts into contemporary fiction, but she has also been acclaimed for her destabilization of gender binaries. With her semi-autobiographical debut novel *Oranges Are Not the Only Fruit* (1985), Winterson became known as a writer with a radical lesbian agenda, but throughout her long career, she has resisted such limiting categorization, insisting, "Enough of the 'lesbian' tag" (Chittenden). In her essay, "The Semiotics of Sex," she explained: "I am a writer who happens to love women. I am not a lesbian who happens to write" (102). Winterson has consistently repeated this message throughout the last several decades: even as constructions of gender and sexuality are central preoccupations of her work, she eschews narrow definitions of sexual identities. *Written on the Body* (1992), perhaps her most famous novel, features a narrator whose gender is ambiguous, and her most recent works focus on the more current understanding of gender fluidity. In one interview she explained that her partner "calls herself post-heterosexual. I like that description because I like the idea of people being fluid in their sexuality. I don't for instance consider myself to be a lesbian. I want to be beyond those descriptive constraints" (Jeffries).

In *The Gap of Time*, the sexual relationship between Leo and Xeno is inextricable from their complex emotional attachment. Both have fathers from broken marriages who leave their thirteen-year-old sons at a boarding school. The other boys go home on weekends but Leo and Xeno are left behind, united in their common loneliness, and "by fifteen they were inseparable" (33). Typical teenage activities—movies, music, and sports—eventually lead to sex:

> One night after target practice they had sex. It was a cliché. Shower. Hard-on. Three-minute handjob. No kissing. But the next day Leo kissed Xeno in the bike shed. He kissed him and touched his face. He tried to say something but he didn't know what it was.
>
> *(33–34)*

In contrast to Shakespeare's "twinned lambs," Leo and Xeno are physically and temperamentally distinct: Xeno is smaller, quieter, and artistic, while Leo is stronger, taller, and combative. But in spite of their association with stereotypical feminine and masculine gender traits, they are afraid that their mutual attraction defines their sexual identity:

> "Do you think about girls when we do it?" said Xeno.

> "Yes," lied Leo.
> And then Xeno worried about being gay.
>
> *(34)*

In the midst of this emotional confusion, their friendship is threatened when Xeno nearly dies in a bike accident, a result of Leo's competitive challenge. Xeno forgives him, but Leo is overwhelmed with guilt and they begin to drift apart: Leo climbs the aggressive career ladder of corporate banking and Xeno lives a transient, bohemian life on the road. Still, their friendship endures into adulthood as they struggle with their individual and mutual identities:

> "Are you gay?" Leo asked suddenly.
> Xeno shrugged. He had girlfriends but no one special. He hadn't fallen in love but he liked women. He liked real conversations.
> Leo hadn't fallen in love either.
>
> *(39)*

Paul Zajac points to the central "area of thematic convergence between Shakespeare's *The Winter's Tale* and Winterson's *The Gap of Time*: the struggle to attain and maintain intimacy" (332). A fear of intimacy is an obstacle between Leo and Xeno but it also threatens their relationships with others. Leo, not typically insightful or reflective, at least attempts to reach some awareness of the problem:

> A man needs understanding because he is existentially alone … That was the difference between men and women, Leo thought. Men need groups and gangs and sport and clubs and institutions and women because men know that there is only nothingness and self-doubt. Women were always trying to make a connection, build a relationship. As though one human being could know another.
>
> *(40)*

The deep love between Leo and Xeno is as important as any sexual attraction, but their internalization of homophobic attitudes and their emotional immaturity impedes true intimacy. Other relationships in their lives—with partners, children, and colleagues—suffer from a similar avoidance of the vulnerability and responsibility that mature relationships demand. MiMi recognizes that Leo "is afraid of being close to anyone" and Xeno admits that he "liked holding hands with women … As long as they didn't get too close. And they always did—or thought they did, or tried to. It was easier with men" (67).

If Leo and Xeno are case studies in a fear of intimacy, they also exhibit a resistance to maturity and aging that is manifest in an obsession with play, like their counterparts in *The Winter's Tale*. Gina Bloom explains that within the context of early modern notions about play and masculinity, Polixenes' rhapsodic memory of their boyhood games and Leontes' emphasis on play with Mamillius "leads to a displaced obsession with youth and recreation" and a "failure to place themselves comfortably within a developmental narrative of manhood," though she further argues that Leontes is ultimately more successful in overcoming this failure than Polixenes (332).

Winterson reproduces the importance of play in *The Gap of Time*, where boyish indulgence in teenage sports and pranks gives way to men's obsession with video games. Many of Winterson's novels show a keen fascination with the ways technology can both isolate humans and create community; here, gaming represents a form of arrested development. Xeno criticizes conventional games: "Gaming is the best technology mated with prehistoric levels of human development ... It's all cars, fights, theft, risk, girls, and reward," which is what Leo prefers (38). But Xeno believes the medium can be elevated with an aesthetic and moral sensibility, and he makes a career designing a game called—in one of Winterson's many meta-devices—The Gap of Time.

The inspiration for this game, we learn later, comes from a story MiMi once told him about a dream the French poet Gérard de Nerval had before he committed suicide. Xeno's sophisticated concept posits a battle between Dark Angels and the Resistance to find the "most important thing in the world," which, in a deft bit of foreshadowing, is a lost baby. At first Xeno designs his game as a "pretty" allegory, but it eventually becomes a space, complete with avatars and the Paris apartment where MiMi is in hiding, where Xeno and Leo can keep track of each other and reenact the events of the past 16 years. When they play, Leo in particular can express his guilt and despair: "Xeno fluttered at the window like a moth. He wasn't her only visitor. Leo came and hurled himself at the glass that would not break. Battered the building with his wings. Promised. Begged. Raged. Wept ... Nothing changed" (209). As Lauren Muccilli argues, "within the landscape of the game, Xeno and Leo are both able to fully express the trauma they experience" but that catharsis "can only occur in the surreal confines of a virtual world" (10).

Virtual reality provides another opportunity not possible in the actual world: the manipulation of time. Xeno explains why this is one of the game's features: "At any point in the game you can deepfreeze an action, an event, a happening, and return to it later—because, perhaps, you can make it unhappen. I suppose that's what I wanted to do, make things unhappen" (196). Leo's similar desire to go back in time is reflected in his obsession with a favorite scene from a Superman movie where the hero flies around the world and bends time to save Lois Lane from dying. Karin Sellberg describes temporal destabilization as a frequent concern in Winterson's works, where she

> repeatedly questions the concept of time and the writing of history. Her fiction not merely challenges sexual and gender difference, but collapses the divide between past and present to create an interstitial space where empowering experiences abound and significant encounters may grow and prosper.
>
> (65)

But any empowerment or therapeutic value that the game's alteration of time may afford Leo and Xeno does not transfer to their lived reality, where "nothing changed." Towards the end of the novel, Xeno tells Perdita that he does not want to go back in time: "I am not wistful for lost youth. There's nothing there I want back. Not the van, the dog, the books, the girls, the boys, or Leo" (168). But his reclusive, static life suggests otherwise: both Xeno and Leo want to rewind time to undo past transgressions and to avoid confrontations in the present. Pauline, who has spent more time than anyone with Leo, puts it bluntly: "He's a typical Alpha Male. They don't grow up, they just get meaner" (60).

As in *The Winter's Tale*, a resistance to growing up is matched by a mistrust of women. Xeno professes to like women but avoids them; Leo's angry misogyny is revealed in his professed hatred for his mother, his sexist insults about Pauline's physical and professional qualities, and his disparaging comments about women in general. Most disturbing is Leo's treatment of MiMi, who fulfills the classic virgin-whore dichotomy for him: he worships her when he feels in control but when his insecurities overwhelm him, he sets out to produce evidence of her infidelity. In one of the most inventive and disconcerting chapters of the book, "Bawdy Planet," Leo convinces his assistant Cam to set up a surveillance camera in their bedroom so he can spy on MiMi and Xeno and gather proof of their adultery, magnifying the "pornographic aesthetics" of *The Winter's Tale*. When he watches video footage in which MiMi, Xeno, and Pauline are getting dressed for a fundraising concert, Leo—who frequently indulges in pornography for entertainment—projects his own outrageous interpretation onto the innocent scene and imagines depraved sexual activity among all three. In his shrewd analysis of this chapter, Paul Zajac points out that "as Leo watches, his possessive jealousy for MiMi meets his repressed sexual desire for Xeno ... and contributes to [his] dehumanization of and disconnection from his wife" (339–340). Just hours after Leo's violent pornographic fantasy, he rapes MiMi, forcing her into the premature delivery of Perdita. Leo persists in his belief that Perdita is the result of MiMi's adultery, and only with Milo's death and MiMi's utter collapse does he begin to recognize his wrongdoing.

If one desired outcome of *The Winter's Tale* and *The Gap of Time* is that adult networks can maturely accommodate same-sex and opposite-sex friendship and romance, that may remain wishful thinking for both texts. Many argue that in *The Winter's Tale*, the heterosexual is privileged in the reunion of Hermione and Leontes while the wifeless Polixenes is sidelined, yet others point to the rapturous reunion between the men and the absence of spoken forgiveness between the royal couple. Regardless, there is little in Shakespeare's play to suggest how the three characters together will negotiate their social and sexual bonds in the future, even when mollifying body language choices in performances may gesture otherwise.

In *The Gap of Time*, Winterson explores this triangle more thoroughly. While Winterson's description of Leo and Xeno's relationship as sexual may make visible what Shakespeare simply kept invisible, her version of the triangular relationship among MiMi and Xeno and Leo is also a bolder rewriting. Even if Shakespeare teases us with Polixenes' "nine-month" stay in Sicily, there is no indication that he and Hermione knew each other before or that their friendship was anything but, as Hermione tells Leontes, "such a kind of love as might become/ A lady like me; with a love even such,/ So, and no other, as your yourself commanded (3.3. 61–63). Winterson, on the other hand, provides a relationship between Xeno and MiMi prior to her marriage with Leo, as well as a reciprocal attraction among the three.

When Leo first sees MiMi performing in a bar in Paris she is a beautiful "boyish woman," and as she sings a song about falling, he thinks of Xeno: "Xeno had fallen … The hospital and Xeno holding his hand. Xeno never blamed him. He never spoke about to Leo who couldn't bear it. Leo who put the distance between them" (52). Leo's feelings for MiMi are mediated through his past with Xeno, and when he decides to propose to her, he sends Xeno as his emissary to Paris, where the two have a romantic meeting and nearly sleep together. Later, Xeno acts as Leo's best man:

> The night before the wedding they went out together, just the two of them, and Leo wanted Xeno to give him away—to be the one handing him over to MiMi. Instead, he gave Xeno the ring … [Xeno] put it on his little finger … and kissed Leo, so swiftly as if it had never happened, on the mouth.
>
> *(53)*

Leo is attracted to both Xeno and MiMi, and Xeno admits his love for both Leo and MiMi. He tells Perdita and Zel:

> I loved them both. Leo and MiMi … I should have married MiMi … . but he wanted her so much … and I thought, what did it matter? We will always be together, the three of us. I will love them both and I will be with them both. If they had wanted it I would have been lovers with them both, too … . Leo is confident and powerful—he's also an asshole—but he knows what he wants and he goes and gets it—that's attractive … We were lovers once—when we were teenage boys. I don't know how real it was for him. But it was real for me.
>
> *(198)*

While we hear less from MiMi, she also explains her love for them both. When she accepts Leo's marriage proposal, she does so partly because Xeno "will be around."

Does Winterson, then, offer any more certainty that homosocial, homosexual, and heterosexual bonds can co-exist than Shakespeare does? The novel's closing scene is indeterminate but perhaps more suggestive than Shakespeare's denouement. For this finale, Pauline has organized a fundraising concert and, after slipping off to Paris to inform MiMi that Perdita has been found, Pauline persuades her to come to London and perform:

A woman is standing like a statue in the light. She's wearing a simple black dress and red lipstick, her heavy hair cut short.

She doesn't move. Then she does.

"This song is for my daughter. It's called 'Perdita.'"

Leo stood up, went into the aisle. From somewhere in the theatre Xeno came and stood beside him. He put his arm around Leo. Leo was crying now, long tears of rain. That which is lost is found.

(267)

Perhaps "that which is lost" is not only Perdita, but the relationship between the men and their love for MiMi. Douglas Lanier observes that the various threads of *The Gap of Time* work to bring all of the characters towards a state of redemption, not only the major characters,

> but even supportive characters … (Shep, Clo, Lorraine, Pauline) … The novel's ending brings together these narrative arcs so that redemption is amplified and shared, though Winterson does not equate redemption with heterosexual union; Clo's new partner, Lorraine, we hear in a passing remark, is transsexual, and we last see Xeno and Leo with Xeno's arm around his weeping friend, with MiMi in effect out of the frame.
>
> *(239)*

Winterson may not be interested in equating redemption with heterosexual union, but she doesn't exclude it as possibility either. As with much of her previous work, *The Gap of Time* works towards a more expansive view of the way relationships might be reconstructed, so that friendship, love, and sexual relationships can co-exist and transcend cultural constraints. But as with *The Winter's Tale*, possibility is not promise.

The Winter's Tale, part two: Lost and found

Any hopeful outcomes at the end of the *The Winter's Tale* depend on the passage of time and Paulina's tireless oversight of Leontes and Hermione, but even more instrumental is the recovery of Perdita. Individual and collective renewal depends on Perdita's survival, for as the Oracle reminds us she determines the continuity of the family and political dynamic. As we contemplate the ending of this play, our focus on Leontes' degree of repentance, Hermione's method of hibernation, or Paulina's means of intervention should not eclipse the crucial reappearance of the daughter and heir that Leontes cast out to her probable death. The recovery of a newborn princess deliberately lost and precariously found is what allows personal restoration and royal stability.

In the first half of the play, Leontes' directs his anger with Hermione and Polixenes to Perdita as well, and his rejection of her is as violent and disruptive as his treatment is of them. Attempted murder of his friend and attempted execution of his queen are proof enough of his manic vindictiveness, but his brutal response to a newborn child is further manifestation of unleashed tyranny. Paulina brings the baby to Leontes in hopes he "may soften at the sight o'th'child" (2.2. 40), but instead he is further inflamed. In one scene alone he refers to Perdita five times as "bastard," in spite of Paulina's insistence on their physical resemblance, which Leontes' finds such a convincing signifier of paternity when he looks at Mamillius. As Aaron Kitch points out, the word "bastard"

> does a significant amount of work in the play as a register of the dangers of adulteration, hybridity, and illegitimacy. The bastard in early modern England was a cultural and political exile, a potentially subversive force connected with the failure to control discourse as well as with illicit sexual union ... [bastardy] also had quite tangible political consequences in early modern society, threatening ... monarchy as an institution based on authentic and pure bloodlines.
>
> *(50)*

We are reminded that both Elizabeth I and James I suffered challenges based on their heredity, and Deanne Williams argues that *The Winter's Tale* specifically "dramatizes a threatened royal girlhood" in producing "perhaps the most stark memorialization of the girlhood of Elizabeth: through Leontes' accusations of Hermione's adultery and his rejection of Perdita, Shakespeare revisits Henry VIII's treatment of Anne Boleyn and her young daughter" (117).

Even if the stakes were higher for royal legitimacy, however, Leontes does not stop, as Henry VIII did, at removing Perdita from the succession: he threatens to kill her, even with his own "proper hands." Leontes first consigns Perdita to death by fire but then orders Antigonus to abandon her in "some remote and desert place," the change of sentence less a sign of leniency than a punishment of Antigonus for defending "the innocent." Even Antigonus believes "a present death had been more merciful." Leontes has convinced himself that Perdita is not his daughter and he insists he will not be responsible for her—"I'll not rear another's issue"—but surely infanticide was not his only recourse.

In her work on early modern accounts of domestic crime and infanticide, Frances Dolan demonstrates how narratives of child murder overwhelmingly blamed mothers and exonerated fathers in spite of contrary historical evidence. *The Winter's Tale*, one of the most well-known early modern tales of child abandonment, participates in this distortion, particularly with its use of euphemisms to provide cover for Leontes' crimes: Leontes and other characters refer to the "loss" of Perdita rather than naming his murderous intentions for what they were. "Dwelling on Leontes' 'losses,' the play prepares for forgiveness by sparing Leontes the direct, criminalized agency associated with murderous mothers and helping us to repress our knowledge of his crucial role in 'losing' his children" (Dolan 167).

Even when Leontes announces his plan for repentance, he ignores Perdita. When he hears of Mamillius' death, only then does Leontes admit "I have too much believed my own suspicion." Believing that Hermione is still alive, he tells Paulina, "I'll reconcile me to Polixenes,/ New woo my queen, recall the good

Camillo ..." (3.2. 151–152). But he says nothing about Perdita, either at this point or later when he vows to visit the graves of Hermione and Mamillius. Nor does he use any of his royal authority, which he has drawn on abundantly, to send out a search party for her. Perhaps in his justification of his treatment of Perdita, Leontes does not feel the need to play any active role in fulfilling the passive grammar of the oracle's final pronouncement: "the King shall live without an heir if that which is lost be not found."

When Perdita is found by a Shepherd on the "seacoast" of Bohemia, it is in circumstances starkly different from Leontes' claustrophobic, misogynistic court. While Antigonus' farewell words—"for thy mother's fault art thou art exposed"— still assign blame to Hermione, the Shepherd displays a healthier attitude towards sex and reproduction as a natural and mutual enterprise. Immediately following his comic exasperation with frisky young men for their follies "and their getting wenches with child," he finds Perdita:

> What have we here? Mercy on 's, a bairn, a very pretty bairn! A boy or a child, I wonder? A pretty one, a very pretty one. Sure some scape. Though I am not bookish, yet I can read waiting-gentlewoman in the scape. This has been some stair-work, some trunk-work, some behind-door-work. They were warmer that got this than the poor thing is here. I'll take it up for pity.
>
> *(3.3. 65–70)*

The Shepherd assumes that the baby is the result of a gentlewoman's illicit activity, but he also refers to the "they" that produced the child. And, unlike Leontes' insistence, "I'll not rear another's issue," the old man simply decides to take her "up for pity." Several lines later, this frank realism gives way to a more poetic and fantastic interpretation of his discovery: after his son reports Antigonus' savage death, the old man replies, "Thou met'st with things dying, I with things new-born." Then, noticing the rich cloth protecting Perdita and discovering the money left in the box, he proclaims, "It was told me I should be rich by the fairies. This is some changeling ... this is fairy gold" (3.3. 101–105).

The Shepherd's transition from realism to supernatural references should not imply that superstition is the province of the lower-classes; Leontes' court is equally imbued with references to old wives' tales and allusions to magic and witchcraft. Scholars in recent years have demonstrated that belief in fairies and folklore traversed class distinctions, even when it co-existed with more rational and scientific beliefs. Folklore offered a means of accounting for that which was either inexplicable or culturally suspect. The motif of the changeling—a child thought to have been secretly substituted by fairies for the real child—could provide cover in both directions: a child with deformities or unusual traits could be explained as the fairies' substitution, while an abandoned child, especially if accompanied by money or resources for its protection, could be explained as the one fairies had stolen. As Mary Ellen Lamb explains,

> the Old Shepherd's attribution of a fairy origin to Perdita functions for Perdita's benefit, his own, and that of her unknown aristocratic mother. Declaring her to be a fairy changeling saves Perdita from lifelong shaming by providing a socially acceptable narrative for her supposed illegitimacy.
>
> *(284)*

Perdita suffers no shame within the pastoral shelter of her childhood until the intrusion of the courtly world in the form of her princely suitor, Florizel. Perdita is assigned fewer lines than Innogen, Marina, and Miranda, the young female protagonists of Shakespeare's other romances, but she grows up to be outspoken, realistic, and wise. Perdita understands Polixenes will not want his son to marry "a poor lowly maid" and warns Florizel that when the king learns of their courtship "you must change this purpose/ Or I my life" (4.4. 38–39). As she predicts, Polixenes is furious to discover that Florizel is wooing a Shepherd's daughter and in his angry tirade, elitism and sexism overlap. He calls Perdita a "fresh piece of excellent witchcraft," a "knack," an "enchantment worthy enough a herdsman," and he wrongly assumes that she has lured Florizel with sexual favors. Any hopes we might have entertained that Polixenes would be the gentler king in the play are disappointed here: he is tyrannical towards his son, condescending towards the Shepherd, and misogynistic towards Perdita. The lessons from the tragic events 16 years earlier have apparently been lost on Polixenes.

Perdita's attitude towards her social status is ambiguous: she resists playing the queen, being "goddesslike pranked up" for the sheep-shearing festival, leading some to suggest that she is not yet prepared for her royal identity. But perhaps she is being defensive about her upbringing rather than self-deprecating, for she is fully aware of the disparity between her station and Florizel's. At the heart of the frequently cited horticultural conversation between Perdita and Polixenes, she adamantly defends that which is natural: Perdita does not want grafted flowers in her garden, while Polixenes argues that mixing cultivated and wild flowers produces new and improved breeds: "You see, sweet maid, we marry/ A gentler scion to the wildest stock,/ And make conceive a bark of baser kind/ By bud of nobler race" (4.4. 92–95). Critics have puzzled over this exchange, for if the botanical process is analogous to social class, we would expect Polixenes and Perdita to take opposite positions, with Polixenes advocating purity over hybridity. Shakespeare is perhaps pointing to Polixenes' hypocrisy, which echoes the scene discussed in *Prospero's Daughter*: flowers can cross-breed but not social classes.

If, however, our attention is redirected to Perdita, who prefers flowers of household use and refuses to grow "streaked gillyvors,/ Which some call nature's bastards," her argument fits within a larger sense of her identity. Her use of "bastard" is no coincidence; though she would not remember how often Leontes used the fraught word to describe her as an infant, the echo is undeniable. Perdita's exclusion of "bastards" from her garden need not imply self-rejection but rather repudiation of the very notion of bastardy. More importantly, Perdita may be suggesting that the natural, and its equation with a lower social class, is beautiful enough without the amelioration of cultivating influences. While it is often assumed the intermingling between a higher and lower class is to the benefit of the latter—what we might colloquially call "marrying up"—Perdita suggests that the "baser kind" can be as susceptible to contamination from the "nobler race" as the inverse. Perdita's subversive challenge to the superiority of social hierarchies is even more evident in her outburst after Polixenes' denounces her:

> Even here undone!
> I was not much afeard; for once or twice
> I was about to speak and tell him plainly
> The selfsame sun that shines upon his court
> Hides not his visage from our cottage, but
> Looks on alike.
> *(4.4. 421–425)*

Though unaware of her royal lineage or her orphan history, Perdita is not scheming for royal status with Florizel, nor is she repudiating her humble upbringing, which might be expected from conventional foundling stories. In recent years, scholars including Barbara Estrin and Marianne Novy have exposed the constraints and misrepresentations of most foundling plots and adoption narratives, which privilege biological origins and undervalue the adoptive experience: "the temporary parents (who do all the work of raising the child) are annulled once the true heir is recovered" (Estrin 200). Estrin argues that in the two poles "of the formulaic foundling plot: everything depends on the initial egress from the royal womb and the concluding recovery of the imperiled dynasty" but that in Act 4 of *The Winter's Tale* Shakespeare focuses on the narrative "middle" and "betters the foundling plot, challenging the primacy of inherited, essentially patriarchal, bloodlines" (220). Perdita is not ashamed of her pastoral identity even as she is fully aware that it poses an impediment in her relationship with Florizel.

Much is made in the play that Perdita is "found," which is as misleading as the notion that she was simply "lost" rather than deliberately left to die. The Shepherd finds her when she is initially abandoned, but Perdita's reappearance in Sicilia 16 years later is the fortuitous result of Camillo's self-serving scheme and the young lovers' willing participation rather than anyone's active search. Nonetheless, it is her return that facilitates Leontes' reconciliation with Camillo and, through her marriage to Florizel, with Polixenes. More importantly, her reunion, first with Leontes and then with Hermione, allows for personal and political continuity. Stephen Orgel reminds us that while modern audiences may focus on the family reunion at the end, such a reaction may be anachronistic: "The tragic loss that Perdita represents was not the loss of her company, or of the opportunity to watch her grow ... but the loss of an heir." Once she is found, "everything returns to its proper place, and royal authority is restored" (*Winter's Tale* 79).

But what of Perdita's adoptive family who raised her for 16 years? Marianne Novy claims that although the Shepherd is nurturing and clearly provides "a better environment for child rearing than the cold and suspicious world of the court," his portrayal in the play is ambivalent: he and his son are simply named "the Shepherd and the Clown," and he nearly disowns Perdita when he is threatened by Polixenes (68). Furthermore, their recent upgrade as the king's "kindred" is played for comic effect when they brag about their new "gentlemen born" wardrobe to Autolycus. Yet, the off-stage meeting of Perdita's two families seems to have been welcoming. A gentleman reports that when Leontes is reunited with "his found daughter," he also "thanks the old shepherd, which stands by like a weather-bitten conduit of many kings' reigns" (5.2. 37–39). The Clown's report is even more enthusiastic:

> The King's son took me by the hand and called me brother; and then the two kings called my father brother, and then the Prince my brother and the Princess my sister called my father father; and so we wept, and there was the first gentlemanlike tears that we ever shed.
>
> *(5.2. 107–111)*

Still, any indication of assimilation of the humble and royal families does not appear in the final gathering in Pauline's art gallery, to which the Shepherd and the Clown do not seem to have been invited. As Novy points out, at the play's end, "Perdita's other family is lost from sight. The characterization of the old Shepherd, at this point, is designed to reduce interest in him and to focus instead on the reunion of Leontes, Hermione, and Perdita" (69). Perdita's story of how she has "been preserved" by one family for another family is a story yet to be told.

The Gap of Time, part two: Lost and found

Perdita's story as a foundling was what first inspired Winterson to "cover" *The Winter's Tale*. The ubiquity of the orphan plot in our literary tradition reveals what Linda Hutcheon calls its "narrative persistence" (4), but adoption also has personal relevance for Winterson and is a recurrent theme in her work. In many of her novels, and particularly in her unflinching memoir, *Why Be Happy When You Could Be Normal?* (2011), Winterson insists that the adoptive experience need not be defined exclusively by trauma, for it can also open possibilities for creativity and self-invention. Though Winterson's reconfiguring of *The Winter's Tale*'s complex web of adult sexual relationships may first strike readers as the more explicit revision, her amplification of Perdita's story also exposes a fundamental "talking back to Shakespeare." Winterson makes two critical interventions in the Perdita plot: first, she subverts traditional cultural paradigms of the adoption narrative in a revaluation of Perdita's nurturing and creative adoptive family, and second, she invests Perdita with significantly more character complexity and autonomy.

Although Winterson otherwise follows the narrative trajectory of *The Winter's Tale* closely, she chooses to place Perdita's abandonment and discovery, which was the mid-point of Shakespeare's play, at the very beginning of her novel. Leo orders his gardener, Tony, to deliver Perdita and a large amount of cash to Xeno in New Bohemia. When a bank tip-off sends thieves after Tony, he puts Perdita in a "BabyHatch," an enclosure attached to hospitals where infants can be left, intending to return for her. Shep, a widowed musician coming home from his work at a piano bar, witnesses Tony's murder by his assailants and notices the nearby BabyHatch lit up; realizing there must be some connection between "the dead man, the baby," he rescues Perdita. Shep later explains,

> I did some research. In Europe, in the Middle Ages ... they had BabyHatches back then. They called them Foundling Wheels; a round window in a convent or monastery, and you could pass a baby inside and hope that God would take care of it. Or you could leave it wrapped up in the woods for the dogs and wolves to raise. Leave it without a name but with something to begin the story.
> *(13)*

Shep picks up Perdita because he does not want to leave the baby to an uncertain fate in a foster care system; like the Old Shepherd, he takes Perdita up for "pity," but he also wants to redeem his guilt over the death of his wife, whose suffering from terminal illness he had ended with a mercy killing: "It's as though I've been given a life for the one I took. That feels like forgiveness to me" (22). Shep ponders the ethics of his decisions throughout Perdita's childhood.

In *The Winter's Tale*, Perdita's childhood is elided in the play's 16-year gap of time, but the affection she shares with her father and brother imply a positive upbringing. Winterson, on the other hand, fully depicts the nurturing care Perdita receives from her brother Clo and her father Shep, who claims, "I am learning to be a father and mother to her" (23). Shep's embrace of his androgynous parental role is another of Winterson's subversions of conventional gender restraints. When he renovates their new piano bar, he

> worked with Perdita strapped to his back. She had been put down once and he was never going to let her be put down again. At night she slept in his room and he told her old stories of love and loss. She was too young to know that's what they were. What she knew was the sound of his voice.
> *(130)*

Along with Barbara Estrin and Marianne Novy, Margaret Homans has reframed our understanding of the adoption narrative in literature and in lived experience. As Homans explains, adoption stories have typically been couched in terms of damage and loss, but other experiences can counter popular theories that insist only the discovery of one's birth parents will fill the void left by the adoption. According to Homans, sentimentalized and misleading representations of "adoption trauma" result from "the commonly unquestioned assumption that genetic inheritance precedes and trumps all other sources of identity formation" (5). Homans briefly discusses how Winterson's memoir captures both the pain and the positive outcomes of her own adoptive experience; in The Gap of Time, Winterson goes even further in imagining an honest, loving, and productive family life for Perdita.

Winterson's Perdita, unlike her counterpart, grows up with the knowledge of her adoption, as Shep explains: "She asks about her mother and I say we don't know. I have always told her the truth—or enough of it. And she is white and we are black so she knows she was found" (23). When Perdita and Zel are falling in love, Zel expresses his sympathy after she tells him she was adopted but Perdita replies that she is not sorry or ashamed, and when she discovers details of her history she assures Shep, "I love our life ... What you made for us" (247). Later, when Shep berates himself for not trying to reunite Perdita with MiMi, Pauline reminds him:

And what kind of a childhood would it have been? The divorce, the horror of everything that happened afterwards. Milo. And Leo would have had Perdita half the time, Mimi the other half, and all the misery of loss and mistake and the two of them not able to speak to each other. Perdita is happy with you.

(257)

This recurrent defense of the adoptive family throughout the novel may seem heavy-handed, but Winterson is intent on countering conventional foundling stories with an alternative experience.

When Xeno tells Perdita about her biological parents, she decides to go to London to find more information, but she approaches her mission without preconceived notions. She disguises herself as "Miranda" when she meets Leo and reserves judgment about whether she will reveal her own identity or seek a relationship with him. Even when Xeno, Shep, and Clo follow Perdita and Zel to London and the truth is revealed, Perdita remains loyal to her adoptive family. In The Winter's Tale, the Shepherd and the Clown are only partially included in the royal family's reunion, but in The Gap of Time, Winterson unequivocally portrays the assimilation between Perdita's two families, cementing it with further alliances in the romances between Shep and Pauline and Clo and Lorraine, Leo's office assistant. When Perdita's two fathers first meet—a reunion that Winterson, unlike Shakespeare, chooses to show—Shep is aware of Leo's suspicion: "Leo, you're one of the guys who makes the world the way it is. I'm one of the guys who lives in the world the way it is. To you I'm a black man you see mostly doing Security and Delivery. And money and power being the most important things to you, you reckon they are the most important things to those who don't have them ... " (247).

Leo does not respond well to the criticism: "You steal my daughter and spend my cash and now you're in my office lecturing me on how to live?" In the midst of this fraught tension between the two men, Perdita is the one who intervenes and initiates conciliation: she "went and stood by Shep and took his hand." After looking at Perdita closely and considering her gesture, Leo eventually offers his hand and says, "'Thank you ... I wish we'd met a long time ago.' Shep took his hand" (248). This is the moment of forgiveness the narrative arc of the romance genre reaches towards, but it is not facilitated here by Leo, or even Pauline, but by Perdita. In *The Winter's Tale*, the role Perdita plays as the agent of reconciliation is critical but largely coincidental; here, Winterson gives her Perdita the capacity to deliberately affect the narrative and its outcomes. Just as with several of the other works considered in this study, Gerard Genette's description of character revision as one of many possible strategies in adaptations applies here: "The revaluation of a character consists in investing him or her—by way of pragmatic or psychological transformation—with a more significant and/or more 'attractive' role in the value system of the hypertext than was the case in the hypotext" (50). Perdita's role in the "value system" is much more visibly enacted in *The Gap of Time*; when she is confronted with her complex family history she gathers information and works towards resolutions.

Winterson's greater investment in Perdita is clear, but her contemporary setting may also allow for more plausible empowerment. In looking at the affinities between Shakespeare's Perdita and young girls in the early modern period, Diane Purkiss points out that teenage girls were

> between childhood and adulthood, but also between two parents, between two cultures, borderers, liminals who walk the margins. As such, they are also marginal to their culture, and this was far truer in the early modern period, which devoted less energy to representing and interpellating them than does our own.
>
> *(58)*

Given a cultural context in which we have begun to value young girls in their own right, Winterson's contemporizing update affords her an opportunity to create a more influential and progressive Perdita.

Not only does Winterson's Perdita reverse the conventional foundling narrative but she exhibits a fuller range of determining personality traits and behaviors. Like her Shakespearean counterpart, Perdita manages the household for Shep and Clo with humor and brisk efficiency; she appreciates female community through her friendship with HollyPollyMolly, triplets who were adopted from China by a local family. But she is also musically talented, familiar with a range of musical genres and comfortable as a performer—perhaps a result of innate talent and MiMi's genetic influence, but mostly Shep's teaching. She is an avid reader and has informed opinions about current events. And, while she is in love with Zel and even takes the initiative in the relationship, she also insists on her independence, telling him at one point, "I'm not your possession." In short, Perdita is now a believable teenage girl, confident in her identity and not "marginal" to her culture.

Just as Perdita opened the novel, she also has the last word. Much has been made of the indeterminate ending of *The Winter's Tale*, and although *The Gap of Time* does not prescribe definite outcomes for its various characters, its conclusion suggests a more hopeful future. The novel's actual events close with MiMi's reappearance and suggestions of various reconciliations, but nonetheless, the story of the adult generation is minimized. After the novel ends, Winterson breaks the fictive boundaries with a paratextual interlude, commenting on her personal relationship with the play and concluding,

> After the nuclear wastes of Leontes' fallout, there is nothing that can be done until the next generation is ready to remedy it—and they too must first escape the necrotic longings of the past, as Perdita avoids death for a second time.
>
> (271)

And so, she gives Perdita, representative of "the next generation," the final say in what is both an epilogue and a prologue to the future. Perdita's words, a combination of lyrical beauty and pragmatic realism, are addressed to Zel and their possible life together, but they also evoke the previous generation's challenges with loving relationships:

> Soon this will become our life together and we have to live in the world like everyone else. We have to go to work, have children, make homes, make dinner, make love and the world is low on goodness these days so our lives may come to nothing. We will have dreams but will they come true?
>
> (272)

She follows with a series of scenarios describing their future life together, all predicated by "maybe," indicating possibility as well as uncertainty: "Maybe we'll hurt each other so much that we will deny that what happened happened" (272).

Julie Ellam claims that regardless of her subject matter, Winterson's work always returns to her unrelenting, foundational belief in the power of love, even as she offers penetrating critiques of its challenges. Perdita acknowledges that she may not be able to improve upon her parents' failures, but she will try:

> I will remember that, although history repeats itself and we always fall, and I am a carrier of history whose brief excursion into time leaves no mark, I have known something worth knowing, wild and unlikely and against every rote ... Though I find my way by flashlight in the dark, I am witness and evidence of what I know: this love.
>
> (273)

Shakespearean romance seeks redemption for past wrongs, but it is also grounded in the hope future generations provide. In this sense, The Gap of Time seems to be talking back to The Winter's Tale, perhaps urging everyone to look even more carefully to the children.

References

Bloom, Gina. "'Boy Eternal': Aging, Games, and Masculinity in The Winter's Tale." *English Literary Renaissance* 40. 3 (2010): 329–356.

Bond Stockton, Kathryn. "The Winter's Tale. Lost, or 'Exit, Pursued by a Bear': Causing Queer Children on Shakespeare's TV." In *Shakesqueer: A Queer Companion to the Complete Works of Shakespeare*, ed. Madhavi Menon. Durham: Duke UP, 2011.

Boose, Lynda. "The Pornographic Aesthetic of *Othello*." In *Othello: Contemporary Critical Essays*, ed. Lena Cowen Orlin. New York: Palgrave, 2004: 22–48.

Chittenden, Maurice. "Interview with Jeanette Winterson." *The Sunday Times*. December 13, 2009.

DiGangi, Mario, ed. *The Winter's Tale: Texts and Contexts*. New York: Bedford St. Martins, 2008.

Dolan, Frances. *Dangerous Familiars: Representations of Domestic Crime in England 1550–1700.* Ithaca: Cornell UP, 1994.

Ellam, Julie. *Love in Jeanette Winterson's Novels*. New York: Rodopi, 2010.

Estrin, Barbara. *Shakespeare and Contemporary Fiction: Theorizing Foundling and Lyric Plots.* Newark: U of Delaware Press, 2012.

Garber, Marjorie. *Coming of Age in Shakespeare*. London: Methuen, 1981.

Genette, Gérard. *Palimpsests: Literature in the Second Degree*. Trans. Channa Newman. Lincoln: U of Nebraska Press, 1997.

Greenblatt, Stephen. *Tyrant: Shakespeare on Politics*. New York: W. W. Norton, 2018.

Guy-Bray, Stephen. *Homoerotic Space: The Poetics of Loss in Renaissance Literature*. Toronto: U of Toronto Press, 2002.

Homans, Margaret. *The Imprint of Another Life: Adoption Narratives and Human Possibility*. Ann Arbor: U of Michigan Press, 2013.

Hutcheon, Linda. *A Theory of Adaptation*, 2nd ed. New York: Routledge, 2012.

Jeffries, Stuart. "Jeanette Winterson: 'I Thought of Suicide.'" *The Guardian*. February 21, 2010.

Kitch, Aaron. "Bastards and Broadsides in *The Winter's Tale*." *Renaissance Drama* 30 (2001): 43–71.

Lamb, Mary Ellen. "Taken By the Fairies: Fairy Practices and the Production of Popular Culture in *A Midsummer Night's Dream*." *Shakespeare Quarterly* 51. 3 (2000): 277–312.

Lanier, Douglas. "The Hogarth Shakespeare Series: Redeeming Shakespeare's Literariness." In *Shakespeare and Millenial Fiction*, ed. Andrew James Hartley. Cambridge: Cambridge UP, 2018: 230–250.

Muccilli, Lauren. "'My Big Game': Virtual Possible Worlds and the Surreal Aesthetic in Winterson's *The Gap of Time*." Unpublished paper.

Novy, Marianne. *Reading Adoption: Family and Difference in Fiction and Drama*. Ann Arbor: U of Michigan Press, 2007.

Orgel, Stephen. *Impersonations: The Performance of Gender in Shakespeare's England*. Cambridge: Cambridge UP, 1996.

Orgel, Stephen, ed. *The Winter's Tale*. Oxford: Oxford UP, 1996.

Purkiss, Diane. "Fractious: Teenage Girls' Tales in and out of Shakespeare." In *Oral Traditions and Gender in Early Modern Texts*, eds. Mary Ellen Lamb and Karen Bamford. London: Ashgate, 2008.

Sanders, Julie. *Adaptation and Appropriation*, 2nd ed. New York: Routledge, 2016.

Sellberg, Karin. "Beyond Queer Time after 9/11: The Work of Jeannette Winterson." In *Women's Fiction and Post-9/11 Contexts*, eds. Sebastian Groes, Peter Childs, and Claire Colebrook. New York: Lexington Books, 2015.

Sparey, Victoria. "Performing Puberty: Fertile Complexions in Shakespeare's Plays." *Shakespeare Bulletin* 33. 3 (2015): 441–467.

Traub, Valerie. "Gender and Sexuality in Shakespeare." In *The Cambridge Companion to Shakespeare*, eds. Margreta de Grazia and Stanley Wells. Cambridge: Cambridge UP, 2001: 129–146.

Williams, Deanne. *Shakespeare and the Performance of Girlhood*. New York: Palgrave Macmillan, 2014.

Winterson, Jeanette. "The Semiotics of Sex." In *Art Objects: Essays on Ecstasy and Effrontery*. New York: Knopf, 1996.

Winterson, Jeanette. *Weight: The Myth of Atlas and Heracles*. New York: Canongate Books, 2005.

Winterson, Jeanette. *Why Be Happy When You Could Be Normal?* New York: Grove Press, 2012.

Winterson, Jeanette. *The Gap of Time*. New York: Penguin Random House, 2015.

Zajac, Paul Joseph. "Distant Bedfellows: Shakespearean Struggles of Intimacy in Winterson's *The Gap of Time*." *Critique: Studies in Contemporary Fiction* 59. 3 (2018): 332–345.

5

MARK HADDON'S *THE PORPOISE* AND WILLIAM SHAKESPEARE'S *PERICLES*

When Hogarth Shakespeare asked Mark Haddon to adapt one of Shakespeare's plays, he turned down the invitation, claiming "I did not have the chutzpah to measure up to one of the big plays, and for that reason, I put it aside." But the idea of revisiting Shakespeare intrigued him and he later began to think about *Pericles* for "completely inexplicable reasons ... I knew that it wasn't terribly good in my opinion ... why measure up to Shakespeare on a good day? Why not take him when he's at a disadvantage, and he's only written half the play, and frankly he's not in top form?" Like Margaret Atwood and Jeanette Winterson, Haddon takes on Shakespeare with a combination of wry humor and respect—and a candid view that the bard deserves corrective intervention. What finally drew Haddon to *Pericles* was not that the play held personal relevance but "because there was a problem to be fixed" (Bogaev and Haddon).

Haddon is best known for *The Curious Incident of the Dog in the Night-Time* (2003), a coming-of-age novel about a young boy who gradually solves a difficult mystery about his family; the book won a stream of major literary awards, has been widely translated, and was in turn adapted for the stage in 2012. But the enormous success of that work should not eclipse the rest of Haddon's colorful career as an artist, a writer and illustrator of children's comic literature, a screenwriter, and an author of novels *A Spot of Bother* (2006), *The Red House* (2012), and now *The Porpoise* (2019). Haddon also published an acclaimed collection of short stories, *The Pier Falls* (2016), which includes several subversive adaptations of such canonical works as the myth of Ariadne and Theseus, the medieval romance *Sir Gawain and the Green Knight*, and a Brothers Grimm fairy tale.

Pericles has not elicited as much interest as other Shakespeare plays, perhaps because the episodic structure and the passivity of its hero disrupt conventional expectations about Shakespearean drama. But in the twenty-first century there has been renewed interest in staging *Pericles*: in particular, Mary Zimmerman's 2004

DOI: 10.4324/9781003166580-6

production with the Shakespeare Theatre Company in Washington D.C. and Trevor Nunn's 2016 production in Brooklyn at the Theatre for a New Audience were both celebrated for their emotional depth and spectacular stagecraft. Film and literary adaptations, though few, have found *Pericles* an apposite framework for current issues. Jacques Rivette's New Wave film, *Paris nous appartient* or *Paris Belongs to Us* (1961), is premised on a disastrous theatrical production of *Pericles* and includes various other intertextual Shakespeare references. The indie film *Pericles by Shakespeare on the Road* (2019) transplants Shakespeare's text into a contemporary landscape overlaid with visual references to immigration and poverty. Ali Smith's recent novel *Spring* (2020) uses *Pericles* as a subtext to corral her account of the global migrant crisis, a young girl searching for her mother in a detention center, and a screenwriter grieving for his friend. What some critics have characterized as "the messiness of the play's materials" provides fertile space for a wide range of imaginative appropriations (Cohen 1161).

Pericles begins with a scene in which the hero discovers the incestuous relationship between the princess he is wooing and her father. This brief episode is quickly dispatched, those characters forgotten, and the play turns to its primary focus on Pericles' labyrinthine adventure from marriage and fatherhood to tragedy, and then to recovery and reunion. The "problem to be fixed," for Haddon, is this very beginning where he

> felt that there was a gap in the play, which was also a moral wrong. The princess at the beginning who is in an incestuous relationship with her father, the King: she is used as a mere springboard to set the larger, melodramatic plot going. She's given no name, she's given two lines, and she is spurned by our protagonist.
>
> *(Bogaev and Haddon)*

Haddon began by addressing the silencing and trauma of the victimized girl and along the way he created a story as capacious and wide-ranging as *Pericles*. By empowering the play's female characters with more voice and more community, by destabilizing notions of pure, canonical Shakespeare, and by transgressing the foundations and parameters of the romance genre, Mark Haddon talks back—"and measures up to Shakespeare on a good day."

Pericles and *The Porpoise*: Brief synopses

For the purposes of adaptive comparison, it is necessary to provide brief synopses of Shakespeare's *Pericles*, most likely written in 1607–1608, and Mark Haddon's *The Porpoise*, published in 2019.

Pericles, Prince of Tyre draws on the Apollonious of Tyre episode from the medieval work *Confessio Amantis* by John Gower, later retold in prose by Laurence Twyne in *The Pattern of Painful Adventures* (c. 1576). In a nod to his own intertextual borrowings, Shakespeare brings in Gower as the occasional choric narrator.

Pericles is suitor to the daughter of King Antiochus, but when he discovers her incestuous relationship with her father, the king threatens his life. Leaving his government affairs to the faithful Helicanus, Pericles sets out on a sea voyage, pursued by Antiochus' hired assassin. In Tarsus, he helps King Cleon and Queen Dionyza rescue their country from a famine, but on the next phase of his journey a storm wrecks his ship on the coast of Pentapolis. There he woos Thaisa, daughter of the good King Simonides. They marry and Pericles then learns of Antiochus' death, so it is safe to return home. Pericles, a pregnant Thaisa, and her nurse Lychorida travel to Tyre; amidst another sea storm Thaisa delivers a baby girl, Marina, but then dies of childbirth complications. The shipmates insist that it is bad luck to keep a dead body on board so Thaisa is buried at sea. She washes ashore at Ephesus and is revived by a physician, Cerimon; assuming her baby and Pericles died in the storm, she becomes a priestess in the Temple of Diana. Pericles, deciding he cannot properly parent a newborn, takes Marina to Tarsus and leaves her with Cleon and Dionyza to raise with their own daughter Philoten.

As Marina grows up into a beautiful, accomplished young woman, Dionyza is jealous that she outshines Philoten, so like an evil fairy-tale stepmother, she orders Marina killed. Marina is instead kidnapped by pirates and traded to a brothel in Mytilene, but she manages to use her skillful rhetoric to preserve her virginity. She convinces several customers, including the governor of the city, Lysimachus, to mend their lewd ways. Pericles returns to Tarsus, eager to reclaim his daughter after several years, but Dionyza convinces him she died. Devastated, he resumes his sea voyage and just happens to land at Mytilene, where he is reunited with Marina. The goddess Diana then appears to Pericles in a vision and directs him to her temple at Ephesus, where he and Marina rediscover Thaisa. The conventional romance ending is completed when Marina is married off—in one of the most unsettling betrothals in all of Shakespeare—to Lysimachus, the governor of Mytilene and former brothel customer.

The Porpoise adheres to the play's general plot but slips back and forth between ancient, early modern, and contemporary time periods. Haddon's novel begins with a small plane crash in which a pregnant woman, Maja, is killed, though her baby girl survives. The counterpart to King Antiochus, the child's father Philippe, is a wealthy art collector, so overtaken by grief that he fashions his privileged life to live with his daughter Angelica in virtual isolation with only a few well-paid, compliant servants. As the years pass Philippe's obsession with Angelica turns to incest. When a private collector, Darius, shows up to sell some artwork, Angelica imagines him as a means of escape from her father. Philippe flies into a jealous rage and threatens Darius: at this point, realities begin to refract. In the novel's imaginary, it is possible that Philippe kills Darius, but it also appears that Darius escapes, manages to board a yacht named *The Porpoise*, and wakes to discover that he has travelled back thousands of years to become Pericles, the prince of Tyre.

The rest of *The Porpoise* toggles between the Pericles tale, much of which parallels Shakespeare's play, and Angelica's continued abuse in the present by her father, which she tries to resist first through escapist literature and a vow of silence, and finally anorexia. Haddon cleverly suggests that Angelica is the one narrating the richly re-imagined travails of Pericles, Marina, and Chloë, the Thaisa counterpart. The story recreates their separate journeys in picturesque detail, with much greater attention given to Chloë's life as a priestess at Diana's temple, its supportive community of women, and Marina's harrowing escape from her murderers. In a meta-textual inter-lude, the tale also stops by early modern London where Shakespeare's ghost escorts George Wilkins, the play's co-author and a notorious London pimp, into the afterlife where he encounters retribution from the women he abused in real life. The finale does not promise a reunion among Marina and her parents but it points readers in that direction, and there is no inclusion of a forced marriage with Lysimachus. In the pre-sent day, Angelica and her father die in a fire, like their Shakespearean parallels; but for Angelica, the ending also alludes to the possibility of a happier transport into a different world with the surreal guidance of a woman in "tunic, boots, quiver," a composite female figure of her own mother Maja and the women she has conjured in her stories, Marina, Chloë, and the goddess Diana.

Pericles, Prince of Tyre: Tell thy story

Pericles provides a useful case study in the vagaries of literary taste: it was enormously popular in its own day, but since then it has been one of the least performed and most reviled of Shakespeare's plays; as its critics like to point out, it was his one play that was not even included in the First Folio. Theatre records and contemporary references attest to the enthusiastic reception *Pericles* had with early modern theatre-goers, and when the theatres reopened during the Restoration it was the first of Shakespeare's plays to be performed (Giddens 173). But by the eighteenth century, interest was dwindling, as the episodic structure and uncertainty over its authorship made it less appealing to readers and audiences. In the nineteenth century the play's frank sexu-ality—incest, attempted rape, prostitution scenes—did not comport with a Victorian sensibility. It was not until the twentieth century that interest was renewed, with some of its alleged flaws then seen as fodder for creative possibility and critical interrogation.

The play's authorship has troubled its reputation as much as its content. In the last two decades, scholars have convincingly demonstrated that Shakespeare colla-borated with other dramatists on several of his plays. This issue of co-authorship should not be confused with the unfounded and usually preposterous claims of the "Anti-Stratfordians" that someone other than Shakespeare—Francis Bacon, the Earl of Oxford, even Queen Elizabeth in her spare time—wrote all of his plays. MacDonald Jackson, Brian Vickers, and others have used historical information and stylistic data to reveal that collaborative practice among early modern playwrights was not uncommon, and that Shakespeare had some degree of input from other authors in several of his plays, including George Peele in *Titus Andronicus*; Thomas Middleton in *Timon of Athens*; John Fletcher in *Henry VIII* and *The Two Noble Kinsmen*; and for our purposes, George Wilkins in *Pericles*.

Shakespeare's co-authorship with Wilkins has engendered more scholarly investi-gation and debate than his other collaborations; this is, in part, because *Pericles* was the first of what are now commonly referred to as Shakespeare's four romances, and thus signaled a pronounced shift in aesthetic direction from his late tragedies. But the anxiety also has to do with Wilkins himself. Because he was a notorious brothel owner and frequently in trouble with the law, Shakespeare's association with him has raised questions. Wilkins was considered "a distinctly second-rate, though by no means talentless writer" who had a brief but productive writing career between 1606–1608 (Duncan-Jones 206). In 1606, he published a translation of a Roman chronicle, *The History of Justine*, which, according to Anthony Parr, is an extensively plagiarized version of an early translation by Arthur Golding (ODNB). Around this time he also published *Three Miseries of Barberie*, a xenophobic account that claims that Muslims were struck by the plague far more than Christians. The following year saw a flurry of activity; he co-authored the scurrilous pamphlet *Jests to Make you Merrie* with Thomas Dekker; he collaborated with John Day and William Rowley on the play *The Travels of Three English Brothers*, a sensationalized account of the contemporary travels of the three Sherley brothers in the Middle East; and he wrote *The Miseries of Enforced Marriage*, which was performed by Shakespeare's company, the King's Men. This play was based on the 1605 scandal of country squire Walter Calverly's violent murder of his two small children and the near-fatal stabbing of his wife. The successful run of the play likely explains why Wilkins had a hand in *Pericles* for the King's Men later that year, but that collaboration was further complicated when Wilkins also published his own prose version in 1608, *The Painful Adventures of Pericles Prince of Tyre*, seemingly for personal profit. At that point, the relationship between Wilkins and the King's Men was severed, so the question is not why Wilkins was invited to collaborate with their theatre company in the first place, but why he was then no longer welcome.

In addition to any ill will that may have been caused by Wilkins' opportunistic gain from *Pericles* with his novelization, there may have been concerns about Wilkins himself. Wilkins owned a tavern-brothel and was known for his violent behavior, for which he was summoned in at least eighteen court cases. According to Katherine Duncan-Jones,

> As well as engaging in the unlicensed sale of food and drink, Wilkins had a persistent habit of violence, presumably when drunk. On one occasion he kicked a pregnant woman in the belly, on another stamped on a woman he had already beaten up so severely that she had to be carried home in a chair. In both cases, the women appear to have been prostitutes, widely regarded as "fair game."
>
> *(206)*

We do not know if Wilkins' criminal behavior affected any personal or professional relationship between him and Shakespeare. In 1612 there was a legal dispute involving a marriage dowry between Stephen Belott and his father-in-law, Christopher Mountjoy, in whose house Shakespeare had lodged; both Wilkins and Shakespeare gave evidence in court, though this does not prove an ongoing friendship between the two men. What we do know is that after 1608 Wilkins had no further collaboration with Shakespeare or with the King's Men. As Charles Nicholl puts it:

> After a brief swagger of literary success a chill settles over his career, and the next we hear of him is at [court] ... bound over for aggression towards the "quean" or prostitute Anne Plesington—and so begins the dark and violent tragicomedy described in the police-record.
>
> *(226)*

Finally, *Pericles* was reprinted in quarto six times prior to 1635, and not one of these editions named Wilkins as co-author. Still, the current scholarly consensus is that Wilkins wrote approximately the first nine scenes of the play and Shakespeare wrote the rest, even if we do not know the exact nature of their collaborative process.

Though *Pericles* has often been faulted for its hero who rules by absence and inactivity, and for its peripatetic plot, the play is a remarkably cohesive and symmetrical journey that begins in loss and suffering and ends in redemption and reunion. Characters, episodes, and themes echo, repeat, and reverberate as the play circles back to its principal concerns: the father–daughter relationship and the marginalization of the maternal in the family dynamic, natural and unnatural manifestations of sexual desire, and the use and abuse of kingly power. All of these concerns coalesce in the opening scene, a brief but blatant portrayal of incest in the royal family and a transgression of socially sanctioned courtship.

In his study about the personal, literary, political, and theoretical presence of incest in the Tudor and Stuart periods, Bruce Boehrer begins with the bold claim, "The English Renaissance is about incest." Boehrer describes how incestuous relationships, even broadly construed, were central to early modern constructions of personal identity and modes of controlling the distribution of wealth, status, and privilege:

> the act of becoming (or maintaining) oneself as one might want to be involves remaking (or preserving) one's family in a form that complements the desired self. Thus the very individuals who connect the strong Renaissance male to other males—mother, daughters, sisters, and so forth—also serve ... as focal points for the strong male's social narcissism, jealousies, and anxieties.
>
> *(5–6)*

For royalty, the pressure to ignore the incest prohibition and keep within the family was particularly intense: given the early modern philosophy of royal absolutism, monarchs did not want to be forced into dependence on external forces, "a foreign wife or husband, an elaborate marriage treaty drawn up between heads of state ... to maintain the royal lineage and the royal myth" (5–6).

The early modern position regarding incest, then, was oxymoronic: on the one hand the desire to keep control over a contained royal or aristocratic family implied some degree of incestuous association, yet the legal, religious, and social prohibitions against it were clear. The conflicts playing out in the social and political arena were inevitably reproduced on the stage; Bruce Boehrer and Lois Bueler have documented over forty plays in this period that deal with incest; it was a recurrent theme in prose romances as well (Boehrer 12). While definitions of incest encompassed a wide range of possible kinship connections beyond what we would call the immediate family, the father–daughter relationship becomes one of the most common and problematic sites of incestuous relations given the wide reach of patriarchal entitlement and possessiveness.

Before we see Pericles' attempt to procure a royal wife so he can secure his own family and dynasty, Gower opens the play describing the corruption in Antioch: "This king unto him took a fere/ Who died, and left a female heir/ So buxom, blithe, and full of face/ As heav'n had lent her all his frace/ With whom the father liking took/ And to her incest did provoke." The jauntiness of the rhyming tetrameter couplets juxtaposed with the perverse subject matter is disconcerting, but even more troubling are the next lines: "Bad child, worse father, to entice his own/ To evil should be done by none" (1.0. 21–28). While the fault is not distributed equally—the father is said to be worse—the attribution of any blame to the "bad child" is unfair as there is no evidence of her complicity. In the only two lines assigned to her, she wishes Pericles success in solving the riddle that is prerequisite to their marriage: "Of all 'sayed yet, mayst thou prove prosperous/ Of all 'sayed yet, I wish thee happiness" (1.0. 102–103). Brief as her words are, they indicate hope that Pericles will take her away from her father. Susan Frye points out that the sources Shakespeare drew on "both begin with the father's *rape* of Antiochus's daughter after her mother's death, while … Shakespeare works to erase the rape of his sources and implicate the daughter in the abomination of her father's physical incest" (45–46). However, while Shakespeare's Gower implicates the daughter, Shakespeare's princess herself gives no evidence of being a willing participant.

Until he reads the riddle, Pericles is oblivious to the signs that something is amiss. King Antiochus' language, filled with imagery of death and decay, is accompanied by visual reminders: a row of skulls on the wall, the heads of the previous suitors who were the "martyrs slain in Cupid's wars." This scene seems puzzling because Antiochus' riddle is hardly difficult to solve because he is encouraging men to discover the very "sin" he is trying to hide, and because either way the suitors answer the riddle guarantees their death. But the elimination of his rivals is precisely Antiochus' goal, and the air of illogic in the scene illustrates ambiguous Renaissance attitudes, which both condemned and perpetuated the problem of incest. Once Pericles discovers the "foul sin," he quickly flees Antioch to avoid its corruption and to protect himself from Antiochus' murderous wrath. This opening scene propels the play's narrative trajectory, Pericles' long journey from error to self-knowledge and compassion through his own trials and the suffering of his family.

What are Pericles' faults in this first catalytic episode? He is not wrong to pursue marriage and the formation of his own family, a dynastic imperative for a young ruler, nor can he be blamed for the incest he uncovered. But insofar as incestuous desire was an extreme manifestation of male control and possessiveness, especially endemic to royalty, Pericles' behavior is not beyond reproach. He greets the princess with objectifying language—she is the "fruit of yon celestial tree," a "fair glass of light," a "fair viol"—filtered through Antiochus' and his own male gaze, and then his admiration immediately turns to disgust when he realizes she has been "played on before her time." Like Gower, Pericles blames her as much as her father: "… and she, an eater of her mother's flesh/ By the defiling of her parents' bed,/ And both like serpents are …" (1.1. 173–175). Pericles' assumption of her guilt may explain his failure to help her escape but it also diminishes his standing as a heroic figure. Furthermore, the perception that the sexualized female body represents a disruptive threat to the body politic does not end in Antioch.

But if the romance genre, in contrast to tragedy, is determined by second chances—though not for everyone—another courtship opportunity soon presents itself; Pericles, journeying the high seas to avoid Antiochus' assassins, shipwrecks on the shores of Pentapolis and learns of a tournament to win King Simonides' daughter. In contrast to Antiochus, Simonides is said to be a decent ruler and an appropriately loving father, eager to make a good marriage for his daughter Thaisa; and unlike the virtually silent princess in Antioch, Thaisa is encouraged to speak out and participate in choosing her husband. But in this "do-over" there are still disturbing parallels: again, Thaisa is presented to the suitors as the object of their worshipful gaze and the prize in their male competition, and her father makes proprietary comments about her sexuality. Then, once she and Pericles fall in love, Simonides feigns disapproval to exert his paternal authority—as Prospero does with Ferdinand and Miranda—until he finally concedes: "It pleaseth me so well that I will see you wed/ Then with what haste you can, get you to bed" (9. 13–14). As Richard McCabe points out,

> Pericles's adventure in the court of Antiochus is presented as a bizarre perversion of familiar courtship rituals with the traditional paternal guardian incongruously cast as a rival lover. Lurking beneath the surface is a suggestion of similar, suppressed tensions in *all* such ordeals as the sexual component of parental love struggles with its own possessiveness.
>
> *(180; emphasis mine)*

Simonides may be a less menacing father than Antiochus and Thaisa is markedly different from the nameless princess in her expression of desire and agency. She woos Pericles with as much candor as Miranda woos Ferdinand, and she tells her father boldly, "I entreat you/ To remember that I am in love,/ The power of which love cannot be confined/ By the power of your will" (9. 80–81). Fortunately, Simonides agrees with Thaisa's choice, and Pericles' second courtship proceeds along the rightful track of marriage and procreation. Soon enough "a babe is moulded" and the formation of the proper royal family is reinforced when news arrives that the improper Antiochus and his daughter are dead and that Pericles, whose identity as king is now revealed, is asked to return to Tyre within a year and assume his throne. Thaisa, though far along in her pregnancy, insists on making the sea voyage with him, cementing her commitment to a new family order. But that transition is quickly interrupted, for on the voyage to Tyre Thaisa dies in childbirth during another storm. Lychorida, midwife and nurse, brings the baby to Pericles and announces both birth and death at once: "Take in your arms this piece of your dead queen" (11. 17–18). The sailors insist that Thaisa must be thrown overboard, and though Pericles accuses them of superstition, he hastily prepares an explanatory letter and includes jewels to pay for her burial should her coffin wash ashore, then says "a priestly farewell to her."

In the past several years, scholars including Janet Adelman, Helen Hackett, Naomi Miller, Gail Kerns Paster, Mary Beth Rose, and others have demonstrated the ambivalence of early modern attitudes towards female sexuality and maternity: on the one hand, procreation was prized as a woman's essential purpose, particularly for queens who needed to provide for dynastic continuity. On the other hand, however, pregnancy, childbirth, and motherhood were seen as polluting and threatening. These attitudes are reflected throughout early modern drama and Shakespeare's late plays in particular where, as Helen Hackett claims,

> the fact that mothers are so often dead or believed dead in these plays, has raised difficult questions as to how far the maternal is being celebrated, falling in with the general theme of rebirth, and how far it is being repressed or excluded.
>
> (Shakespeare's *26*)

Certainly in *Pericles*, there is scant celebration of the maternal, for within the long arc of the play, the span of Thaisa's marriage, pregnancy, and death is compressed, as if the fertile female body cannot be expunged quickly enough. As Janet Adelman points out, "Whatever the overt sympathy extended to Thaisa in childbirth, the play proceeds to treat her as though her maternity had made her taboo or tainted, allowing her to return only after a long period of penitential cleansing" (199). Nor is her wifehood given much attention: Jeanie Grant Moore explains that in the source texts Shakespeare drew on, Thaisa's death in childbirth is described in more prolonged detail, but here, "When Pericles' grief and his reluctance to have his wife thrown overboard are noticeably minimized in this way, the audience is denied the picture of a close marital bond" (39). Thaisa's coffin is recovered and after she is revived by the physician Cerimon she quickly embraces her solitary life, but the fact that she will live as a priestess only reinforces the need that she must be cleansed of a disease that signifies "the sullying female sexual and reproductive processes, and she is 'treated' in a temple appropriately designated to the worship of the pagan goddess Diana's admirable state of perpetual virginity" (Peterson 254).

If Pericles' opportunity to construct his royal family is thwarted by the elimination of Thaisa, he still has an heir, his "poor inch of nature." Pericles orders the sailors to head to Tarsus—where he had earlier rescued the kingdom of Cleon and Dionyza from famine—"for the babe/ Cannot hold out to Tyre. There I'll leave it/ At careful nursing" (11. 76–77). Pericles remains with Marina in Tarsus until his twelve-month deadline to return to Tyre nears and he then returns alone to stabilize his kingdom. The prevailing criticism of Pericles for leaving his newborn daughter in foster care may be anachronistic: Marianne

Novy reminds us that the early modern period was a time of "multiple parenting," and though the spatial and temporal separation in this case is extreme, it was not uncommon for aristocratic and royal children to be raised in other households (238–241). Still, Pericles' decision to leave Marina behind may not entirely be explained by childrearing practices or political exigencies, nor does it help advance his narrative of progress in dynastic terms. Many critics have suggested that a more compelling reason Pericles leaves Marina is to avoid the snare of incest that seems to threaten many paternal relationships; as Deanne Williams claims, "When he later finds himself in the same position as Antiochus, a widower raising a daughter, he arranges things to make sure he doesn't fall into the same pattern … it is not so much that Pericles abandons his daughter to be raised by others following the death of his wife" but that he leaves to preserve her independence and literally avoid the act of incest (102–103). Whether Pericles is abdicating his paternal responsibility, acting soundly, or avoiding temptation, his ability to reassume his throne at this point cannot accommodate the sexual temptation or dangerous maternity that females represent.

Pericles does think of Marina as his heir, for he asks that she be given "a princely education." Cleon and Dionyza, indebted to Pericles for his earlier help to their kingdom, educate their charge well, but as the years pass Marina becomes more attractive than their own daughter, Philoten. Dionyza grows so jealous on Philoten's behalf that she arranges for Marina's murder. Once Lychorida dies, thus removing the only protective maternal presence in Marina's life, Dionyza orders her servant Leonine to carry out the killing. But Marina begins telling him about her life "when I was born," and in the delay her story telling causes, pirates come ashore, kidnap her, and sell her to a brothel in Mytiline.

This rapid turnaround of events may seem outlandish even within the romance genre's atmosphere of exaggerated episodes, but piracy, sex trafficking, and the prostitution industry were not unknown in early modern England. Marina is a prize because of her virginity, and the brothel owners Pander and Bawd are excited about the profit they will make from her, for "such a maidenhead were no cheap thing." But in an impressive display of fortitude and rhetoric, Marina protects herself and directs her customers to a more virtuous life. Her princely education was likely not intended for this purpose, but her persuasive tactics serve her well, much to the dismay of her employers who quickly realize that their new investment is bad for business. When the governor of the country, Lysimachus, arrives, Bawd scolds Marina to do no more "virginal fencing" and remember that he is their most important client and "an honourable man"—so Marina appeals to him on the basis of that honor: "My life is yet unspotted/ My chastity unstained ev'n in thought./ Then if your violence deface this building/ The workmanship of heaven, you do kill your honour,/ Abuse your justice, and impoverish me" (19. 103–106). After a prolonged appeal, Lysimachus is convinced: "Though I brought hither a corrupted mind/ Thy speech hath altered it" (19. 121–122).

Lysimachus pays more than his usual fee but Bawd and Pander are furious when he leaves "as cold as a snowball, and saying his prayers, too." Pander orders Boult, a brothel worker, to rape Marina: "Crack the ice of her virginity, and make the rest malleable" (19. 158–159). When Marina defends herself and urges Boult to seek better employment, his reply reminds us that prostitution was an industry, in part, driven by poverty: "What would you have me do? Go to the wars, would you, where a man may serve seven years for the loss of a leg and have not money enough in the end to buy him a wooden one?" (19. 195–198).

Furthermore, children were frequently its victims. Duncan Salkeld describes how *Pericles* reflects the actual problem of early modern sex trafficking in children in England: "In this play Shakespeare and Wilkins depict the world of pimps and bawds as dangerous and cruel, especially for young people, for caught up in the midst of this appalling exploitation is a young child, Marina" (Courtesans 61).

If Marina is only 14, Lysimachus' questions disturbingly suggest that even younger girls were exploited—"How long have you been in this profession? ... Did you go to it so young? Were you a gamester at five, or seven?" (19. 64–70). *Pericles*, Salkeld argues, shows "Shakespeare at his most socially engaged ... neither Shakespeare nor Wilkins was escapist. Theirs is the only play of its kind to recognize the suffering of some early modern children in garrets and chambers just beyond the playhouse walls" (London 89).

Marina is exceptionally adept at meeting every threat against her on its own terms. Boult's concerns are economic, so she offers him a business plan. Marina the gifted storyteller, Marina the angel in the house of iniquity, now becomes Marina the entrepreneur:

> Here's gold for thee.
> If that thy master would make gain by me,
> Proclaim that I can sing, weave, sew, and dance,
> With other virtues which I'll keep from boast,
> And I will undertake all these to teach,
> I doubt not but this populous city will
> Yield many scholars.
>
> *(19. 193–199)*

Marina's plan to open a finishing school for Renaissance women is successful, and she gives her earnings to the brothel owners. The play's negative characterizations of women up to this point—incestuous daughter, dead mothers, evil queen, cold-hearted bawd—are finally countered by Marina's fearless independence and pragmatic agency.

In *The Tempest* and *The Winter's Tale*, Miranda and Perdita play significant roles in bringing about family harmony and political restoration, but Marina is even more instrumental in activating the play's resolution, not only because she is remarkably accomplished but because her father is in such a dire state. Pericles was finally on his way to Tarsus to bring Marina home, but he arrives just after her abduction and Dionyza convinces him she died. Pericles travels on for months and when the ship happens to stop in Mytilene, he is still overcome by regret and sorrow. Lysimachus welcomes the visiting king and learning that his grief has rendered him silent, he sends for the charismatic talker Marina to "win some words of him." In contrast to the silenced princess of Antioch, Marina is admired and valued for her speech. In an extraordinarily emotional scene, Pericles at first rebuffs Marina, resisting any attempts to intrude on his self-imposed isolation. Gina Bloom argues that

> in closing his ears to protect himself from further dangers, Pericles has shut out knowledge as well, including the essential knowledge of his state's political disorder ... for with the deaths of his loved ones, Pericles has lost his opportunity to produce an heir to the throne.
>
> *(129)*

But as Marina gently persists in recounting her experiences, Pericles listens and fires questions at her—urging her to "tell thy story"—and with each revelation he grows more animated and hopeful. When Pericles is finally convinced of her identity, he is ecstatic: "Now blessing on thee! Rise. Thou art my child" (21. 199). Rejuvenated, he calls for his royal robes, signaling his readiness to resume his political responsibilities as well as his proper role as father. By the end of *Pericles*, "both fatherhood and daughterhood have been redefined, with fathers no longer the tyrannical agent of terror, but eager listeners, and daughters no longer the victimized objects of patriarchal will, but self-sufficient storytellers" (Williams 107).

The stability of the royal family also requires Thaisa's resurrection, facilitated when the goddess Diana appears to Pericles in a vision and orders him to Ephesus. In a second dramatic reunion, Cerimon reveals to Pericles that Thaisa, who has been serving as a nun at Diana's altar, is his wife. Pericles and Thaisa are overjoyed to discover each other alive, and Thaisa and Marina meet for the first time since the ill-fated childbirth. In a parallel to his reunion with Marina, Pericles asks to know every detail of Thaisa's recovery, "how this dead queen re-lives," and to whom he owes gratitude "for this great miracle." Royal authority is reasserted with signs that Pericles has been enlightened and humbled by his suffering and can now appropriately embrace his roles as compassionate husband, appropriate father, and confident king.

But Pericles' transformation and the harmonious ending come at a cost for Marina when he abruptly announces he will marry her off to Lysimachus. The previously independent and voluble Marina speaks only one line in the final scene—a greeting to her mother—but says nothing about her betrothal, and her silence does not necessarily convey consent. For his part, Lysimachus earlier admitted that he would marry Marina if only she were not lowborn but "came of gentle kind or noble stock"; now, once the impediment of her social status has been removed, he is eager to marry a princess. Apologists for Lysimachus' elitism may claim that he is simply reflecting hierarchical conventions of the time, but in the other two romances we have considered, Ferdinand and Florizel's attractions to Miranda and Perdita are not predicated on their social class. More important is that, in spite of his alleged conversion, Lysimachus was a regular client at a brothel where sexually transmitted diseases, as Pander and Bawd joke, are accepted as an occupational hazard. Margaret Healey reminds us that "for early modern playgoers child prostitution and syphilis were very real and allied diseases" and they would have seen Lysimachus as corrupted by this "tragic and widespread disease" (101). Even though their reunion takes place at the temple of the virgin goddess Diana, the specter of sexual corruption has not been eliminated by the end of the play— except that the threat of contamination is now located in the male presence.

Furthermore, with the announcement of Marina's marriage to Lysimachus comes the news that Simonides has died, so Pericles decides that he and Thaisa will rule Pentapolis, and Marina and Lysimachus will rule Tyre; Pericles has passed his own kingdom to his daughter and agreed to rule jointly with his wife in the kingdom she inherited, suggesting a fairly progressive articulation of royal author- ity. But this solution also ensures that the tempting presence of his daughter will not threaten the royal stability Pericles has achieved:

> Marina will never know him, since they will rule in different lands. Many see the reunion scene as restorative for Pericles since they believe it sets to rest his unresolved Oedipal desires ... but [her marriage] can also be seen as another of Pericles' escapes; the absence of his daughter will allow him to avoid ever confronting the Oedipal problem.
>
> *(Moore 42)*

As in *The Winter's Tale*, the romance genre's eagerness to celebrate the king's recup- erated family and political continuity does not fully resolve the problems of royal entitlement and sexual anxiety that produced so much suffering and trauma in the first place, or the fact that the recovery may not be experienced equally by everyone.

The Porpoise: Women who weave stories

Towards the end of *The Porpoise*, an assassin executing his order to kill a young girl is overtaken in a dark forest by a group of women with arrows and javelins:

> If he had been asked what would frighten him most at night in the hills he would have said a hungry bear, or a band of armed men perhaps. But this scares him more than anything he could imagine ... The world turned upside down. The weak given power.
>
> *(234)*

In this retelling of *Pericles*, these warrior women remind us that women who talk back to Shakespeare can include female characters as well as female authors. Mark Haddon's novel is the one work in this study by a male writer, and it is arguably the most explicitly feminist in reversing the minimization of women in its source text. In *The*

Porpoise, Haddon invests his female characters with more vibrant personalities, more interiority within the narrative arc, and more authority in telling their own stories.

In several interviews, Mark Haddon explains that the catalyst for his adaptation of *Pericles* was the portrayal of the abused princess in the opening scene. Haddon objected to her role as simply a convenient device to initiate the larger, melodramatic plot. Furthermore, she is nameless, she is only ascribed two lines, "and she is spurned by our protagonist, who is the first person outside the family to realize what is happening to her. He was initially attracted to her. When he realizes that she is being sexually abused, he simply runs away." This moral failure seemed urgent for Haddon, who adds that a book "… works, or at least it only works for me, if there's a necessity to it. If something feels as if it needs to be fixed" (BBC).

The Porpoise begins to fix the problem in *Pericles* by recognizing that the presence of incest cannot so quickly be erased, emblematic as it is of the fraught sexual politics that persist throughout the play. After making visible the causes and the damage of the incestuous relationship, the novel incrementally expands to give voice to the silenced female characters, create a strong community of female protectors, and reassess conventional constructions of masculinity. In the process of this ambitious agenda, Haddon challenges definitions of the romance genre that rely on an unequivocal restoration of the patriarchal status quo.

In Haddon's contemporary setting, Antioch's counterpart is Philippe, an international art collector whose pregnant wife, a beautiful actress, dies in a plane crash, though her baby survives. Philippe wraps himself in reclusive mourning but is shocked that a man of his status should have to endure such suffering: "Philippe is not so naïve as to believe that money can alter the brute facts of life but he has always assumed that it can postpone and ameliorate" (18). In his grief and self-absorption he begins to justify the incestuous possession of his daughter Angelica, the worst of many manifestations of his sense of entitlement:

> When does Philippe's touching move from innocence into something more sinister? … He cares for her unconditionally in a way that no one else will ever be able to care for her … Nor, as she gets older, will he be able to bear the thought of sharing Angelica with another man … He will refrain from full intercourse until he is fourteen. He thinks of this as a kindness.
>
> *(34)*

Though the house staff suspects impropriety, they are paid well enough to pretend ignorance. Bruce Boehrer argues that there is a parallel between early modern and contemporary articulations of incest: "the political imperatives of Tudor family structure are reiterated in contemporary family arrangements that privilege the male, and that these family arrangements, in their turn, generate and/or augment paternal incestuous desire" (5). Echoing the rationale for the incestuous behavior in *Prospero's Daughter*, paternalism and privilege intersect in Philippe's insistence that his actions are protecting Angelica, his possession.

The Porpoise is shaped around multiple perspectives so we are privy to Angelica's interiority, not just Philippe's. Angelica at first believes that what Philippe does to her is normal: "How would she know any different? ... Some of the things he makes her do are disgusting and some of them are painful, but ... only as she gets older is there a growing sense of something wrong" (37). Angela's victimization is exacerbated by her extreme loneliness. Philippe has isolated her from any friends or family and he has bribed the servants into denial. With no outside support or counter explanation for her experience Angelica is left to try to understand it herself, and she begins to wonder if her lack of resistance makes her an accomplice. She immerses herself in reading for escape and solace, and the literature of fantasy and mythology that she prefers begins to shape how she sees the world.

As she grows into an attractive teenaged girl, older men begin to notice her on the rare occasions she and Philippe appear in public; Philippe is jealous and paranoid that "she is looking for a white knight, someone to hoist her onto his saddle and bear her away" (41). That potential white knight comes in the form of Darius, the son of one of Philippe's fellow traders in the art world. When his father suddenly dies and Darius is unsure if he has been left any money, he decides to make a quick profit by selling a set of Hockney etchings to Philippe. Darius shows up unannounced and Angelica is so excited to see a rare visitor that she is "already in thrall of an imagined future in which he takes her away from all of this, and the knowledge that the fantasy is ridiculous does nothing to sour its addictive sweetness" (44). Philippe orders her to her room but Darius, every bit as confident and privileged as Philippe, insists that Angelica remain and she decides "for once, to hell with her father" (45).

Darius senses, however, that in spite of his initial attraction to her, something is amiss and he first puts the blame on Angelica, who now seems "needy and fragile." When he realizes that the real problem is Philippe's dangerous sexual jealousy, he leaves to avoid becoming involved. But Darius differs from Pericles who fled from Antioch—though Darius has led a dissolute life of privilege and womanizing, he sees Angelica's plight as a moral dilemma and decides he must help her escape after all:

> But a teenage girl is suffering and he finds that for once he can't walk away. That desperate look she gave him as he turned and left. He had acted dishonorably and far from being a victory his departure had in fact been a shameful admission of defeat.
>
> *(48)*

When Darius returns, Philippe chases him into the woods and attacks him with a heavy cast-iron poker. A violent struggle ensues and Darius is severely injured; after this episode, the novel departs from its single linear trajectory, as we are told that either "Darius is dead, or he escaped and ran away." At this point, Haddon turns the narrative authority over to Angelica: she goes to her room and enters the world "between dream and story ... She is weaving another world" (56–57). In Angelica's telling, Darius finds his way to an emergency room and then, with the help of friends, he flees for his life on a yacht and wakes up the next day as Pericles, and she begins recounting his continuing journey.

In restoring voice to Angelica, the counterpart to the wronged princess of Antioch, Haddon does not adopt the most convenient and obvious corrective by simply granting her more dialogue and presence. Haddon's strategy in assigning Angelica more control over her speech takes two interesting and seemingly opposite forms: on the one hand, from this point on she refuses to speak out loud and, on the other hand, she becomes the teller of a richly detailed tale of female-centered heroism. After years of being a powerless victim of her father's desire, she learns that the one way she can exert control is through language: she will decide when and how to use her words.

Once escape with Darius is no longer possible, Angelica stops talking, and the more her silence angers her father, the more empowered she feels: "She has always deferred to her father, always done what he tells her to do, but as this silence extends the balance begins to shift" (82). Angelica's silence at first might not seem agentic, but she quickly realizes how thrilling it is to finally have some control. Silence is typically equated with passivity and submissiveness, understood to be the opposite of expression as an act of human agency. But as Christina Luckyj points out in her work on early modern women's silence and speech, there is a difference between being silenced and being silent. Even in the early modern period silence was understood as a potential means of defiance: "Contrary to its own agenda of keeping women and silence in their places, early modern misogyny invests feminine silence with significant power and danger … Feminine silence can be constructed as a space of subjective agency which threatens masculine authority" (Luckyj 60). Although women were typically admonished to be "chaste, silent, and obedient," the desired outcome of male dominance over women's speech was not always silence: the goal was to dictate women's use of language to serve patriarchal needs, whether that meant silence or compliance. So in spite of the cajoling and threats from her father, Angelica continues to remain silent in her external reality and instead turns inward, for "there is only one story she wants to tell now" (83).

Perhaps Haddon's most radical departure from *Pericles* is to give Angelica ownership of the story, a blank canvas where her creativity can be exercised. Because Philippe did not want the prying interference of school officials and teachers, Angelica has been largely taught by tutors and by her own private reading, where she finds comfort and companionship. She loves older stories,

> those that set deep truths ringing like bells, that take the raw materials of sex and cruelty, of fate and chance, and render them safe by trapping them in beautiful words. And every night, when her father comes to her room, she recites silently to herself the magic words which bring one of those other worlds into being and wanders there, far from the body he is using for his pleasure.
>
> (38–39)

She especially loves mythology and the "darker tales about women who weave stories"—Arachne, Minerva, Helen—and as she constructs her own story, weaving becomes a recurrent trope for female creativity and expression.

As Angelica cloaks herself in silence externally, inwardly she unleashes the full force of her voice as she becomes the creator of stories as well as the receiver:

> She is both teller and listener. She forgets, sometimes, where the page ends and her mind begins. She recounts these tales to herself in idle moments, inevitably changing them a little every time and comes to believe, in some occult way, that these are stories of her own invention ...
>
> *(39)*

If the impetus for her story was to tell her newly imagined version of Darius as Pericles, her adventurous romance soon expands to create powerful women and to imagine herself in new roles affiliated with Marina, Chloë, and the leader of the female community, the goddess Diana.

Our contemporary association between female readers and the romance genre dates back to the early modern period when, it is often assumed, romance fiction was largely intended for and associated with an emerging, newly literate female readership. However, a distinction must be made between current definitions of romance as narratives concerned largely with heterosexual courtship, marriage, and domesticity, and the broader early modern concept of romance as a genre comprising exotic travel, fantastic elements, and wondrous coincidences. Helen Hackett urges a more cautious view about the notion of early modern romance fiction as primarily female-driven by reminding us that these works, with a few exceptions, were authored by male writers and often had a male readership in mind as well, though she acknowledges that a female audience was significant (*Women* 21–25). Tina Krontiris argues that early modern romance was an "oppositional genre" because "by its portrayal of daring heroines the romance often encouraged women to ignore social restrictions" and "by its construction of an ideal world, the romance ... could make the female reader critical of her position in the real world ..." (55–56). Krontiris adds that the romance genre offered experiences to women that were typically unattainable in real life, citing the ubiquity of Amazons and warrior women as an example. Joyce Boro also argues that early modern women read romances not necessarily for the "eroticized experiences," as supposed by their male contemporaries; rather, because romances often included adventurous and courageous female protagonists, they offered modes of behavior that

> were in stark opposition to that of the ideal woman—stationary, domestic, chaste, silent, and obedient—which women were consistently encouraged to emulate ... it is incontestable that the genre was gendered as feminine and that it offered a recognizable imaginative space of female agency.
>
> *(190)*

Pericles incorporates many of the elements of romance that were present in its sources—far flung travels, supernatural interventions, and twists of fate—but its general focus remains on the experiences of the eponymous hero. Although *The Porpoise* preserves the contours of the *Pericles* framework, Angelica's immersion in the "old tales" about women, and the lack of nurturing female presence in her own life, leads her to imagine an alternative iteration of her own story that centers less exclusively on Pericles and distributes more attention to Marina, Chloë, and other female characters.

Current research in literary trauma studies, a field that has emerged in the last few decades, can also illuminate why and how Angelica, as a victim of incest and rape, authors her story. Led by pioneer Cathy Caruth, the first generation of trauma studies scholars aligned with prevailing trends in psychological research that described trauma as so devastating that the victim was unable or unwilling to remember or articulate it, a notion referred to as "traumatic amnesia" that became foundational to trauma studies. However, imaginative or figurative literature was thought to be a vehicle that could give expression to trauma when ordinary, discursive language was inadequate: "Literary verbalization … still remains a basis for making the wound perceivable and the silence audible …" (Hartman 259). More recently, scholars including Michelle Balaev and Joshua Pederson have argued against the theory of amnesia, claiming that trauma is quite memorable and describable; that this recognition is necessary to give agency to the survivor; and that a variety of linguistic registers as well as literary forms can have healing power. For Angelica, remembering her trauma was never in question; her challenge was in discovering how she wanted to express and transform her experiences. Once she decides to adopt an external silence and weave an internal story, the knowledge that she can control her own language is empowering:

> She is surprised to discover how strong it is, the simplest of weapons, one that has been lying unused within her reach all this time. She takes up less space than she once did, but she is not reduced … She was a branch, now she is a blade. She can cut through anything. She cannot be broken.
>
> *(109)*

The call now in literary trauma studies is to focus less on the unsaid and more on the content and multiple forms various textual narratives of trauma can produce. As Pederson points out, critics should recognize that "authors may record trauma with excessive detail and vibrant intensity. Indeed, we may need more words—not fewer—to accurately represent its effects in text" (339). Many psychologists now argue that while victims may in fact have intense memories of trauma, these memories may be altered, so spatial and temporal contexts may change as well and lived reality may seem unreal. This phenomenon may be evident in the types of literary forms used to express trauma: "Literature—and perhaps modern literature most convincingly—is capable of capturing the effects of this condition … evocations of confusion, shifts in place and time, out-of-body experiences, and a general sense of unreality" (Pederson 340). If the alternative life Angelica wants to imagine for herself is served by the female-driven romance genre, so too is the narration of her trauma served by the slipstream form her story takes that juxtaposes realistic detail and prolonged descriptions with multiple perspectives, temporal shifts, and a sense of dislocation. Many critics now concur that in trauma fiction "novelists frequently draw on the supernatural ... the real can no longer appear directly or be expressed in a conventional realist mode" (Whitehead 84).

Given the sustained sexual abuse Angelica has suffered from her father, it is not surprising that hers is also a feminist narrative populated by strong female characters and a community that provides sanctuary from male predators. As Angelica imagines herself as Marina, she also conjures her mother in the form of Chloë, the Thaisa counterpart, who has "thick blond hair and blue, blue eyes ... [and] a tiny half-moon scar on her cheek," a description that duplicates what she knows of her actual mother. In *Pericles*, Thaisa is more fully realized than the nearly silent princess of Antioch, but in *The Porpoise*, Chloë commands even more attention than Thaisa. Suitors still come to Pentapolis to vie for her hand, but now she has brothers whose own marriages relieve any pressure for her to be the sole provider for dynastic continuity and a mother whose presence mitigates any incestuous undertones. Simonides is a fond, indulgent father who admits that Chloë has an independent spirit because he "allowed her to read books," and when he notices that she and Pericles are falling in love

> what he feels mostly is a terrible sadness at the forthcoming loss of the only person in the palace who can tease him and disobey his orders and make him laugh and to whom he can talk with complete freedom.
>
> *(132)*

Chloë's loving partnership with Pericles is described at length, a realistic portrayal of a companionate marriage so seldom represented in Shakespearean drama. When Pericles hears that Antiochus has died and it is safe to return to Tyre, Chloë insists on accompanying him, even though she is in the advanced stages of her pregnancy. When she dies in childbirth during the tempest, her fear is portrayed as well as Pericles' grief.

In *Pericles*, Thaisa is buried at sea in one scene, and in the next her recovered casket is pried open by Cerimon, the physician at Ephesus. In contrast, *The Porpoise* depicts Chloë's horrific experience in between, as she wakes up trapped in the coffin and

> the awful truth begins to dawn ... No one is coming to rescue her. She is a strong woman but she has been cosseted her whole life. She is more frightened than she has ever been, more frightened than she believed possible.
>
> *(166)*

In one of the most harrowing episodes among many related in the novel, Chloë is battered around in the coffin, barely able to breath and afraid that she is losing her mind. Though she is eventually discovered and revived by Kerimon, she is aware of the impact of her traumatic experience: "In truth she does not need a doctor. Her bruises will heal. Her nose will set of its own accord, if a little off-centre. But something important has broken in her mind and it will never heal completely" (189). Chloë fully understands what happened to her, but she does not speak to Kerimon for several days, and she does not tell him her story until much later when they have developed a trusting friendship. The parallels with Angelica are evident: Chloë also had to accept that "no one was coming to rescue her" and she too must decide how she will remember her trauma and how she will speak of it.

Michelle Balaev describes how an extreme experience of trauma "can challenge previous formulations of the self and a sense of an integrated identity" and lead to a reconstruction of a "relational self" (26–27). Chloë's first words to Kerimon are "My name is Emilia": she already feels separate from her previous existence and decides to redefine her new, post-traumatic life. In the past she was spoiled and wealthy, but now she learns to be content with simplicity:

> She does not even know whether the child survived. If they did they will grow up cosseted and pampered and have nothing in common with Emilia, not unless they pass through a similar ring of fire which strips away the privilege and the presumption.
>
> *(190–191)*

Seeking purpose in her life, Emilia becomes a caretaker to the elder Kerimon, a beloved sage who writes and interprets documents for the villagers, and she takes over his work when his health fails. In an echo of Angelica's fascination with the creative act of weaving, Emilia also learns the activity she disdained in her pampered life, and "she is a good student this time around, she takes more care, she has more patience … She is starting to learn how one weaves figurines, landscapes, stories" (204).

Emilia is interested in some ruins she finds on one of her walks, an old temple once dedicated to Diana. Kerimon gives her the resources to have it renovated and townspeople begin coming to visit. Though she "never becomes the priestess in any official sense" she is seen as the town confidante, nun, and therapist, and she finds satisfaction in being useful. This sense of serving others is a frequent trope in trauma literature, where

> suffering caused by traumatic events offers the opportunity to construct new meaning or reformulate consciousness to the extent that the protagonist is not simply viewed as infected or transporting a diseased self to others … many fictional representations portray the traumatized protagonist as someone who has special knowledge or unique, positive powers that can help others.
>
> *(Balaev 27)*

When Kerimon dies, he leaves her his property and she continues a fulfilling life as the local wise woman.

In *Pericles* and *The Winter's Tale*, pregnant women undergo a purification ritual of childbirth, death, resuscitation. Thaisa's burial at sea is a similar journey that continues in Ephesus, where evidence of childbirth and marriage is erased as she adopts her new life as votaress in Diana's temple:

> Thus she enacts the fantasy of a desexualized body, a woman without a womb ... Crucial for the continuation of the lineage, Shakespeare's mothers seem to necessitate such a chirurgical or mnemonic loss of parts of themselves ... in order that they may perform the role they are assigned in the final purification of the family plot.
>
> (Garbero 106–107)

But in *The Porpoise*, Emilia's life is not portrayed as simply a period of limbo until she can take her place in the "family plot": she grieves for her husband and daughter, but she has also fashioned a beautiful life for herself that has value defined outside of wifehood or motherhood.

In Marina, Angelica constructs her alternative self: they are the same age, they both have dark skin and hair the color of mahogany, and they both love to read and create imaginary worlds. But Marina has the independence and voice that Angelica does not have in her daily life, and most importantly, she is free from the taint of an incestuous father. Still, Marina has suffered and her life is also traumatic; she lost her mother during childbirth and was put in foster care as a newborn by her father, though she did have a surrogate mother in her nurse: "If she has no father she has Lychorida." When she dies years later, Marina grieves, especially because Lychorida told her stories—another association between women and storytelling—and was her only link to her "supposed prehistory."

Marina and Phoebe grow up as loving sisters, and their favorite game is to create fictional worlds "where there are cyclopes and centaurs and wolves and birds big enough to carry off adult goats" (227). But in spite of their intimate bond, Phoebe is jealous of Marina's more tragic backstory: she "cannot imagine herself as the center of a story. Marina is a story in herself" (227). Marina does not dwell on the sorrows of her lost parentage but, like Angelica, she understands her life through a literary framework:

> In truth, though Marina is sometimes melancholy, she rarely thinks about her parents. They are characters from a romance. Her mother died giving birth, her father saved the city then lost his mind and became a scattering of tall tales.
>
> (228)

Like her counterpart in *Pericles*, Marina is intelligent, resourceful, and almost preternaturally observant, a trait that has perhaps resulted from her orphaned state: "She understands other people, she watches, she analyzes. She knows that she does not belong here, that she does not belong anywhere, that she can take nothing for granted" (229). When Dionyza decides that Marina's beauty and intellect are threatening to Phoebe she hires a servant, Lucius, to assassinate her. Lucius kidnaps her in the middle of the night, binds and gags her in a traveling bag, and intends to take her to a farm where she will be fed to pigs. Nobody sees them escape the palace except an eagle owl that seems to communicate with the forest world, for eventually Marina senses a sympathetic presence outside. High in the hills are twenty young women who "rise from sleep," put on their tunics and hunting boots and take up their bows and javelins:

> In the shadows between the trees stand twenty red deer ... At the head of the pool the twenty-first woman rises. She is taller by a head than all of them ... the virgin herself ... the hunting goddess, goddess of trees and animals, goddess of deer and oaks and high places.
>
> *(232)*

Then Marina hears the women whooping with the animals of the forest, startling the horses and overturning the cart, and trapping Lucius underneath. He dies a slow death, horrified with the knowledge of "the weak given power. The revenge they could justify if they had the means at their disposal" (234). Marina rolls from the cart and is freed by a woman who cuts her binding ropes:

> It is hard to make anything out in this low light and Marina has seen her own reflection only in rudimentary mirrors and on the surface of still water, but the woman looks like her ... Marina is giddy with the strangeness of the encounter.
>
> *(236)*

Angelica's narrative, a wishful alternative to her own story, creates for Marina a cohort of women so powerful and supportive that she identifies with them physically as well as spiritually, particularly Diana, the "strongest of them all."

This female rescue narrative differs from the masculine savior paradigm, for once freed, Marina is left alone to continue her journey and prove her own resilience:

> She must conserve her energy until the moment when it can be most profitably spent. She will be angry, she will be ugly. She will get through this and she will be revenged upon those who have done it to her.
>
> *(232)*

After days and nights of fugitive struggle in the woods, she finally makes her way to Diana's temple where Emilia finds her, disheveled and starving. There is no epiphanic recognition between mother and daughter, but Emilia feels that there is something "otherwordly" about the girl and she is eager to care for her: "Time is repeating or rhyming, the girl arriving in the way that she herself arrived, out of nowhere, nameless, half conscious" (276). They slowly learn to trust each other and Marina wishes she could stay, but she fears she is being hunted by Dionyza's soldiers and does not want to endanger Emilia. In an echo from *Pericles*, Marina offers to read, transcribe, or tutor in exchange for money that she will need to continue her journey.

Careful readers will note at this point an important departure *The Porpoise* takes from *Pericles*, for in the play Marina escapes her assassin only to be kidnapped by pirates and sold to a brothel. Haddon's elimination of this episode is not because he is avoiding the gritty realism of the prostitution scenes. Indeed, for all of its supernatural effects and wondrous coincidences, *The Porpoise* is filled with realistic detail: animals slaughtered mercilessly in sacrificial rituals, corpses piling up during the plague, mistrustful travelers violently attacking each other. Haddon boldly confronts the specter of prostitution so crucial in *Pericles*, and the related issue of co-author George Wilkins' professional crimes, instead by allowing the women he abused the revenge that Marina had vowed against her tormenters.

Mid-novel, the narrative suddenly shifts to early modern London and in an authorial commentary, Haddon acknowledges the co-authorship debate over *Pericles* and suggests that perhaps Wilkins was primarily responsible for the play's scenes of sexual abuse. Shakespeare is not entirely exonerated, for when Wilkins dies of a heart attack, his ghost is ordered to appear and escort him into the afterlife: "'Good morning, George,' says the silhouette. 'This will doubtless come as something of a surprise'" (107). Shakespeare and a stupefied Wilkins, in their afterlife transparency, begin a long walk to the Thames. In a novel steeped in geography and place, London is described with a keen cartographer's eye, as buildings, monuments, neighborhoods, and streets are named—Cripplegate, Cheapside, Silver Street—as though the city is proclaiming its concrete longevity compared to Wilkins's ephemerality. At the jetty the two men board a black wherry with a waterman who leads them down the tumultuous river in a "Virgilian manner."

Shakespeare's ghost and the waterman eventually disappear and Wilkins is left alone "in a tiny boat many miles from land … He knows he will not be rescued," an echo of Angelica's dilemma and Chloë's plight at sea (162). After a terrifying night alone, Wilkins notices movement: "this is the moment when they start to rise slowly from the water, one by one, around the boat" (163). Dark creatures approach the boat and he gradually recognizes them: "One of them is Ann Plesington, or some demon wearing her body… He beat her with a strap and one of the blows hit her face and left her permanently scarred." More and more figures emerge from the water, a virtual roll call of the women Wilkins actually abused in his life as brothel owner and pimp:

> Rebecka Chetwood. Dorothy Lumbarde. Magdalen Samways … No longer countable, though he recognizes every one of them. Judith Walton. Allison Packham. Susanna Medeley whom he kicked in the belly when she was pregnant … and only now does he see the child who died in her womb … Joane Chatwyn whom he took by force. Isabelle Fletcher whom he took by force. Frideswide Chase who died when three men used her for their pleasure …

(*163–164*)

And the list goes on. The women surround the boat, forcing Wilkins to confront his treatment of them, but still he is not repentant; he brags that he gave them employment and complains that it is too hard to bear that "the sex too weak to have dominion in the physical world are possessed of demonic powers in the other," a sentiment shared by Marina's would-be assassin (164).

If, as Shuli Barzilai points out, "sometimes revenge is justice," what follows is Wilkins' just punishment given his refusal to admit to any wrongdoing in his life (320). After a group of women helped free Marina in the forest, her desire to seek revenge for herself grew to include other wronged women, for suddenly another figure appears in the water whom Wilkins does not recognize: "She is sixteen or so, Barbary skin and mahogany hair ... the kind of girl who would never work for him ... who wears damask and lawn and sleeps under clean sheets and washes her soft hands between courses" (164–165). Marina is not named, but the physical identification is clear; as a terrified Wilkins watches, she opens her mouth, and it is ringed with knife-life thorns. While the rest of the women hiss loudly, she lunges at him and bites, "spikes locked in hard enough for him to be hoisted off his feet and dragged forward, his ankles banging clumsily on the prow as he is hauled down into the cold and dark" (165). Haddon's replacement of the brothel scene with this tour de force of retribution and revenge gives these otherwise notorious women in history justice; and for Angelica, a sexual abuser is finally punished.

In her work on representations of revenge in classical and early modern literature, Marguerite Tassi argues that because revenge narratives typically reflect entrenched norms of masculine behavior, it may seem that such stories are "almost excessively masculine" in their focus and concerns. However, Tassi demonstrates, from classical literature,

> female characters articulate claims for revenge, often on rational and moral grounds, expressing passions associated with vengeance—moral outrage and anger, indignation and resentment, vindictiveness and retributive hatred. Like men, women often desire justice for "honour's injury" and articulate the need to move beyond grief into the realm of action, where they can see injustice paid back.
>
> *(18)*

While the Marina of *Pericles* outwits her wrongdoers, she does not actively seek revenge, but the Marina of *The Porpoise* is a vivid example of the type of female character Tassi describes, one who wants to "see injustice paid back." A widely accepted feature of Shakespearean romance is its preference for forgiveness and justice over revenge, even if traces of revenge still intrude. *The Porpoise* challenges this notion with its suggestion that one size of retribution does not fit all, that there is a time for forgiveness and a time to move "into the realm of action," particularly against someone as cruel and unrepentant as George Wilkins.

The previous discussions of *The Tempest* and *The Winter's Tale* are a reminder that the reconstitution of royal authority and family is a hallmark of Shakespearean romance. How does Angelica accommodate Pericles as patriarchal monarch into her more female-centered narrative? If the positive outcome of the romance genre relies on the male protagonist achieving some measure of awareness about his flaws or wrongdoings, then what has this Pericles learned? Though his sins may be less egregious than those of Leontes and Prospero, Pericles manages challenges and temptations largely through avoidance and misreading. He takes the newborn Marina to Tarsus for care and education but "there are whole days when Pericles forgets he has a daughter" (185). He returns to Tyre but, in contrast to the play, he does not assume the throne; in another of the novel's promotions of female power, Pericles is ousted by his sisters, and he is forced to admit that they are better fit to rule. For the next 14 years, he becomes a trader, traveling on land after all of his mishaps at sea, but more importantly, coming to terms with his mistakes:

> For the first few years he is haunted daily by thoughts of the daughter he abandoned, berating himself constantly for his dereliction, his cowardice, trying to palliate the hurt by reminding himself that he would have made a desperately poor father.
>
> *(217)*

As he works through his grief for his wife and daughter, the threat of female sexuality and incest still troubles him: "In lonely drunkenness he has paid to lie with women but seldom finished the act, their face overlaid suddenly with the remembered face of Chloë or, worse, the invented face of Marina" (216).

As with so many other characters in the novel, Pericles' link to the past is in the stories he hears along his travels: some are about a king from Tyre who went mad, and "he hears, every so often, of a city ruled by sisters" (217). After years of trying to repress memories of Marina, he heads to Tarsus to find her, but when he arrives, it is too late:

> His wife died in childbirth because he refused to take the advice of her parents. Their daughter died because he did not have the strength to look after her himself. A kingdom was lifted from his hands in the way that a precious object is carefully lifted from the hands of a clumsy child. He has thrown away everything of value in his life.
>
> *(146)*

Pericles is so devastated by grief and regret that, half-suicidal, he finds a boat and throws himself at the mercy of the seas. In keeping with the romance genre's generous coincidences, he washes ashore at Ephesus, but it is not a joyous arrival. He is nearly dead, and then some young boys violently attack and mutilate him. By the time he is found and taken to the home of the local healer—Emilia—he is a man physically and emotionally broken. The extreme suffering Pericles endures, as harsh as the trauma of Chloe and Marina, becomes an equalizer in their relationship.

Just as Pericles arrives at Emilia's, she and Marina are close to achieving an intimate bond, but they are still unaware of each other's identity. Marina is frightened when she hears of a stranger's arrival and she contemplates running away, but Emilia decides that it is her moral duty to help the stranger:

> The tattooed man lying on the ground rolls his head toward Emilia. He opens his left eye. The right is so swollen and bloodied that it refuses to open … He is in pain … Tattoos or not he has a soul. And he is damaged, like the girl, like herself … They are all missing something. She cannot turn him away.
>
> *(287)*

Their story ends there, with no certainty of recognition or reunion, but with cautious hope. Chloe and Marina have reunited first, shifting the balance in the family triangle and de-centering the predominance of the paternal in the romance genre.

As fitting for the novel's hybrid structure, Haddon, via Angelica, offers us two endings. In the present time, as in *Pericles*, Angelica and her father die in a fire. But as Philippe tries to save his own life, he is still entitled, selfish, and unrepentant:

> If the nurse does not rescue her then Angelica will die. A sick panic overwhelms him. How will he live with himself if he did nothing to save his daughter? But in the middle of his horror he sees an opportunity to escape a terrible quandary. If Angelica dies she will take her story to the grave. She can no longer destroy them both.
>
> *(292)*

But Angelica also envisions an alternative ending, a better transition into another life. Weakened by her illness, "emaciated and bone-white … Angelica no longer has any reason to remain alive … But the animal body will not give in so easily." She tries to rise from her bed, but suddenly someone appears at the door. Like Wilkins, a figure comes to escort her, but this is a benevolent force: "A woman is standing beside the bed. Tunic, boots, quiver. She seems familiar but Angelica cannot remember when or where they last met. The woman reaches out. 'Come. Take my hand'" (294). In the imaginary Haddon allows Angelica to construct, she is finally able to join a safe and supportive community of powerful and loving women.

References

Adelman, Janet. *Suffocating Mothers: Fantasies of Maternal Origin in Shakespeare's Plays.* New York: Routledge, 1992.

Balaev, Michelle. *The Nature of Trauma in American Novels.* Evanston: Northwestern UP, 2012.

Barzilai, Shuli. "How Far Would You Go? Trajectories of Revenge in Margaret Atwood's Short Fiction." *Contemporary Women's Writing* 11. 3 (2017): 316–335.

BBC Radio 3 Podcast: Mark Haddon and Anne McElvoy. April 28, 2020.

Bloom, Gina. *Voice in Motion: Staging Gender, Shaping Sound in Early Modern England*. Philadelphia: U of Penn Press, 2007.

Boehrer, Bruce. *Monarchy and Incest in Renaissance England: Literature, Culture, Kinship, and Kingship*. Philadelphia: U of Penn Press, 1992.

Bogaev, Barbara and Mark Haddon. *Shakespeare Unlimited*. Podcast. Episode 131. October 29, 2019.

Boro, Joyce. "John Fletcher's Women Pleased and the Pedagogy of Reading Romance." In *Staging the Early Modern Romance*, eds. Mary Ellen Lamb and Valerie Wayne. New York: Routledge, 2008: 188–202.

Cohen, Walter. "Introduction to Pericles." In Greenblatt, Stephen, ed. *The Norton Shakespeare*, 3rd ed. New York: W.W. Norton and Co., 2015: 1161–1167.

Duncan-Jones, Katherine. *Ungentle Shakespeare: Scenes from His Life*. London: Arden Shakespeare, 2010.

Frye, Susan. "Incest and Authority in Pericles, Prince of Tyre." In *Incest and the Literary Imagination*, ed. Elizabeth Barnes. Gainesville: U Press of Florida, 2002: 39–58.

Garbero, Maria del Sapio. "Shakespeare's Maternal Transfigurations." In *Maternity and Romance Narratives in Early Modern England*, eds. Karen Bamford and Naomi Miller. New York: Routledge, 2016: 93–118.

Giddens, Eugene. "Pericles the Afterlife." In *The Cambridge Companion to Shakespeare's Late Plays*. Cambridge: Cambridge UP, 2009: 173–184.

Hackett, Helen. "'Gracious Be the Issue': Maternity and Narrative In Shakespeare's Late Plays." In *Shakespeare's Late Plays: New Readings*, eds. James Knowles and Jennifer Richards. Edinburgh: Edinburgh UP, 1999: 25–39.

Hackett, Helen. *Women and Romance Fiction in the English Renaissance*. Cambridge: Cambridge UP, 2000.

Haddon, Mark. *The Porpoise*. New York: Doubleday, 2019.

Hartman, Geoffrey. "Trauma Within the Limits of Literature." *European Journal of English Studies* 7. 3 (2003): 257–274.

Healy, Margaret. "*Pericles* and the Pox." In *Shakespeare's Late Plays*, ed. Jennifer Richards. Edinburgh: Edinburgh UP, 1999: 92–107.

Krontiris, Tina. *Oppositional Voices: Women as Writers and Translators in the English Renaissance*. New York: Routledge, 1997.

Luckyj, Christina. *'A Moving Rhetoricke': Gender and Silence in Early Modern England*. Manchester: Manchester UP, 2011.

McCabe, Richard. *Incest, Drama, and Nature's Law: 1550–1700*. Cambridge: Cambridge UP, 1993.

Moore, Jeanie Grant. "Riddled Romance: Kingship and Kinship in *Pericles*." *Rocky Mountain Review of Language and Literature* 57. 1 (2003): 33–48.

Nicholl, Charles. *The Lodger: His Life on Silver Street*. New York: Penguin, 2007.

Novy, Marianne. "Multiple Parenting in *Pericles*." In *Pericles: Critical Essays*, ed. David Skeele. New York: Garland Press, 2000: 238–248.

Parr, Anthony. "George Wilkins: Playwright and Pamphleteer." In *Oxford Dictionary of National Biography*. In print and online: September 23, 2004.

Pederson, Joshua. "Speak, Trauma: Towards a Revised Understanding of Literary Trauma Theory." *Narrative* 22. 3 (2014): 333–353.

Peterson, Kaara L. "Shakespearean Revivifications: Early Modern Undead." *Shakespeare Studies* 32 (2004): 240–266.

Salkeld, Duncan. *Shakespeare Among the Courtesans: Prostitution, Literature, and Drama, 1500–1650*. New York: Routledge, 2012.

Salkeld, Duncan. *Shakespeare's London*. Oxford: Oxford UP, 2018.

Tassi, Marguerite. *Women and Revenge in Shakespeare: Gender, Genre, and Ethics*. Selinsgrove: Susquehanna UP, 2011.

Whitehead, Anne. *Trauma Fiction*. Edinburgh: Edinburgh U Press, 2004.

Williams, Deanne. *Shakespeare and the Performance of Girlhood*. New York: Palgrave Macmillan, 2014.

6

EMILY ST. JOHN MANDEL'S *STATION ELEVEN* AND WILLIAM SHAKESPEARE'S *KING LEAR*

Emily St. John Mandel's novel *Station Eleven* opens with a global pandemic that causes swift and epic devastation, so when the coronavirus exploded in early 2020, it was one of the books frequently mentioned, along with Albert Camus's *The Stranger*, Daniel Defoe's *A Journal of the Plague Year*, Geraldine Brooks' *Year of Wonders*, Lin Ma's *Severance*, and other works referred to as plague literature or contagion fables. Another author frequently cited was Shakespeare, with a popular meme admonishing us to be as productive as he was during isolation. When much of the world went into lockdown in the spring and singer Rosanne Cash tweeted, "Just a reminder that when Shakespeare was quarantined he wrote *King Lear*," Mandel herself was one of the first to respond: "Fair point, but I bet he had childcare."

Shakespeare may not have composed *Lear* exactly during the months of a plague outbreak, but given their frequency and the consequent death toll in early modern England, the specter of the deadly disease could never have been far from his mind. While Mandel wrote her novel a few years before the Covid-19 catastrophe, it is set in the aftermath of even more widespread contagion and fatalities. But if a plague informs the creation and the background of both *Lear* and *Station Eleven*, it is not their primary focus. Rather, both works are occupied with how humanity reacts to the non-human world and to each other after destructive forces have been unleashed.

King Lear compels us to engage with grand metaphysical issues, as it moves in concentric circles from fraught family relationships to larger anxieties about monarchical government to yet more encompassing questions about the human condition and our place in the cosmos. Edgar's final pronouncement about "the weight of this sad time" leaves us contemplating the totality of the play's wreckage, as he echoes Albany's acknowledgement that "Our present business is general woe." Albany and Edgar allude to the slight possibility of restoration and redemption, though what that new world order might look like is left to our imaginations.

DOI: 10.4324/9781003166580-7

Indeed, whether *King Lear* offers any hope at all is one of the abiding arguments surrounding this play.

Mandel's novel could be said to begin where *King Lear* leaves off, in a world of massive chaos. In *Station Eleven*, the ruin is caused by a lethal virus rather than human arrogance and error, though it is left unclear whether the pandemic itself should be seen as a random event or as the result of globalization and human interference with the environment. But the novel picks up at the moment the disaster erupts, and the ending of Shakespeare's tragedy sets the tone with the opening lines: "The king stood in a pool of blue light, unmoored. This was act 4 of *King Lear*, a winter night at the Elgin Theatre in Toronto" (1). This King Lear suddenly collapses on stage, the first of many deaths as the "Georgia flu" destroys most of the world's population within weeks: thus begins a slow and harrowing journey towards recovery and the reclaiming of civilization.

A critical and commercial success upon its publication in 2014, *Station Eleven* is something of a departure for Mandel. Her first three novels, *Last Night in Montreal* (2009), *The Singer's Gun* (2010), and *The Lola Quartet* (2012), are generally considered thrillers or noir fiction; her most recent book, *The Glass Hotel* (2020), is also a crime novel surrounding an international Ponzi scheme. While *Station Eleven* exhibits the same non-linear structure, multiple narrative perspectives, and page-turning plotlines as her previous works, its affinity is with such recent post-apocalyptic novels as Omar El Akkad's *American War* (2017), Peter Heller's *The Dog Stars* (2012), or Cormac McCarthy's *The Road* (2006).

At the heart of *Station Eleven* is its interfacing with *King Lear* and with Shakespeare's world in general, but, unlike most of the works in this study, it is not an explicit adaptation of the play. Like *The Tempest, King Lear* has inspired numerous portrayals and retellings since its initial performance, the most famous being Nahum Tate's Restoration play that allows Lear and Cordelia to live and puts her and Edgar on the throne. Tate's optimistic version was so popular that it replaced Shakespeare's *Lear* on stage for nearly the next two centuries. But most adaptations in film and literature in the last several decades have not mitigated *Lear*'s overwhelming bleakness. In the latter half of the twentieth century, influential films by Peter Brooks, Grigori Kozintsev, and Akira Kurosawa preserved both the grandiosity and tragic vision of the play. Even more recently, popular television shows such as *Empire* and *Succession* have used the structure and implications of *King Lear*'s family drama to enact generational and sibling rivalries and power struggles. In literature, perhaps it is not surprising that so many of the revisions have been by women, given the unsettling gender politics of the play: Jane Smiley's Pulitzer prize-winning *A Thousand Acres* (1991); Sophie Mackintosh's *The Water Cure* (2018); Elizabeth Nunez's *Even in Paradise* (2016); and Preti Taneja's *We That Are Young* (2017) resituate the Lear plot in different time periods and locations but have in common a critique of the play's misogyny and patriarchal entitlement.

Among *Station Eleven*'s ensemble of characters are autonomous, powerful women, but this novel is not as directly occupied with feminist concerns as with a broader examination of how humans interact in the face of extreme adversity.

Unlike *King Lear*, which exposes an abusive and unchecked monarchy, and unlike many contemporary post-apocalyptic novels that critique social systems, Mandel gives minimal attention to any human follies that may have directly led to the disaster. Indeed, its tragic impact derives more from its seeming randomness; where humans are held accountable is not as much in causing the pandemic but in how they respond to it. Mandel's a-linear narrative describes the pre-catastrophic world and the immediate aftermath of the contagion, but the novel's main emphasis is on the period years later as the few remaining survivors work to reconstruct the social contract and a sustainable future. Referring to her novel as a love letter to our world, Mandel is primarily interested in how we can recuperate and build upon the best in human achievements. Thus, the precarious but gradual optimism of *Station Eleven* talks back to the darkness and despair of *King Lear*.

King Lear and *Station Eleven*: Brief synopses

For the purposes of adaptive comparison, it is necessary to provide brief synopses of Shakespeare's *King Lear*, first performed at King James's court in 1606, and Emily St. John Mandel's *Station Eleven*, published in 2014.

King Lear begins in early Britain with an aging ruler's unusual decision to retire from the throne and divide his kingdom among his three daughters, their portions contingent upon their proclamations of love for him. The eldest two daughters, Goneril and Regan, satisfy Lear with their flattery, but Cordelia, his youngest and favorite, refuses to participate in this public spectacle and remains silent. Lear is furious and banishes her, along with his beloved servant Kent who tries to dissuade Lear from his rash behavior. The King of France, present to woo Cordelia, takes her as his queen and they leave the kingdom to be divided between Goneril and Regan and their husbands, Albany and Cornwall. The sisters initially unite against their father's foolish behavior and when Lear finds their care of him insufficient, he quickly regrets his faith in them. Their disagreements escalate and an enraged Lear is left wandering outdoors in the midst of a dangerous thunderstorm with his fool and Kent, who has returned in disguise to watch over him.

A parallel plot involves the faithful Earl of Gloucester and his two sons, Edgar and Edmund, his illegitimate son. Edmund, aggrieved over his unfair treatment as a "bastard," contrives discord between Gloucester and Edgar. Gloucester is led to believe Edgar is conspiring against him, so Edgar is forced to flee for his life; he disguises himself as a poor beggar, Tom o'Bedlam. When Gloucester tries to defend Lear, Regan and Cornwall punish him with a violent blinding and Cornwall is killed in the process. Only later does Gloucester, like Lear, realize which of his children is truly loyal. Edmund also causes further division when he promises himself to both Goneril and Regan, and in their rivalry over him, Goneril poisons Regan and then kills herself. Cordelia learns that the family rifts have exploded into full-blown war and returns from France with an army. Though she briefly reunites with Lear and he asks her forgiveness, they are both captured and Cordelia is hanged. Heartbroken, Lear dies. In a duel, Edgar kills Edmund, and he and the kind-hearted Albany are left to reassemble the broken kingdom.

If the devastation at the end of *King Lear* is astonishing, so are the unfathomable fatalities that open *Station Eleven*, beginning with Arthur Leander, the actor who dies suddenly while performing as Lear. Within weeks, ninety-nine percent of the world's population succumbs to the virus. Most of the novel then flashes forward 20 years later to the survivors in North America who have formed small communities. One of these, a group of actors and musicians called The Travelling Symphony, visits settlements where they perform classical music and Shakespeare. Kirsten Raymonde, one of the members, was an eight-year-old actress playing the role of Cordelia as a child when Arthur collapsed. Now an expert knife-thrower, Kirsten is one of the group's fiercest protectors, and she scavenges abandoned homes along the road where she searches for anything useful, along with old tabloids that may refer to Arthur. She also treasures some graphic novels that Arthur gave her called *Station Eleven* and *Dr. Eleven*; they allude to *The Tempest* and were written and illustrated by Miranda, one of Arthur's three ex-wives.

When the troupe travels back to a village to reunite with Charlie, a former member who had remained behind to have her baby, they find her and her partner missing and the village taken over by a fanatic and violent cult leader called the Prophet, who rapes young girls for his collection of wives. They quickly head towards the Severn Airport, now a settlement known as the Museum of Civilization, but they are followed by the Prophet's men who abduct part of their group. Kirsten and her friend August become separated from the rest, but when they are almost at the Museum they encounter the Prophet's men who have killed one of their members and are holding another, Sayid, hostage. They manage to free Sayid and kill the kidnappers, but the Prophet catches up with them. In the ensuing melee, he is killed by one of his own men. Kirsten, August, and Sayid make their way to the airport where they find Charlie and the rest of the troupe. One of the inhabitants, Clark, curates a collection of artifacts such as credit cards and iPhones to memorialize "the time before"; in one of the many interconnections among various characters of the novel, it turns out that Clark was a friend of Arthur's. He knew Arthur's wives, he figures out Kirsten's relationship to Arthur, and reveals that the Prophet was Arthur's only son, Tyler Leander, who had become a religious zealot in the early years after the pandemic. The novel ends with Clark taking Kirsten up to the airport's watch tower to see a town in the distance with electric lights, an enormous step towards rebuilding modernity. Kirsten and the troupe then resume their travels, and she leaves Clark with her copy of *Dr. Eleven* for his collection, signaling that Shakespeare, in text and performance, will continue to be a vital part of the new world.

King Lear: This little world of man

Like so many of Shakespeare's works, *King Lear* is itself an adaptation. The play draws on a number of sources including *Holinshed's Chronicles*, Sir Philip Sidney's pastoral romance *Arcadia*, Edmund Spenser's epic poem *The Fairie Queene*, and Samuel Harsnett's anti-Catholic tract on exorcisms, *A Declaration of Egregious Popish Impostures*. The play even echoes a familiar folk tale in which a king banishes his daughter for saying she loves him like salt; it is only when he tastes his bland, unseasoned dinner that he realizes the value of her words. Shakespeare may have also had in mind a recent London scandal involving a lawsuit brought against Sir Brian Annesley by his two eldest daughters; they were attempting to declare him insane and claim more inheritance but he was defended by his youngest daughter, coincidentally named Cordell (Duncan-Jones 185–190). But the source that Shakespeare reworked most explicitly was the anonymous play *The True Chronicle History of King Leir*, performed by the Queen's Men in the early 1590s but not published until 1605.

In all of his plays, Shakespeare's genius is evident in the transformation and incorporation of his sources into a work solely his own. In the transition from *Leir* to *Lear*, Shakespeare maintained much of the primary plot and many of the main characters, but he deftly added a parallel plot, replaced archaic rhyming couplets with eloquent blank verse and prose, and perhaps most significantly, replaced the earlier play's positive outcome with an ending of utter annihilation (Skura 132–134). Furthermore, Shakespeare was known to apply the adaptive process even to his own work, as demonstrated in the two versions of *Lear* that have led to so much vigorous textual scholarship. Of the 36 plays gathered in the First Folio of 1623, 18 had been previously published in individual short quartos, and there are often discrepancies between the two versions that indicate revision by Shakespeare, members of his company, or printers. In the case of *Lear*, the differences in language and line attribution between the 1608 quarto and the Folio text are significant, and though it cannot be proven how much of that rewriting was done by Shakespeare himself, scholars have made a convincing case for his authorial interventions. Most editors today choose to conflate the two texts in the interest of preserving as much of the language and substance as possible; this chapter will refer to this combined text.

King Lear focuses on the fall of its eponymous monarch and the concomitant destruction of the family and royal systems that he heads: with the demise of the king comes the ruin of the world surrounding him. The intersection of the personal and the public may have seemed inevitable given the early modern view set out by Shakespeare's own ruler, King James I, in his 1598 treatise *The True Law of Free Monarchies*. James's extensive analogy comparing the role of a king over his subjects to that of a father over his children begins: "By the law of nature the king becomes a natural father to all his lieges at his coronation" (Rhodes 262). This assumption of such comprehensive rule was given even more force by the concept of divine right monarchy, a notion that a ruler was directly appointed by God and mirrored his omnipotence. This was another belief heartily endorsed by James who had also written about it in *Basilikon Doron*, his 1599 training manual for his son Prince Henry, where James assured his heir that God "made you a little God to sit on his Throne, and rule over other men" (Rhodes 211).

As father and as king, Lear's peremptory demands in the play's opening set the tone for the precipitous descent that follows. By the end of the first act, he disowns his beloved Cordelia for not sufficiently flattering him when he demands that his daughters compete for his favor. Lear's anger is so extreme that he curses Cordelia with the chilling words "Better thou hadst/ Not been born than not t'have pleased me better" (1.1. 232–233). He then banishes his beloved servant Kent, the only other person on stage who refuses to enable Lear's foolish behavior. Soon after, Lear, who wants to retain the privileges but not the responsibilities of kingship, becomes furious that the treatment he is receiving from Goneril and Regan is insufficient for his royal status and he excoriates them in some of the most hateful rhetoric in any of Shakespeare's plays. He berates them in extremely misogynistic terms, striking at the core of their sexuality and womanhood: he appeals to the Goddess Nature to curse Goneril with sterility: "Dry up in her the organs of increase/ And from her derogate body never spring/ A babe to honor her ..." (1.4. 246–248) and calls them both "unnatural hags." Several scholars, including Janet Adelman, Lynda Boose, Coppelia Kahn, and Kathleen McLuskie, have discussed the deep-seated psychological and political insecurity that drives Lear to attack his remaining daughters: in spite of any impatience and cruelty they have exhibited towards him at this point, his denunciation of them displays a fearsome loathing of women grounded in his sense of extra-ordinary patriarchal entitlement.

Given Lear's presumption of his total and absolute power, his decision to abdicate and divide the kingdom comes as either a surprise or a sign of his growing irrationality. Division, in its many personal and political manifestations, is the defining feature of this tragedy. Within the first few lines of the play, Gloucester refers to "the division of the kingdom," and shortly after Lear enters and announces, "Know that we have divided/ In three our kingdom" (1.1. 35–36). Lear's declaration to divide his kingdom would have signaled alarm to his early modern audience, particularly given that King James was obsessed with an opposite agenda in uniting the crowns of England and Scotland under the banner of Great Britain. As James Shapiro points out, "For Jacobeans inundated by pageantry, polemic, and gossip about the proposed union, any play that turned to Britain's distant past to explore the consequences of a divided kingdom would have been seen as part of this conversation" (40). James had already advised Prince Henry against just such division as Lear proposed: "By dividing your kingdoms, ye shall leave the seed of discord among your posterity" (Rhodes 239).

The discord that Lear sows begins with Cordelia's punishment and continues with a kingdom that will now be divided into two instead of three, starkly illustrated when the king throws his crown to Cornwall and Albany with a command impossible to execute: "This coronet part between you" (1.1. 137). The territorial division that Lear disastrously initiates is quickly echoed in an exhausting list of familial divisions: Lear is divided against Cordelia, Cordelia divided against her sisters, Lear divided against Goneril and Regan, Goneril and Regan divided against each other, Cornwall against Albany, Albany against Goneril, Gloucester against Edgar, Edmund against both father and brother. It is an overwhelming series of ruptures from which no one recovers. The notion of division also applies to Lear himself, whose identity becomes increasingly fragmented and unstable to himself and others. Frustrated with his fallen state, which he persists in blaming on his daughters, Lear asks, "Does any here know me? ... Who is it that can tell me who

I am?," to which the Fool trenchantly replies, "Lear's shadow" (1.4. 206–212). Without the trappings of kingship, Lear's sense of self is dissolving, and when confirmation of his own superior status is not reflected back to him, he fears that he is going mad.

Many critics cite the mid-point of the play, when a furious Lear rushes into the stormy night and Regan "shuts up" her doors after him, as the pivotal moment in his evolution, the impetus that drives him towards compassion and a humble recognition of his failures as king, father, and fellow human, even as his sanity is challenged. Any epiphany, however, is not immediate, for he first rails to the storm about his victimhood, "Here I stand your slave,/ A poor, infirm, weak, and despised old man," and later insists, "I am a man more sinned against than sinning" (3.2. 19–20 and 59–60). On the other hand, he displays some concern for his Fool's well-being: "Come on, my boy. How dost, my boy? Art cold?/ I am cold myself … I have one part in my heart/ That's sorry yet for thee" (3.2. 72–73). This uncharacteristic thoughtfulness prompts a further realization as he thinks of the more vulnerable people who regularly endure poverty and harsh weather:

> Poor naked wretches, wheresoe'er you are
> That bide the pelting of this pitiless storm,
> How shall your houseless heads and unfed sides,
> Your looped and windowed raggedness defend you
> From seasons such as this? O I have ta'en
> Too little care of this.
>
> *(3.4. 27–32)*

This may be the closest Lear comes to acknowledging that he has neglected his responsibilities to his subjects and that severe poverty and homelessness are the result. At this point, Lear meets Edgar disguised as Tom, naked and shivering in just a loincloth and blanket and repeating, "Poor Tom's a cold." In a gesture of solidarity, Lear begins to unbutton his clothes as though to share them with Edgar, until his Fool stops him. When Lear later finds the wounded Gloucester, he shares his new-found realization about his condition:

> When the rain came to wet me once, and the wind to make/ me chatter, when the thunder would not peace at my bidding,/ There I found 'em, there I smelt them out. Go to, they/ are not men o' their words. They told me I was everything./ 'Tis a lie. I am not ague-proof.
>
> *(4.6. 101–105)*

In spite of the fact that Lear exhorted the thunder to fury instead of "peace," he begins to see that his kingly status does not make him immune to the hardships suffered by others. Craig Dionne's excellent reading of Lear's move from "the ostentatious court to the denuded heath" in this scene highlights this gradual, if limited, knowledge:

King Lear's heath is where the king must face the essence of the human ... a world of want and scarcity, a place where survival means coming to terms with what makes all humans equivalent in the most radical sense, by showing us "unaccommodated existence," that is, precisely *without* those symbols of status Lear posed as the essence of human identity.

(145)

But does Lear's sympathy for Tom and the Fool and his awareness of his own vulnerabilities ultimately transform him into a more compassionate being, attuned to the suffering of humankind? Does he emerge from his experience in the storm understanding himself as a fellow human being belonging to a larger community instead of a privileged occupant at the peak of a social hierarchy? Some of the wisdom he displays in his conversation with the blinded Gloucester suggests a decided difference from his previous narcissism, but it may not be as transformative as is often claimed. Lear still sees himself as the one wronged, he still harps on his daughters, and Tom's still a'cold—in other words, nothing substantially changes. Lear's mistake, he believes, is that he simply trusted the wrong daughters, not that his egotistical greed was in any way responsible for the ruin he caused. He thinks he is still "every inch a king," while Gloucester responds more perceptively with "O ruined piece of nature!" Chris Fitter points to the limitations of Lear's allegedly new-found kindness and argues that it

appears intransitive: it is confined to self-unbuttoning. He seeks the savage relish of the shared nadir, in a kind of pantomime of victim status. Neither here, nor at any point hereafter in this drama, will the royal enlightenment extend to remedial practicality.

(ELH 840)

When Lear prays to the gods to "Expose thyself to feel what wretches feel,/ That thou mayst shake the superflux to them/ And show the heavens more just" (3.4. 34–36), Fitter adds that "Lear's language of dropping from above ... suggests a process wherein individuals are physicked by pity yet vertical structures remain intact. 'Shake the superflux to them' commends a compassion definitively aloft, distributing *de haut en bas*" (*ELH* 837). This more conventional and token approach to charity or almsgiving, Fitter argues, is in contrast with Gloucester's more pragmatic call for social re-ordering: "So distribution should undo excess,/ And each man have enough" (4.1. 72–73). In Gloucester's recognition and in the exposure of social injustices, some critics see the play gesturing towards a more radical dismantling of the political status quo, but the degree of Lear's own personal and social awakening continues to be subject to debate.

Just as the storm on the heath has been examined as Lear's push towards a more compassionate humanity, it has also been seen as the episode that reorients his place within the larger universe, a position vastly different from the more comfortable indoor sanctuary of court. Unfortunately, however, it is not a given that Lear's encounter with the "wrathful skies" leads him to humility in face of the greater forces of the non-human world. He variously appeals, commands, and sympathizes with the tempest, alternately seeking confirmation of his own victimhood and grasping at his diminishing authority. One gentleman explains to Kent that Lear is outdoors

> Contending with the fretful elements,
> Bids the wind blow the earth into the sea ...
> That things might change or cease ...
> Strives in his little world of man to outscorn
> The to-and-fro conflicting wind and rain.
>
> *(3.1. 4–8)*

Lear's raging against the violent weather makes for riveting theatre, but as Gabriel Egan argues, "Lear's exposing himself in the storm appears rather more of a melodramatic gesture that exploits his body's capacity to bear a meaning to his enemies" (145). Nonetheless, while Lear's experience out on the heath may not meaningfully transform his entitled selfhood, its centrality means that we cannot ignore the many other ways the play exposes the connections, or disconnections, between the human and the non-human world. As a growing body of ecocriticism demonstrates, *King Lear*'s attention to the world at large extends far beyond the storm, including its abundance of animal imagery, its attention to astrological influences, its (mis)appropriation of land and resources, and its exposure of human consumption and prodigality.

As discussed in Chapter 2 on *Prospero's Daughter*, viewing Shakespeare ecocritically now commands a particular urgency as we reckon with our past and present exploitation of the environment. This interdisciplinary approach is wide-ranging but some of its most fundamental principles that require us to break from past practices are relevant here. First, ecocriticism urges us beyond assuming that literary depictions of the non-human world are synonymous with soothing pastoral beauty—what Steve Mentz refers to as "sentimental eco-writing" (*Ecocritical* 167). In early modern literature, the pastoral genre occupies an important aesthetic and political place, but much literary analysis has privileged beautiful, non-threatening, and even stylized portrayals of the non-human world over more agentic and realistic representations. Certainly, the depictions of the outdoor world in *Lear* defy idyllic innocence; even post-storm, Lear's run through the fields crowned in wild "cuckoo flowers" is more an indication that he is "as mad as the vexed sea" than a sign of bucolic stability.

This leads to a second principle of ecocriticism: that we view representations of the non-human world less symbolically and more literally, focusing on their actual and historical contexts. In particular, meteorology in Shakespeare's plays—a topic given scant attention prior to the rise of ecocriticism—is now the subject of critical conversation as volatile as the climate it considers. While not denying that the weather phenomena in Shakespeare can carry metaphorical meaning, signal supernatural forces, or provide the excitement of special effects in the theatre, ecocritics also remind us that there was an "instance of some storm in every Shakespearean

play" and they had realistic equivalence (Jones 2). Philip Armstrong explains that
during Shakespeare's lifetime, a period known as the Little Ice Age brought
weather as unpredictable as what we are now experiencing in the twenty-first
century: "Shakespeare would have grown to maturity surrounded by a generational
sense that a previously fecund, temperate, and reliable natural environment had
been replaced by freezing temperatures, blighted harvests, and sudden, wild storms"
(107). Even more than the cold, it was the uncontrollable variability of the weather
that Shakespeare's contemporaries would have understood—and feared. Randall
Martin points to the consequences that the turbulent climate change had for the
most vulnerable people: "Frigid and flooded conditions of the 1590s devastated
English regional landscapes and animal populations" and failed harvests led to
"widespread famine and unemployment. Experience of these real life miseries
intensified audiences' affective responses to the hunger and homelessness" in *King
Lear* and other plays (10). The effects of dangerous weather were exacerbated by
the widespread practice of enclosure: land formerly available for the raising of food
was now fenced off to raise sheep for the profitable wool industry, and food insecurity became an even greater threat (Archer 519). Thus, both human and non-
human forces overlapped to pose very real threats, and while Lear the fallen king
may never fully comprehend these effects, the thousands of starving Tom o'Be-
dlams in his kingdom, reduced to eating "the swimming frog, the toad, the tad-
pole, the wall-newt … [and] cow-dung for salads," certainly do.

The third principle of current ecocritical theory particularly relevant to *Lear*
cautions us to reconsider the word "nature," commonly used to describe a distinct
outdoor world of flora and fauna. This usage ignores the fact that we are also part
of nature and reinforces a binary separation in which human beings see themselves
as outside of nature rather than an integral component. This more inclusive view of
"nature" was perhaps better understood by early modern people for whom the
division between human and non-human was not as pronounced. As Jean Feerick
points out, "For the premodern world of which Shakespeare was a part, the social,
the cultural, and the human were still perceived to be *inside* nature, not separated
from it and abiding by a discrete set of principles" (36). This does not suggest,
however, that Shakespeare's contemporaries saw themselves in harmony with the
non-human world, but that they understood themselves as a small cog in the
capacious and powerful wheel of "Nature." Indeed, the word "nature" and its
variants "natural" and "unnatural" appear in *Lear* over 40 times, far more than in
any other of Shakespeare's plays; it is used broadly to describe the outdoors and
climatic events, inherent and transgressive characteristics of human beings; roles in
the social hierarchy; and a goddess that Lear desperately invokes. Leah Marcus
notes that

> *King Lear* is the only tragedy in which characters make a habit of conversing
> both with nature herself and with elements of the natural world, and in which
> that world, on occasion, may be said to talk back to them. Indeed, the word

"Nature" is almost always capitalized in the folio text as though to signal its unique status in this particular play.

(422)

But although the natural world may talk back to humans in *King Lear*, it does not always tell them what they want to hear.

For if *King Lear* the play, though perhaps not King Lear the individual, displays a more intimate and integrated understanding of humankind's position on the planet, how is that relationship articulated? Steve Mentz argues that, especially in *Lear*, we should not expect that such intimacy leads to congenial interdependence, for *Lear* especially "reminds 'green' readers how difficult and disorderly living in a mutable eco-system can be ... [it] mocks human faith in an orderly universe." Mentz claims that the world's "stubborn exteriority" and instability defies any human desire to be comfortably incorporated with it:

> Lear learns to distrust old ideas about natural order. In presenting this crisis of legibility, Shakespeare's play gestures toward a re-configured, less sympathetic but perhaps still survivable, relationship between bodies and nature ... King Lear's opaque world of catastrophe and crisis bears an uncomfortable resemblance to the place in which we are learning to live now.
>
> (Shakespeare *146*)

Lear has lost his sense of identity as a king and a human being, he has abandoned faith in many human relationships, he cannot find solace in the natural world, and he finds the gods to whom he appeals indifferent. His disillusionment infects the rest of the play, leaving us to ask if this is the "promised end" or if there is any promise forward—if not for Lear, then for the rest of humanity. For indeed, the sweeping devastation at the end marks not just the fall of one man, but the erasure of an entire family and political order, juxtaposed with the poverty and suffering that afflict the larger society. The tragedy, however, is not in the demise of a single tyrant led to believe he could command both the human and non-human world around him at his pleasure; the tragedy is that once he has ruinously divided his family and his entire kingdom, there is no alternative offered in its place. Margot Heinemann argues that the division of the kingdom itself is not the problem:

> the *division* as such does not in fact cause the war and barbarity that we see. The sole rule of Goneril, the eldest, would scarcely make for peace and harmony, and the single rule of Cordelia could only be secured if primogeniture were ignored.
>
> (78)

Nonetheless, such extreme contention among people does not bode well for any political and social order, even if there is no ready apparatus to reform an imperfect monarchy or to provide for a new shared system of governance. Indeed, the few good men left at the end—Albany, Edgar, and Kent—seem at a loss as to how to proceed. Kent enigmatically disqualifies himself from the proposed triumvirate and future management of the country falls on the reluctant Edgar and Albany.

In the absence of a consoling natural world, divine intercession, or an improved political structure, humans are left to fall back upon themselves, to work with one another for the greater good. In a play in which human action is so dominated by betrayal, cruelty, and rivalry, it is difficult to locate cooperative possibility and ethical behavior, but such occasions are not entirely absent in *King Lear*. Though some have faulted Cordelia for naiveté or conflicting national allegiances, while others have praised her as the apotheosis of Christian self-sacrifice, most agree that Cordelia embodies compassion and honesty, virtues in short supply elsewhere in the play. Like Cordelia, Edgar is wrongfully judged by his father, yet he risks his life to save a wounded Gloucester from death and despair. Kent, the one character initially brave enough to speak truth to power, courageously returns from his banishment to protect the king who wronged him and keep him from doing further damage. Albany objects to his wife's cruelty to her father, albeit in harshly misogynistic terms, for which Goneril accuses him of being a "milk livered man." And though Gloucester is capable of his own misjudgments, he too defends Lear, and loses his sight because of it. Forgiveness and loyalty, requisite for the successful functioning of a human community, are present, though as Tom Clayton points out, "Loyalty as such is not a virtue in this ethically circumspect play" where one could justify any behavior as "just following orders," to a tyrannical leader (189). But in spite of how deserving Lear may or may not be, these demonstrations of courage and loyalty are all exercised as moral resistance against even worse acts of barbarity.

Perhaps the most remarkable example of humane behavior comes from a character so secondary he is nameless, only referred to as "First Servant." After Regan and Cornwall have locked the doors of Gloucester's home against Lear, they turn to grill their host about Cordelia's plans to return with a French army. They bind him and assault him with a series of questions and threats, even more intent on retaliatory punishment than extracting information. When Gloucester steadfastly defends Lear, Cornwall brutally gouges out one of his eyes, one of the most shocking and violent moments in the entire Shakespearean canon, while Regan urges her husband to also pluck out the other eye. Just as swiftly, one of Cornwall's servants steps forward to intervene:

> Hold your hand, my lord.
> I have served you ever since I was a child,
> But better service have I never done you
> Than now to bid you hold.
>   *(3.7. 71–74)*

In the ensuing struggle, the servant stabs Cornwall, whose wounds later prove to be fatal, and Regan in turn kills the servant. Stephen Greenblatt argues that Shakespeare's audience would have endorsed this "serving man who stands up for human decency," his radical act driven not by personal motives or political ambition but a desire to prevent cruelty towards a fellow human being. Two more nameless servants then vow to help the blinded and outcast Gloucester, one to lead him on his journey to Dover and the other to "fetch some flax and whites of eggs/ To apply to his bleeding face" (3.7. 104–105). Greenblatt acknowledges that such "fundamental ethical responsibility ... and other moments of comfort and solidarity [are] all comparably modest," but nonetheless, "these small gestures are the core of the play's moral vision" (NYRB).

Ethical behavior is not always rewarded, as evidenced by the deaths of Cordelia and Cornwall's servant, though Albany, Edgar, and Kent survive. Unfortunately, in a world marked by so much annihilation, the prospects for "this little world of man" are bleak, and might only be redeemed by the solace provided when human beings recognize that their individual little worlds will only survive within a larger world of cooperative humankind.

Station Eleven: Rebuilding a world

Post-apocalyptic fiction is not a new phenomenon, but the last two decades have seen a resurgence in what Andrew Tate calls "popular contemporary narrative haunted by dreams of a future that is a place of ruin." *Station Eleven*, appearing in 2014, joins this "exceptionally depressing literary universe," but as much as it shares common ground with the genre, its determined optimism sets it apart (3). Considered a cross-over work between genre and literary fiction, *Station Eleven* won an Arthur C. Clarke Award for Science Fiction in 2015 and was shortlisted for both the National Book Award and the PEN/Faulkner Award. But *Station Eleven* also sits alongside works of adaptation and appropriation, looking backward to Shakespeare, and *King Lear* in particular. In an interview, Mandel explained how her reading about Shakespeare's life and work informed her novel:

> ... it seemed to me that there were some natural parallels between Elizabethan England and the post-pandemic landscape of the book, the most obvious being that in Shakespeare's time, theatre would so often have been a matter of these small companies of traveling players setting out on the road. I liked the symmetry in the idea that I was writing about a time when such a company might again set out, the age of electricity having come and gone.
>
> *(Griffith)*

Though Mandel acknowledges Shakespeare's influence, *Station Eleven* is not an explicit adaptation of *King Lear*. A reminder of Julie Sanders' distinction between literary adaptation and appropriation is useful here: whereas an adaptation typically signals its relationship with an informing source text through closer adherence to character and plot, an "appropriation frequently effects a more decisive journey away from the informing text ... and the embedded relationship [between the two texts] ... can seem more sideways or deflected" (35–36). In contrast to the more adaptive works in this study, *Station Eleven* can be seen then as an appropriation: it does not closely parallel the plot trajectory of *King Lear* and most of its characters do not have clear counterparts, but it specifically challenges the play's moral vision. In the novel's imaginary, Shakespeare's plays are fundamental to the gradual reclamation of humanity.

The one character in *Station Eleven* who invites immediate comparisons is Arthur Leander, an actor whose performance of Lear opens the novel:

> The king stood in a pool of blue light, unmoored. This was act 4 of *King Lear*, a winter night at the Elgin Theatre in Toronto. Earlier in the evening, three little girls had played a clapping game onstage as the audience reentered, childhood versions of Lear's daughters, and now they'd returned as hallucinations in the mad scene. The king stumbled and reached for them as they flitted here and there in the shadows. His name was Arthur Leander. He was fifty-one years old and there were flowers in his hair.
>
> *(1)*

But if Leander, in whose last name "Lear" is contained, holds the spotlight on page one, he is dead by page two, the first of the many fatalities that provide the backdrop for the novel. Director Peter Brook insists that we should "rid ourselves of the notion that because the play is called *King Lear* it is primarily the story of one individual" and instead view it not "as a linear narrative but as a cluster of relationships" (91). Yet Lear, in all of his commanding egotism, has remained stubbornly at the center of critical attention to the play. In *Station Eleven*, however, Arthur Leander is less a singular tragic hero than the character who connects "the cluster of relationships" among the many characters, even if unintentionally.

Arthur Leander grew up on a small island off the coast of British Columbia, dropped out of college in Toronto and began a series of acting jobs. With his growing success, due to his good looks and good fortune as much as talent, Arthur becomes increasingly materialistic, shallow, and egotistical. He is married and divorced three times: to Miranda, a young woman from his home town whose passion is illustrating graphic novels; Elizabeth, a beautiful starlet and mother of his one child, Tyler; and Lydia, another attractive woman described as a copy of the second. He treats his wives as disposable, cheats on all of them, and neglects his son. Arthur's most visible parallels to Lear are in his extreme narcissism and his emotional distance from his friends, his son, and his wives. His most intimate relationship is with a childhood friend, Victoria, to whom he writes letters that remain unanswered. By his own admission, his uses his letters to "Dear V" as a sort of diary; it is in keeping with his self-centered character that he wants an audience for his thoughts, but the correspondence is entirely one-sided.

By the end of the novel, Arthur meditates on his failures:

> The way he'd dropped Miranda for Elizabeth and Elizabeth for Lydia and let Lydia slip away to someone else. The way he'd let Tyler be taken to the other side of the world. The way he'd spent his entire life chasing after something,

money or fame or immortality or all of the above. He didn't even really know his only brother. How many friendships had he neglected until they'd faded out?

(327)

Arthur dies filled with regrets, but like Lear, any epiphany comes too little too late.

Arthur's death is fitting, for any reconstruction of this post-pandemic world cannot accommodate the self-serving individual. A trademark of Mandel's novels is their organization around the coincidental and the deliberate threads that tie an ensemble of characters together. In *Station Eleven*, there is no dominant protagonist but a web of connections among Arthur, his son Tyler, his friend Clark Thompson, his first wife Miranda Carroll, Kirsten Raymonde, Jeevan Chaudhary, and others. Jeevan was a paparazzo who haunted Arthur and Miranda in Los Angeles during their marriage, but he exchanges that "parasitic" role to become a paramedic. He was in the audience the night Arthur collapsed on stage and after trying, unsuccessfully, to resuscitate him, he consoles Kirsten, the eight-year-old girl playing Cordelia. Kirsten briefly meets Miranda backstage on another occasion and one of Miranda's comics will become one of her prized possessions in the following decades. Clark, Arthur's college friend, is on his way to Toronto for Arthur's funeral when his plane is diverted and he ends up at the Severn Airport with Arthur's second wife and son, Elizabeth and Tyler. Kirsten encounters Tyler years later, but in his new identity as The Prophet, and when she finally reaches the former airport, now the Museum of Civilization, she meets Clark. This is only a partial list of the many interconnections among characters but it illustrates Mandel's careful narrative architecture that weaves people together, even as the fabric is usually visible only to the reader. Moreover, the motif of connectivity is a marked contrast to the divisiveness and strife that dominates *King Lear*.

The emphasis on connection has a particular urgency in this post-catastrophe world that demands that people work together for their very survival. This is not to say such cooperation is unique to "Year Twenty," but the need is more transparent. Indeed, shortly after the flu strikes, Jeevan looks out the window at the nearly deserted streets of Toronto, and he realizes

> how human the city is, how human everything is. We bemoaned the impersonality of the modern world, but that was a lie, it seemed to him, it had never been impersonal at all. There had always been a massive delicate infrastructure of people, all of them working unnoticed around us, and when people stop going to work, the entire operation grinds to a halt.
>
> *(178)*

Collaborative human labor was critical to the operation of the modern world, but it is even more necessary in the aftermath of disaster when the survivors must forge relationships with strangers and establish new communities. In spite of the faith Mandel places in humankind's ability to work together, she does not romanticize it, and she recognizes that mutuality and cooperation may result from need rather than inherent virtue. As Craig Dionne explains:

> As a species, the ability to identify with others, what early evolutionary psychologists called "reciprocal altruism," the ability to empathize with kin, family, and strangers who can aid in labor involved in hunting and gathering, increased our chances of survival and, over time and through natural selection, this trait defined the human.
>
> *(135)*

In one of the settlements Kirsten's troupe visits in the earlier years, she is interviewed by a local archivist who asks about her deepest response to the changed world. Kirsten replies, "I think of killing," echoing Lear's infamous "Kill, kill, kill, kill, kill!," his anguished howl of retaliation against the threatening world. But as the survivors approach their second decade, such rage is decreasing:

> Civilization in Year Twenty was an archipelago of small towns. These towns had fought off ferals, buried their neighbors, lived and died and suffered together in the blood-drenched years after the collapse, survived against unspeakable odds and then only by holding together into the calm ...
>
> *(48)*

The primary group the novel follows is the Traveling Symphony, an imperfect but workable collective of artists and musicians, which Kirsten joined so she could perform Shakespeare: "The problem with the Traveling Symphony was the same problem suffered by every group of people everywhere since before the collapse, undoubtedly since well before the beginning of recorded history." Mandel follows with a litany of petty grievances and then adds:

> But what made it bearable were the friendships, of course, the camaraderie and the music and Shakespeare, the moments of transcendent beauty and joy when it didn't matter who'd used the last of the rosin on their bow or who anyone had slept with ...
>
> *(47–48)*

Some of the secondary characters are not even named, referred to as "the first flute" or "the fourth guitar," a strategy that may minimize their individuality but emphasizes their contributions to a larger mission. Beyond their artistic roles, everyone in the troupe has additional tasks: foraging, keeping watch, tending the horses that pull their rusted pickup trucks. When one cynical member of the group quotes Sartre's claim that "Hell is other people," Kirsten responds with "Hell is the absence of the people you long for" (144).

The other settlement central to the novel is the Museum of Civilization and it has also evolved into a functioning community, now of some 300 people. Along with many of its other inhabitants, Clark ended up there when his plane was diverted during the first days of the pandemic. Like Kirsten, Clark realized early on that cooperation born of necessity could emerge from mutual suffering:

> He'd lost his oldest friend, but if the television news was accurate, then in all probability everyone here with him in the airport had lost someone too. All at once he felt an aching tenderness for his fellow refugees, these hundred or so strangers ...
>
> *(241)*

From the beginning, he was instrumental in organizing its operations—assigning people to gather firewood, collect water, salvage materials from nearby homes, plant crops, and hunt deer—but he also encourages people to share their past experiences and forge a new sense of community.

In *King Lear*, where acts of mutual caring and decency provide the only stay against abusive power, the nameless servant's resistance to Cornwall is a notable demonstration of moral courage. A similar moment takes place towards the end of *Station Eleven*, after Kirsten and August have rescued Sayid from the prophet's kidnappers. They have almost reached the airport when the prophet and his men overtake them. August and Sayid manage to hide in the underbrush but Kirsten is exposed. As the prophet is about to shoot her, he recites a line from the first issue of *Station Eleven*. Kirsten, astonished that someone else is familiar with it, responds with more lines: "We long only to go home ... we dream of sunlight, we dream of walking on earth" (302). It is not clear whether the prophet recognizes that Kirsten is also quoting from Miranda's comic book, but one of his followers, a young boy, is moved to tears by what he is hearing and witnessing. The prophet then adjusts his rifle to shoot Kirsten:

> The shot was so loud that she felt the sound in her chest, a thud by her heart. The boy was in motion and she wasn't dead, the shot hadn't come from the prophet's rifle. In the fathomless silence that followed the sound, she touched her fingertips to her forehead and watched the prophet fall before her, the rifle loose in his hands. The boy had shot the prophet in the head.
>
> *(303)*

August quickly kills the Prophet's other two men, but the boy, so shocked at what he had done, shoots himself. It is a dramatic and fast-paced episode, but this critical and unexpected act of one human defending another also diverts the narrative from further tragedy by eliminating a fanatic tyrant.

But even in this world so pressured by the urgency of survival, sheer cooperation and good will, whether compassionate or transactional, are not enough. Kirsten's favorite saying, tattooed on her body and painted across the lead caravan, comes from an old *Star Trek* episode: "Because survival is insufficient." Beyond physical existence alone, the desire for a more meaningful life persists. This is what the Traveling Symphony tries to provide through their performances of music and theatre, and Shakespeare in particular:

They'd performed more modern plays sometimes in the first few years, but what was startling, what no one would have anticipated, was that audiences seemed to prefer Shakespeare to their other theatrical offerings. "People want what was best about the world," Dieter said.

(38)

In *Station Eleven*, Shakespeare is offered not only as what is "best about the world," but because Mandel is explicitly drawing a connection between her characters' post-apocalyptic experience and Shakespeare's early modern world:

> *Pestilential*, a note in the text explains, next to the word *contagious*, in Kirsten's favorite of the three versions of the text that the Symphony carries. Shakespeare was the third born to his parents, but the first to survive infancy. Four of his siblings died young. His son, Hamnet, died at eleven and left behind a twin. Plague closed the theatres again and again, death flickering over the landscape.
>
> (57)

When the plague closed the London playhouses, acting companies took to the road, as they do here. In addition to performing *King Lear* and *Hamlet*, the troupe often decides to put on *A Midsummer Night's Dream* when they think their audiences need something more upbeat. The conditions under which they perform are harsh and spare, but the performers take their mission seriously. When Kirsten scavenges homes, she looks for clothes they can repurpose because

> what they were always doing, was trying to cast a spell, and costuming helped; the lives they brushed up against were work-worn and difficult, people who spent all their time engaged in the tasks of survival ... Kirsten thought it meant something to see Titania in a gown, Hamlet in a shirt and tie.
>
> (151)

Everyone turns out for the performances when they visit the settlements:

> What was lost in the collapse: almost everything, almost everyone, but there is still such beauty. Twilight in the altered world, a performance of *A Midsummer Night's Dream* in a parking lot ... And now in a twilight once more lit by candles, the age of electricity having come and gone, Titania turns to face her fairy king.
>
> (57)

Does Mandel overstate the redemptive power of art? While the post-pandemic world has begun to stabilize by Year Twenty, conditions are still precarious—can Shakespeare really make any difference in people's lives? The players continually wrestle with whether or not what they were doing was noble:

There were moments around campfires when someone would say something invigorating about the importance of art, and everyone would find it easier to sleep that night. At other times it seemed a difficult and dangerous way to survive and hardly worth it, especially at times ... when they were turned away at gunpoint from hostile places ... when they were cold and afraid ... when the heat was unrelenting.

(119)

Mandel celebrates the impact of their mission but does not idealize its significance. One of the musicians "hated Shakespeare" and "found the Symphony's insistence on performing Shakespeare insufferable" (303). The players grumble about having to memorize lines and rehearse while they are so preoccupied with the tasks of daily survival, and they wonder if audiences are simply interested in their appearances for the rare diversion they provide. But the grateful response after every performance—standing ovations, people smiling and weeping—reaffirms their sense of purpose.

Still, Mandel's privileging of Shakespeare over other cultural productions could be seen as yet another manifestation of deifying and essentializing Shakespeare. A recurrent concern of this study, and a focus of Nunez's *Prospero's Daughter* and Atwood's *Hag-Seed* in particular, is the call to decentralize Shakespeare's position as a cultural icon—an act not of erasure but of repositioning. Philip Smith argues that in *Station Eleven*, "we find affirmation of an essentialist Shakespeare ... shown to effortlessly bridge historical and cultural gaps—to unite past and future—because he speaks directly to the essence of that which is human." Smith warns that Mandel's notion of restoration through Shakespeare is reproducing the British colonialist enterprise that assumed that "Shakespeare had the potential to impart British civility to a local populace and to drive cultural development," and that the troupe's performances risk re-enacting the relationship between the colonizer and the colonized (298–299). We need to interrogate the cultural status we have granted Shakespeare and the misappropriation of his work for political ends, but the aims of Mandel's players are far less calculating and grandiose. What the Traveling Symphony does is more akin to the rural tours Shakespeare's acting company made to entertain their fellow countrymen who could not make their way to the London playhouses, rather than the deployment of Shakespeare to advance British imperialism in later centuries. Kirsten and the other performers do not see themselves or their artistic agenda as inculcating a civilizing superiority—they are primarily trying to bring some respite to desperate and hardscrabble lives, whether through a Shakespeare play or a Brandenburg concerto. Furthermore, Shakespeare is accorded no privileged status amidst the other remnants of popular culture—comic books, old sitcoms, *Star Trek*, and tabloids—that the survivors also cherish.

People in *Station Eleven* struggle to create meaningful lives within humankind, but as in *King Lear*, any kind of rebuilding also depends on their co-existence with the non-human world. Noting the relevance of *King Lear*'s catastrophic world to our current environmental challenges, Steve Mentz insists that we should "resist the older temptations of living 'in' or 'with' nature ... [for] the world in ecological crisis may not resemble a pastoral garden so much as a sea in flood" (*Shakespeare* 146–147). In *King Lear*, the non-human world is marked by human misappropriation, but as Lear discovers on the heath, it remains remarkably impervious to human demands. Much of the action in *Station Eleven* takes place in open space that is largely indifferent to human activity, as they gather, hunt, and raise their food or travel from place to place. But even more than in *King Lear*, this outdoor world is covered in human footprints. Almost every description in the novel of the non-human world is inflected with traces of human activity: "The lakeshore road was a complicated patchwork of broken pavement and grass" (127); "now the town was a meadow with black ruins standing. A sea of pink flowers had risen between the shards of buildings" (127), "The road curved towards the distant shine of the lake and disappeared behind the trees. The highway was miles of permanent gridlock, small trees growing now between cars and thousands of windshields reflecting the sky. There was a skeleton in the driver's seat of the nearest car" (144).

Evidence of an invasive human presence is seen throughout *Station Eleven*, even more visibly than in *King Lear*, but both works remind us that people have left massive scars on the planet, signs of blight and waste.

If Shakespeare had to deal with erratic weather and freezing temperatures in his own lifetime, Mandel's world is also marked by the climate change we suffer now. Rising temperatures are one manifestation of this human-made phenomenon, and it provides an oppressive backdrop for the survivors:

> Twenty years after the end of air travel, the caravans of the Traveling Symphony moved slowly under a white-hot sky. It was the end of July, and the twenty-five-year-old thermometer affixed to the back of the lead caravan read 106 Farenheit, 41 Celsius ... The heat wave had persisted for a relentless week.
>
> *(35)*

Martin Paul Eve argues that *Station Eleven* is deeply concerned with global warming:

> While *Station Eleven* never touches directly upon the unfolding disaster of human-made climate change, the comic book-within-a-book world of Doctor Eleven (drawn in Mandel's novel by Miranda and read by Kirsten) is one that is submerged beneath the waters of the ocean.

The future planet that Miranda imagines—and from which the novel takes its name—is described as broken, damaged, and "almost all water," which, as Eve notes, is "the exact future prediction of current climate research" (Eve). Pieter Vermuelen agrees that the novel engages "with crucial elements of the Anthropocene imagination—extinction, epidemics, energy depletion, survival—in ways that are relevant for our understanding of cli-fi" (12). It is no coincidence that the speech Mandel cites from the troupe's *Midsummer Night's Dream* performance is Titania's topical description of early modern weather disturbance:

> Therefore the winds, piping to us in vain, as in revenge, have sucked up from the sea contagious fogs … Therefore the moon, the governess of floods, pale in her anger, washes all the air, that rheumatic diseases do abound … And through this distemperature, we see the seasons alter.
>
> *(57–58)*

Titania is warning Oberon that their private quarrels and the turmoil in the fairy world are the cause of the disastrous weather—and indeed, many of Shakespeare's audience may have believed that—but this also appears to be an explicit reference to the severe draughts and meteorological unpredictability of the 1590s, when the play was first performed.

Mandel does not explicitly critique human contributions to climate catastrophe, but the "unfolding disaster" of severe weather hovers throughout the novel. Similarly, she does not make clear the extent to which the pandemic itself was caused by human behavior. In an interview, Mandel claims that it is not her intent to "chide" people for their behavior and that she has found other post-apocalyptic novels "heavy-handed about the perils of nuclear power and the follies of man. I've always been wary of novels whose aim is to impart a specific lesson …" (Griffith). Nonetheless, even if Mandel is not scolding or overtly drawing a causal relationship between profligate contemporary lifestyles and the catastrophic virus, it is impossible to ignore the conditions she describes. One of most prominent motifs in the novel is the obsession with air travel. The Museum of Civilization, the primary settlement featured in the novel, is established at a former airport and characters recall airplanes from the "time before" with a reverent nostalgia, but the virus also spreads as quickly and lethally as it does because of airplanes. Mandel portrays both the economic and emotional benefits and the severe environmental costs air travel has brought to modernity. Sharon O'Dair claims that Mandel clearly understands the correlation between our modern petro-dependency and other viruses

> to infer that environmental stress, population growth, and air travel underlie the pandemic Georgia Flu and the apocalypse; forests and jungles are cut for agriculture and cattle ranches, humans live in proximity to animals, viruses jump from one species to another and are jetted across the globe. Our way of life, the carbonized world that was lost, causes the pandemic and the apocalypse.
>
> *(21–23)*

O'Dair adds that "along with having children, air travel is the biggest carbon sin humans commit" (21–23).

In the world of *Station Eleven*, the damage has been so massive that humans are forced to return to a pre-industrial lifestyle, their lives of hunting, foraging, and planting putting them in close proximity to the land. The novel requires us to think about the inverted relationship between the "old" world of modernity and the present "pre-modern" world, where the wistful longing for airplanes sits alongside the knowledge that they helped ruin the planet and kill us with viruses. This painful reckoning over the consequences of our choices is evident in an inventory where she catalogs what has been lost, though she calls it "An Incomplete List":

> No more ball games played out under floodlights. No more porch with moths fluttering on summer nights. No more trains running the surface of cities on the dazzling power of the electric third rail. No more cities. No more films ... No more pharmaceuticals. No more flight ... No more Internet. No more social media, no more scrolling through litanies of dreams and nervous hopes and photographs of lunches, cries for help and expressions of contentment ... no more reading and commenting on the lives of others, and in so doing, feeling slightly less alone in the room.
>
> *(31–32)*

This is a world much diminished and marked by negation, as is *King Lear*. Bradon Smith points out that in this list

> many of these are no longer possible specifically because they rely on an abundance of cheap energy. Through this eulogy for a lost high-energy society, Mandel reveals the extent to which contemporary Western culture is epitomized by and dependent on our energy production and consumption, highlighting in particular the dependence of its forms of cultural production.
>
> *(145)*

Like Sharon O'Dair, Smith reminds us that our reliance on fossil fuels has had as many negative consequences as the elegiac list of things that are missed.

Perhaps the novel then leaves the survivors—and readers—with a draconian choice: either a life deprived of the life supports and conveniences that electricity can provide, or a return to our former petro-dependent habits, ultimately destructive for both the human and non-human world. At the end of the novel, Clark takes Kirsten up to a traffic control tower for a surprise. She looks through the telescope and sees "In the distance, pinpricks of light arranged into a grid. There, plainly visible on the side of a hill some miles distant: a town, or a village, whose streets were lit up with electricity" (311). As Bradon Smith argues,

> Kirsten is excited at the end of the novel about traveling to see this newly electrified settlement, but the novel gives us no assurances that this is a positive development. The reader is kept in the dark about how this electrification has been achieved—a return to the old system of fossil fuels or a new, cleaner energy system?
>
> *(150)*

Whether humans will create more environmentally responsible and sustainable forms of energy is not specified, but as Vermuelen notes, *Station Eleven* arguably "opens new avenues for cli-fi—avenues that are less spectacular and apocalyptic than usual" (16). Perhaps this "less apocalyptic" tone allows for rebuilding a better energy future that would respect both the human and the non-human worlds.

Readers and critics have noted that as much as *Station Eleven* is a profoundly post-apocalyptic novel, its optimism is uncharacteristic of the genre. According to Andrew Tate, *Station Eleven* does not give in to the disdainful and misanthropic tone of similar works in that the survivors refuse

> to capitulate to despair or aggressive rejection of community ... the novel takes the risk of believing that an ethical, cooperative version of society might be achievable. The nightmare of ruined worlds, it suggests, are vital to our collective imagination, but there are alternatives, if we do not capitulate to the idea that the future has already been written.
>
> *(135–137)*

In *King Lear*, the tragic outcomes, so rooted in entrenched political and patriarchal systems, seem ordained from the beginning, and the bleak future already written. In *Station Eleven*, Mandel talks back to this inevitable nihilism and suggests that even in the aftermath of global devastation, people have the capacity to rewrite a new future.

References

Adelman, Janet. *Suffocating Mothers: Fantasies of Maternal Origins in Shakespeare's Plays*. New York: Routledge, 1992.

Archer, Jayne. "The Autumn King: Remembering the Land in *King Lear*." *Shakespeare Quarterly* 63. 4 (2012): 518–543.

Armstrong, Philip. "Preposterous Nature in Shakespeare's Tragedies." In *The Oxford Handbook of Shakespearean Tragedy*, eds. Michael Neill and David Schalkwyk. Oxford: Oxford UP, 2016: 104–119.

Boose, Lynda. "The Father and the Bride in Shakespeare." *PMLA* 97. 3 (1982): 325–347.

Brook, Peter. *The Empty Space: A Book About the Theatre*, 2nd ed. New York: Scribner, 1995.

Clayton, Tom. "'The Injuries that they themselves procure': Justice poetic and pragmatic, and Aspects of Endplay." In *King Lear: New Critical Essays*, ed. Jeffrey Kahan. New York: Routledge, 2008: 184–207.

Dionne, Craig. *Posthuman Lear*. Santa Barbara: Punctum Books, 2016.

Duncan-Jones, Katherine. *Ungentle Shakespeare: Scenes from His Life*. London: Arden Shakespeare, 2001.

Egan, Gabriel. *Green Shakespeare: From Ecopolitics to Ecocriticism*. New York: Routledge: 2006.

Eve, Martin Paul. "Reading Very Well for Our Age: Hyperobject Metadata and Global Warming in Emily St. John Mandel's Station Eleven." *Open Library of Humanities* 4. 1 (2018).

Feerick, Jean. "Economies of Nature in Shakespeare." *Shakespeare Studies* 39 (2011): 32–42.

Fitter, Chris. "'So Distribution Should Undo Excess'": Recovering the Political Pressure of Distributive and Egalitarian Discourses in Shakespeare's *King Lear* and Early Modern England." *ELH* 86. 4 (2019): 835–863.

Greenblatt, Stephen. "Shakespeare and the Uses of Power." *New York Review of Books*. April 12, 2007.

Griffith, Colin. "When the Dust Settles: An Interview with Emily St. John Mandel." *Tethered by Letters*, April, 2015.

Heinemann, Margot. "Demystifying the Mystery of State': *King Lear* and the World Upside Down." *Shakespeare Survey* 44 (1992): 75–90.

Jones, Gwilym. *Shakespeare's Storms*. Manchester: Manchester UP, 2014.

Kahn, Coppelia. "The Absent Mother in *King Lear*" In *Rewriting the Renaissance: The Discourses of Sexual Difference in Early Modern Europe*, eds. Margaret Ferguson, Maureen Quilligan, and Nancy Vickers. Chicago: U of Chicago Press, 1986: 33–49.

Mandel, Emily St John. *Station Eleven*. New York: Knopf, 2014.

Marcus, Leah. "*King Lear* and the Death of the World." In *The Oxford Book of Shakespearean Tragedy*, eds. Michael Neill and David Schalkwyk. Oxford: Oxford UP, 2016: 421–436.

Martin, Randall. *Shakespeare and Ecology*. Oxford: Oxford UP, 2015.

McLuskie, Kathleen. "The Patriarchal Bard: Feminist Criticism and Shakespeare." In *Political Shakespeare: New Essays in Cultural Materialism*, eds. Jonathan Dollimore and Alan Sinfield. Ithaca: Cornell UP, 1985: 88–108.

Mentz, Steve. "Tongues in the Storm: Shakespeare, Ecological Crisis, and the Resources of Genre." In *Ecocritical Shakespeare*, eds. Lynne Bruckner and Dan Brayton. Burlington: Ashgate, 2011: 155–172.

Mentz, Steve. "Strange Weather in *King Lear*." *Shakespeare* 6. 2 (2010): 139–152.

O'Dair, Sharon. " ... The Great Globe Itself ... Shall Dissolve: Art After the Apocalypse." In *Routledge Handbook of Shakespeare and Global Appropriation*, eds. Christy Desment, Sujata Iyengar, and Miriam Jacobson. New York: Routledge, 2019: 15–24.

Rhodes, Neil, Jennifer Richards, and Joseph Marshall, eds. *King James VI and I: Selected Writings*. New York: Routledge, 2016.

Sanders, Julie. *Adaptation and Appropriation*, 2nd ed. New York: Routledge, 2016.

Shapiro, James. *The Year of Lear*. New York: Simon and Schuster, 2015.

Skura, Meredith. "Dragon Fathers and Unnatural Children: Warring Generations in *King Lear* and Its Sources." *Comparative Drama* 42. 2 (2008): 121–148.

Smith, Bradon. "Imagined Energy Futures in Contemporary Speculative Fictions." *Resilience: A Journal of the Environmental Humanities* 6. 2–3 (2019): 136–154.

Smith, Philip. "Shakespeare, Survival, and the Seeds of Civilization in Emily St. John Mandel's *Station Eleven*." *Extrapolation* 57. 3: 289–303.

Tate, Andrew. *Apocalyptic Fiction*. London: Bloomsbury Publishing, 2017.

Vermeulen, Pieter. "Beauty That Must Die: *Station Eleven*, Climate Change Fiction, and the Life of Form." *Studies in the Novel* 50. 1 (2018): 9–25.

7

MAGGIE O'FARRELL'S *HAMNET* AND SHAKESPEARE'S FAMILY IN FACT AND FICTION

The parish register of Holy Trinity Church in Stratford, England records that in August of 1596 four children died: three were newborns and the other was William and Anne Shakespeare's eleven-year-old son Hamnet. But there are no documents that inform us further about this tragic loss: we do not know the cause of his death, or its effect on his surviving parents and his two sisters, Susanna and his twin Judith, or how his father may have translated his grief into any of the plays he would write in the years that followed. The profusion of Shakespearean biographies, which inevitably amplify the known facts about his life with historical context and speculation, say almost nothing about the death of his only son.

For decades, this silence haunted writer Maggie O'Farrell, who fills the void with her novel *Hamnet*, winner of the prestigious Women's Prize for Fiction shortly after its publication in 2020. O'Farrell is an Irish novelist who has written seven previous novels and a powerful memoir about her own experiences with trauma and grief: *I am, I am, I am: Seventeen Brushes with Death. Hamnet* is her first novel set in the early modern period, but she has explained in numerous interviews that her curiosity about Hamnet Shakespeare began 30 years ago when an English teacher mentioned his name in passing; she was struck by the similarity between his name and the title of his father's most famous work. O'Farrell has also discussed her concern that Hamnet has been overlooked:

> You know, in one of these big sort of 500-page biographies of Shakespeare, Hamnet is lucky if he gets a mention, maybe two mentions. And it always felt to me that Hamnet the boy wasn't well-known enough.
>
> *(NPR)*

The other works in this study are fictional adaptations or appropriations engaged in a dialogue with one of Shakespeare's plays. In *Hamnet*, O'Farrell entertains a

DOI: 10.4324/9781003166580-8

possible link between Hamnet's death and *Hamlet* the play, but her novel primarily talks back to several centuries of facts and hypotheses that have accumulated around Shakespeare and his family. O'Farrell began her project to devote more attention to Hamnet's short life and early death, and to consider what his loss might have meant to an early modern family that lived with the constant fear of child mortality from the plague or other illnesses. But as she was immersed in her research, O'Farrell also became intrigued with Hamnet's mother, Anne Hathaway Shakespeare. If there is a relative silence surrounding Hamnet, the opposite is the case for Anne, who has been speculated about endlessly, variously sanctified and vilified. O'Farrell found the legends about Anne "astonishing" and wanted to provide an alternative to her many unfair portrayals (Folger). *Hamnet* also invites us to consider a range of other issues: the relationship between artists' personal lives and their art, the costs of Shakespeare as cultural icon, and the ethics of appropriation in a historical novel.

Early modern England has proven fertile ground for novelists and playwrights. Aside from the best-selling romances by authors such as Philippa Gregory and Alison Weir, much highly acclaimed literary fiction turns to the sixteenth century. Most notable in recent years are Hilary Mantel's *Wolf Hall* trilogy (2009–2020) about Thomas Cromwell and Henry VIII, and Arthur Phillips' *The King at the End of the World* (2020) about the end of Elizabeth I's reign. With all of their personal drama and political intrigue, the Tudors—called by some popular fans the "hot dynasty"—have fascinated novelists and screenwriters. Shakespeare himself has also been the subject of many fictional adaptations, including Robert Nye's *The Late Mr. Shakespeare* (1999), a memoir by an invented player in the King's Men, Arthur Philipps' *The Tragedy of Arthur* (2011) about a previously unknown play by Shakespeare, and Jude Morgan's *The Secret Life of William Shakespeare* (2014), a historical novel that carefully interweaves Shakespeare's personal and professional lives. Bill Cain's play, *Equivocation* (2009), exposes the paternal and artistic angst that emerges as Shakespeare writes *Macbeth*, and Lauren Gunderson's play, *The Book of Will* (2018), explores his life and art though the preservation of his work in the First Folio. Among the many film and television biopics, John Madden's popular romantic comedy *Shakespeare in Love* (1998) portrays an ambitious and lovestruck playwright at the beginning of his career in London, while Kenneth Branagh's *All is True* (2018) is a nostalgic depiction of his final years in Stratford with his family and friends.

Both Hamnet and Anne Shakespeare might have been entirely lost to history if it were not for William Shakespeare's unparalleled literary celebrity, so any explorations of their lives must begin with his. What we know about his life in Stratford and London has been established, interrogated, and reshaped into countless biographies and there are no signs that this interest is waning. The basic facts are familiar: in 1564 William Shakespeare was born to Mary Arden Shakespeare and John Shakespeare, a glovemaker and the bailiff of Stratford for several years until he fell into some disgrace. At age 18, Will was formally betrothed to Anne Hathaway, then 26. She came from Shottery, a village outside of Stratford. Her father had died the year before and left her a small dowry. They married in November 1582 and six months later, in May of

1583, their daughter Susanna was born. Their twins, Hamnet and Judith, were born in 1585.

The following period, from 1585–1592, is referred to as "the lost years" because there is little solid evidence about Shakespeare's activity during that time, but by 1592 he was established in London as a promising playwright and actor. During the next few years when the theatres were closed because of the plague, he published two narrative poems, *Venus and Adonis* and *The Rape of Lucrece*, which he dedicated to the Earl of Southampton. In the following years, he performed in plays in both public venues and at court, but he turned most of his attention to writing plays for his own company, the Lord Chamberlain's Men, which became the King's Men upon James I's accession.

Though his primary residence was in London, he maintained ties with his family in Stratford. A year after his son Hamnet died in 1596, he purchased New Place, one of the largest houses in Stratford, and invested in other properties there as well as in London. He died in Stratford in April of 1616; seven years later, his fellow players, John Heminges and Henry Condell, gathered most of his plays together into one volume, now known as the First Folio.

There is considerable information that can flesh out the bones of this spare summary—references to William Shakespeare by his contemporaries, theatre archives, real estate records and other legal documents pertaining to his family and his network of friends and business acquaintances in London and Stratford, and his last will and testament—but there is still much that is unknown. We have no letters written by him to colleagues, family, or friends, and we have no diary or personal writings that share his emotional life or illuminate his artistic process. But many historians would add that we know more about him than many of his contemporaries even as we lament the gaps in the record we do have.

What is disputed is not so much the evidence that is available as how those facts should be understood, and the ensuing interpretations are often vigorously contested. Given the finite information available, critics, historians, filmmakers, and writers have tried to fill in the blanks with an imaginative deployment of research about early modern social and cultural conditions. Biographical interest in Shakespeare persists in an attempt to explain and understand the world's arguably most well-known writer, as though the more we know about the man the better we can unlock the mysteries of his works. We know the dangers—or at least the extreme limits—of the biographical fallacy, but still, we try to extrapolate the life from the works and the works from the life. What we conclude often tells us more about the Shakespeare we want to believe existed and about our own cultural imperatives.

The proliferation of Shakespeare biographies did not begin in earnest until almost a century after his death with Nicholas Rowe's account in 1709, but by the twentieth century biographies of Shakespeare increased so rapidly that since the 1990s, one has been published almost every year. Among the many significant authors that focus on Shakespeare's life story through either a macro or micro approach are Peter Ackroyd, Katherine Duncan-Jones, Stephen Greenblatt, Peter Holland, Park Honan, Charles Nicholl, Lois Potter, Samuel Schoenbaum, James

Shapiro, and Stanley Wells, but this list captures only a small portion of an embarrassment of riches.

The most useful scholarly studies of Shakespeare's life are grounded in a common body of evidence that is then situated within a larger historical, literary, theatrical, or political context. No matter the agenda of any particular biography, most of them contend with the same basic questions about his education, the years he spent between his marriage at 18 and his presence in London several years later, his friendships, his sexuality, his love life, his religion, his professional collaborations, and his financial portfolio. Although these biographies necessarily resort to the conditional safety net of "might have, "most likely," and "probably," some indulge in more speculation than others. Many of these conjectures are fairly solid: for example, since it was common practice for young boys in Stratford to attend grammar school, it seems quite likely that young Will Shakespeare did as well, even if we do not have any verifying records. But it is a wilder leap to assume that because he was involved in the theatre, he must have had numerous promiscuous affairs or died of syphilis, or that because he became financially secure, he could afford rich foods and therefore died of obesity or excessive drinking. Graham Holderness' brilliant *Nine Lives of William Shakespeare* (2011) negotiates the fraught relationship between fact and inference by providing nine "micro-biographies" of different aspects of Shakespeare's life. In each chapter, the known evidence is followed by an account of the subsequent assumptions and received legends, and finally a clever fictional reconstruction, including a Sherlock Holmes riff, a parody of a seventeenth century historical document, and a utopian fable. Holderness does not discount the validity of any of these approaches—from fact, to semi-fact, to fiction—as long as each is defined transparently.

Our collective knowledge of Shakespeare's immediate family also comprises documentary evidence, interpretation, and imaginative reconstruction, but the historical record is perhaps richer than we might expect because of the relative prominence of the Shakespeare family in Stratford. John Shakespeare was a whittawer—a craftsman who made leather goods and gloves—and for a time, a civic leader, eventually serving in the town's highest office as bailiff. His wife Mary Arden, daughter of a prosperous farmer, brought an inheritance to the marriage that may have enabled her husband in his property purchases and that he may also have squandered. William was the third of their eight children, three of whom did not survive to adulthood. By the time William was a teenager in the late 1570s, his father's fortunes rapidly declined: evidence points to John Shakespeare's illegal wool trading and the mismanagement of investments that led to hefty debt. Other factors may have been his alcoholism and his clandestine Catholicism, though these charges are less substantiated. Nonetheless, Shakespeare's father lived a long life, dying in 1601, and his mother died in 1608, both of them most likely in their early 70s.

Of Shakespeare's own children we know that Susanna, the eldest, was born in 1583 and may have been educated at a local petty school, along with other Stratford girls whose attendance is documented; her signature on two documents indicates a degree of literacy. In 1607 she married the physician John Hall and they had one child, a daughter Elizabeth, born in 1608. Susanna appears in the Stratford records two other times, provoking further questions about the family's religious affiliation and her social standing: in 1606 she was charged with not having taken communion on Easter Sunday, and in 1613 she and her husband sued a fellow citizen for his slanderous claim that Susanna had committed adultery with another Stratford man and contracted a sexually transmitted disease; they won their suit. Susanna died at age 66 in 1649.

Judith was born in 1585 with her twin brother Hamnet and may also have attended school like her sister; though a legal document from later years bears her mark in place of a signature, she may have been able to read if not write. She married Thomas Quiney in February of 1616; the Quiney and Shakespeare families were closely affiliated. The wedding, just two months before her father's death, was shrouded in scandal because Quiney had recently impregnated another woman, Margaret Fuller. Quiney admitted his paternity and was forced to perform public penance, but Fuller and their child died during childbirth. Judith and Thomas went on to have three children and a marriage that lasted several decades until her death at the age of 77. The timing and revisions of Shakespeare's hastily assembled will that leaves the bulk of his estate to Susanna may indicate that Shakespeare had lost some confidence in the future of Judith's marriage.

Because of his early death, we know the least about Hamnet Shakespeare. Graham Holderness' biography wryly summarizes the bare evidence:

> Everything we know about Hamnet Shakespeare is that he was baptized on 2 February 1585, Stratford-upon-Avon, one of a pair of twins; and buried 11 August 1596. He was eleven years old. He was born; he lived; he died. And one more thing: he happened to be the only son of the most famous writer in history.
>
> (Shakespeare Circle *101*)

It is also widely assumed that Hamnet and Judith Shakespeare were named after Catholic recusants and close family friends in Stratford, Hamnet and Judith Sadler. Hamnet Sadler was one of the five men who witnessed Shakespeare's signatures on his will, and Shakespeare remembered him with a gift to purchase a memorial ring, though his name in the will is spelled with the interchangeable form "Hamlet."

We also know relatively little about Anne Hathaway; there is no extant birth record for her, but the inscription on her grave suggests that she was born in 1555 or 1556. Her father, Richard Hathaway, was a yeoman farmer and a close acquaintance of John Shakespeare, so the marriage of their children was in part a match between two families of long-standing association. After their marriage, Anne and William may have followed common practice and lived in the elder Shakespeare homestead on Henley Street, but again, there is no evidence to confirm this. A year after Hamnet died, Shakespeare bought New Place, the second largest house in Stratford, where Anne would have lived with Susanna and Judith, at least until their marriages. The house was large enough that Shakespeare's parents and siblings and other boarders may have also lived there for periods of time. Recent archeological discoveries show evidence that brewing was likely a household occupation and, perhaps, business (Orlin, *Shakespeare Quarterly* 447), and findings of pottery and ceramics remnants suggest a measure of prosperity (Scheil 65).

While Anne is mentioned in so few documents, there is one reference to her that has garnered far more attention than it may warrant: the infamous bequest to her in her husband's will of his "second best bed with the furniture"—and nothing else. Scholars attempting to interpret this brief reference have examined common practices in early modern wills, typical estate transfers, and the connotations of "second best," to determine whether Shakespeare meant the gift as a gesture of endearment or a slight, while others remind us that the several last-minute changes to his will point to an unfinished product, and that the interlineated line in question may not have even been in Shakespeare's hand.

What the will tells us about Anne or her marriage only leads us back to the words that haunt so much of our biographical sleuthing: we simply do not know. Anne died in 1623, the same year the First Folio appeared, but we do not know if there is any connection between those two events. She is buried in Holy Trinity Church in Stratford next to her husband, with an epitaph in Latin written from the perspective of a child celebrating her "Mother ... who gave me milk and life."

Facts, semi-facts, and fiction: The dehumanizing of Anne Hathaway Shakespeare

Perhaps the most extreme fabrications in the copious biographical histories of Shakespeare involve his sexuality and his love life, both marital and allegedly extramarital, so it is not surprising that suppositions about Anne Hathaway are also clouded by gossip, slander, and wishful thinking. Until recently, little of the focus on Anne has been driven by interest in her as her own person, but rather as the wife who was either the obstacle or muse to her husband's prodigious creative genius. Fictional and historical representations of Anne fall rather swiftly into three patterns and all betray gendered stereotypes: she is either the beloved and patient Penelope who tended the home fires in Stratford and inspired from afar, or the promiscuous adulteress responsible for her husband's bitter distrust of women, or the aging and unattractive nag whose shrewishness drove him to London—the latter two categories sometimes strangely overlapping.

Katherine Scheil's excellent cultural history, *Imagining Shakespeare's Wife: The Afterlife of Anne Hathaway* (2018), examines the depictions of Hathaway from the early eighteenth century to the present that have served the various creators in imagining the kind of wife necessary for their vision of Shakespeare: "Shakespeare's Stratford wife can humanize Shakespeare as a mortal man, but she can also make him conventional rather than subversive, and the domestic, maternal, familial associations that Anne represents have been both embraced and suppressed" (xvii). In the later eighteenth century, when Shakespeare was celebrated as a virile ladies' man whose sexual energy infused his romantic literary productions, Anne was largely absent from these portrayals since "a wife undercuts a narrative of a lusty, sexually active urban Shakespeare, turning him into an adulterer rather than an impassioned Romeo" (24–25). But by the nineteenth century, Victorian sensibility demanded a morally fit Shakespeare, a family man; thus began the mythologizing of his exemplary wife, a devoted and faithful Anne. As Scheil points out, however, the idealization of Anne, her courtship, and marriage was driven as much by the cold profits of tourism as by literary forces. By the nineteenth century, Hathaway descendants and the Shakespeare Birthplace Trust had re-branded the Hewlands Farm where Anne grew up as the "Anne Hathaway Cottage," and it remains to this day an essential part of the commercial Shakespeare industry. The picturesque property is staged with artifacts, relics, and tour guides intended to re-enact the story of the young lovers' pastoral courtship and idyllic romance.

Against this commercial and sentimental promotion of Anne, which continues today in gift shops and imitation cottages around the world, are numerous negative portraits from the last several decades, some of which have had troublesome staying power in popular culture. One of the most disturbing portrayals is Anthony Burgess' novel, *Nothing Like the Sun*, first published in 1964, translated widely and frequently reprinted since then. Burgess' fictional description of Anne, echoed in his 1970 biography of Shakespeare, entitled Shakespeare, is rendered in language as aggressive and repellent as the character he creates: she tricks the poor Will into marriage with her "filthy lust" and leaves him depleted and embittered. His revulsion increases over the years when he discovers "the groaning old crone" committing adultery with his brother. Burgess also imagines Shakespeare's various infidelities, but they are considered the excusable indiscretions of an artistic genius, while Anne's transgressions render her monstrous. The novel, bursting with cruel sophomoric jokes, was endorsed by scholar Harold Bloom as "Burgess' best novel" and "also the only successful novel ever written about Shakespeare" (386).

Misogyny in literary criticism is not a new phenomenon, even if its tenacity seems so jarring in the wake of late twentieth-century feminism. Perhaps even more disappointing is how much the portrayal of an emasculating or sexually repulsive Anne Hathaway persists. Stephen Greenblatt's prominent endorsement of the 2013 reprint of Burgess' *Nothing Like the Sun* as "wildly inventive" should not come as a surprise after his own ruthless depiction of Hathaway in his best-selling *Will in the World: How Shakespeare Became Shakespeare* (2004). Greenblatt refers to Shakespeare's marriage to Anne as "a disastrous mistake" that was "doomed from the beginning" and imagines that when he "lay dying, he tried to forget his wife," but then assigned her "the second best bed" as a sign of his utter hostility towards her. He further imagines that Shakespeare's graveside epitaph also signaled his contempt: "Bleste be ye man yt spares thes stones/ And curst be he yt moves by bones" may mean more than anxiety that his remains would be relocated: "he may have feared still more that one day his grave would be opened to let in the body of Anne Shakespeare" (148). It is not only male scholars who have been dismissive of Anne Hathaway. In her iconoclastic and often fascinating biography, Katherine Duncan-Jones speculates that Shakespeare's interest in Anne stemmed merely from "a combination of boredom with the sexual curiosity natural to his years" and that he felt "reluctant" about the marriage resulting from this "dalliance." She assumes that "he and Anne went to live in the Henley Street house where the flock of children expanded with alarming speed" (22), though at a time when many marriages produced large families, three children hardly constitutes "a flock." Duncan-Jones admits that the union might at some point have been a "lovematch," but she concludes that Shakespeare would have felt trapped by "his unwanted seven-year apprenticeship to domesticity" and was eager to escape to his career in London.

Anne as symbol of the stifling dullness of the countryside has been perpetuated in popular culture. John Madden's Academy Award-winning movie of 1998, *Shakespeare in Love*, still delights audiences with its charm and wit, but it preserves the notion that the male writer's creative output is dependent upon an exciting lust and love life. When the winsome but angst-ridden young playwright is frustrated by his writer's block, his therapist urges him to see the connection between his enervation and his sexual inactivity, which Shakespeare describes as: "Four years and a hundred miles away in Stratford. A cold bed too, since the twins were born. Banishment was a blessing." Other than this brief reference to Anne, she is absent from the film; in screenwriter Tom Stoppard's adaptation, it is Anne who is banished so we do not have to wrestle with the uncomfortable fact of Shakespeare's adultery with his beautiful muse, Viola. In his recent book, *Shakespeare in a Divided America* (2020), James Shapiro describes the filmmakers' struggles over how to land the appropriate ending that would preserve the promise of Shakespeare's artistic future and his reputation as a faithful husband; Anne remains invisible, Viola is sent off to adventures in the new world, and Shakespeare is left to revel in his thrilling love of a woman who demands nothing from him but their shared immortality through his writing.

Hamnet: A novel of the plague

This is a broad overview of the factual and fictional body of Shakespearean history that Maggie O'Farrell talks back to through *Hamnet*. The center of the novel is Hamnet Shakespeare's death from the plague in 1596, but the narrative also looks back to the decade earlier, when his parents married, and then forward a few years later to the staging of *Hamlet* in London. It is the loss of this eleven-year-old boy that instigates the extended imagining of his life in Stratford with his siblings and grandparents, his loving but distant father, and most of all, his eccentric and free-spirited mother. In the novel, O'Farrell refers to Anne as Agnes or Annis, explaining that because her father, Richard Hathaway, named her that way in his will, "I decided to follow his example" (Author's Note). Naming her Agnes also distinguishes her from a history of problematic characterizations of Anne.

With a novelist's talent for setting a scene, O'Farrell begins by describing Hamnet playing on a summer's day with Judith when she suddenly feels unwell. He searches frantically for his mother but Agnes is a mile away at Hewlands tending to her bee-hives and medicinal plants. By the time she arrives, it is clear that the pestilence is to blame. Anne is known as a healer and she is devastated when her remedies are ineffective. In an unexpected twist, Judith in fact survives, but Hamnet, who had naively offered to switch places with his twin, falls ill as well and dies.

From this tragic moment, the novel turns back to the meeting of Agnes and Shakespeare. O'Farrell imagines the courtship as loving, mutual, and practical, for both of them viewed marriage as a means of escaping their restrictive homes. Agnes, who thrives in the outdoor world and is preternaturally savvy about flora and fauna, chafes under the constraints of her stepmother. Shakespeare suffers under the iron fist of his temperamental father and expectations that he helps with a family business in which he has no interest. He is an occasional Latin tutor with no particular promise, but Agnes at least has a small dowry; she is the catch, not the burden. But a few years into their marriage, Agnes senses her husband's restlessness, and she encourages his move to London to expand his father's business. With his gradual immersion instead into the theatrical world, he makes fewer trips home to Stratford and they begin to grow apart.

When Hamnet dies, his parents are overwhelmed by the loss, but Agnes slowly reassumes her role as mother and local healer and sage. A year after Hamnet's death, Shakespeare buys New Place, a large house and property where she immerses herself in bee-keeping, brewing, and gardening. When Agnes hears that her husband is staging a new work called *Hamlet*, she is furious he did not tell her that he wrote a play named after their dead son. In an apt if fanciful finale, Agnes persuades her brother Bartholomew to ride with her to London to confront her husband and see the play; seeing the two Hamlets on stage, father and son, helps her understand how her husband's grief and her son's legacy have been transformed through art.

The appeal of *Hamnet* is not simply that it reconstructs a chapter in the life of one of the world's greatest cultural icons, for many similar attempts have floundered. Whereas so much historical fiction can be heavy-handed, one of O'Farrell's gifts is her seamless incorporation of her knowledge of the early modern world; as Geraldine Brooks writes, O'Farrell is deft

> at keeping her research subordinated to the story. We're not force-marched through a manual on 16th-century glove-making techniques or an exegesis of illegal practices in the Tudor wool trade. But we can smell the tang of the various new leathers in the glover's workshop, the fragrance of the apples racked a finger-width apart in the winter storage shed ...
>
> *(16)*

Nor does the novel fall into the trap of recreating the kind of dialogue and diction that Lois Potter refers to as "embarrassingly pseudo-Elizabethan" (259). *Hamnet* respects biographical information and historical accuracy while avoiding both archaisms and anachronisms. Some scholars make a distinction between the two modes of biographical and historical fiction, but the descriptors are often used interchangeably, a practice followed here as O'Farrell is interested in drawing a fuller portrait of Anne Shakespeare and her son as well as conveying a sense of life in late sixteenth-century England.

But how should we think about *Hamnet* as an act of talking back? Biographical or historical fiction is a form of adaptation that draws not from a prior literary text but from actual historical events and real people—so do we hold it to a more prescriptive standard? Or since we maintain that the creative license of literary adaptations should not be hampered by circumscribed fidelity to their sources, do we allow the same liberty if the intertextual relationship is between a verifiable historical record and a work of fiction? It could be argued that historical fiction, by definition, is inherently more restricted.

Fictional adaptations are free to relocate their retellings temporally and spatially: the other works in this study all transpose their stories into a largely contemporary world, with the exception of *Desdemona*, which takes place in the afterlife. But if a work is going to revisit a particular period, it is necessarily bound to that time. More specific restrictions, however, may not be as definitive, for what we call "history" is not necessarily neutral. The historical record is objective only to a point and then open to interpretation: witness, for example, Shakespeare's will where the existence of the "the second-best bed" line is indisputable, but its implications are not. Furthermore, as we have seen even with someone as well-known as Shakespeare, the record is always incomplete, filled with lost years and unanswered questions. This is where the novelist can enter with a certain responsibility to historical accuracy and known facts, but also the freedom to interpret and create a compelling narrative around their subject.

In the end, fiction is fiction, and as much as that is obvious, it bears repeating when it comes to a novel like *Hamnet* and its kin. Michael Lackey describes the resistance many scholars and readers have had to bio/historical fiction, arguing that it is an oxymoron, so practitioners have had to repeatedly remind their audiences that they are writing fiction and that "what we get in a biographical novel, then, is the novelist's vision of life and the world" and not necessarily a verifiably "accurate representation of an actual person's life" (7). What is useful here is transparency, which can be provided in author's notes, prefaces, or supplementary interviews and writings, explaining what she has drawn from her sources and what she has invented. Jerome De Groot discusses how this "habit of authorial paratextual commentary upon the process and development" of their works has become common practice for novelists who feel compelled "to articulate their practice to their readership," though not all practitioners of historical fiction are so honest (8). We might argue that simply labelling a work "fiction" should be sufficient, but given the erosion of respect for the distinction between fact and fiction we have seen in our time, such clarity can be an ethical gesture.

To return then to our question, how does *Hamnet* fit in with other works that talk back to Shakespeare? Julie Sanders reminds us that just as "the retrieval of lost voices or lost histories is a motif" common to so many adaptations and appropriations, this "shared purpose can also be identified in much contemporary historical fiction" (179–180). Many of the adaptations considered in this study give more voice and agency to marginalized characters in their source texts; similarly, O'Farrell has explained how she was driven to fill in the gaps surrounding Hamnet

Shakespeare and to provide a corrective to the vilification of Anne Hathaway. In this sense, as De Groot reminds us, historical fiction "can report from places made marginal and present a dissident or dissenting account of the past ... [it] can quarrel with particular historical narratives" (140–145). *Hamnet* is a loving portrayal of a family broken by grief and loss: on the surface, it hardly seems radical or dissident. But it does "present a dissenting account of the past," particularly in regards to Anne Hathaway Shakespeare as mother, wife, and early modern woman.

Coinciding with the rich outpouring of feminist criticism in Shakespeare studies in the late twentieth century was an influential body of scholarship in early modern history that aimed at recovering the lives of women across geographical, economic, and social boundaries. Following Virginia Woolf's imaginary construction of a Judith Shakespeare in *A Room of One's Own*, historians demonstrated that there was in fact a Judith Shakespeare, and so many more women who made valuable contributions, private and public, to early modern culture and society. The work of Patricia Crawford and Sara Mendelson, Joan Kelly Gadol, Carole Levin, Betty Travitsky, Wendy Wall, Merry Weisner-Hanks, and many others, brought to light the achievements of individual women neglected by history, but perhaps more importantly, resisted essentialist and monolithic claims about "woman" and examined the diversity of situations and lived experiences of a plurality of ordinary women.

One of the first goals in recognizing early modern women was to acknowledge the value of lives that were largely private and domestic, although portraying women relationally—as mothers, wives, daughters—can also make it difficult to recognize them as individuals in their own right. O'Farrell embraces this challenge, for her characterization of Agnes is of a woman whose loving commitments as daughter, sibling, mother, and wife do not hamper her individuality. In *Hamnet*, Agnes is the protagonist and Shakespeare the secondary player. He is never actually named but referred to variously as father, husband, brother, tutor. This strategy could be seen as elevating his importance—is his greatness such that his name cannot be uttered?—but the effect in fact is to de-center him. He is not dismissed, but his portrayal as more ordinary is also humanizing, a welcome counter to the bardolatry that has elevated him to universal stardom.

O'Farrell's fuller portrait of Agnes is grounded in the important contributions she makes to her family and community, even if they are not as celebrated and visible as her husband's achievements. Agnes grows up as a Cinderella-like figure; her mother dies early and is replaced with a jealous stepmother whose hostility is unleashed when Agnes' father dies. Agnes works hard in the household, but she is more compatible with the outdoor world, training her kestrel and gathering medicinal plants. Agnes is aware of her reputation for eccentricity; when "the young Latin tutor" first sees her at the farm where he has come to give lessons to her stepbrothers, he thinks:

> She has a certain notoriety in these parts. It is said that she is strange, touched, peculiar, perhaps mad. He has heard that she wanders the back roads and forest

at will, unaccompanied, collecting plants to make dubious potions. It is wise
not to cross her for people say she has learnt her crafts from an old crone ...

(32)

The gossip is exaggerated, but he is intrigued. Their brief courtship is one of
mutual attraction, but it also offers both Agnes and Will an alternative to their
current situations with their domineering families. Agnes

grows up feeling wrong, out of place, too dark, too tall, too unruly, too opi-
nionated, too silent, too strange ... she grows up too with the memory of
what it meant to be properly loved, for what you are, not what you ought to
be ... and if she meets it again ... she will seize it again as a means of escape, as
a means of survival.

(49–50)

Shakespeare also feels confined by his overbearing and often physically abusive
father, so Agnes draws on her medical knowledge for the timing of conception
and, as O'Farrell presents it, she and William's first pregnancy is deliberate, a way
of entering into more autonomous adulthood.

From the beginning, their union is companionate, but after a few years, Agnes is
aware that her husband is depressed, struggling with his limited prospects in Stratford and the demands to work under his father's rule:

Is it to be, he asks himself, that they remain here, in this town, forever? Is he
never to see any other place, never to live elsewhere? He wants nothing more
than to take hold of Agnes and the baby and run with them, as far as they are
able to go.

(132)

So she contrives a plan that would send him to London to expand his father's
business, but aware that John "wouldn't listen to a woman in this matter," she has
her brother Bartholomew pose the idea to her father-in-law. When Bartholomew
asks her if she is willing to live separately from her husband for long periods, Agnes
admits it will be difficult, but "If London could save him from this misery, it is
what I want" (162).

This version defies the prevalence in Shakespeare historiography that his "shotgun"
marriage was either an accident or a trap, and is consistent with the alternative view
Lena Cowen Orlin proposes. Anne's supposedly scandalous pregnancy, Orlin argues,
does not account for the urgency we associate with their marriage: "demographic
research has demonstrated that as many as thirty percent of early modern brides were
pregnant when they wed," and as long as a church wedding was involved there was
little social stigma. Orlin suggests instead that the marriage was a means of avoiding an
apprenticeship that Shakespeare's father may well have arranged for him:

Let us suppose that Shakespeare did not want to spend his life—or any more months than he already had done—as a Stratford artificer. The wedding would have been a means of escaping the life that had been organized for him.

(Oxford 56)

In *Hamnet*, Shakespeare begins by selling gloves to the London playhouses and then finds work in the theatre world himself. As his professional career takes off, he and Agnes inevitably grow further apart, their marriage dependent on his occasional letters home and increasingly fewer visits. How often Shakespeare actually went home to Stratford is one of the pressing unknowns in the biographical record. In the seventeenth century, John Aubrey reported that Shakespeare's neighbors claimed he "was wont to go into Warwickshire once a year." James Shapiro estimates that he most likely went more often than that, particularly when theatres in London were closed during Lent or because of the plague, but the trip was arduous: a grueling three days on horseback through often impassable roads and inclement weather (*A Year in the Life* 230–241). While we do not know what homecomings were like for either him or his family, O'Farrell reconstructs them in the novel. Susanna thinks about the times when her father came home:

Twice, three, four, five times a year. Sometimes for a week, sometimes more … I come whenever I can, he told her, the last time he was here … He had been packing to leave again—rolls of paper, close with his writing, a spare shirt, a book he had bound with cat gut and a cover of pigskin. Her mother gone, vanished, off to wherever she went, for she hated to see him leave.

(55)

While her husband spends most of his time in London, Agnes is busy helping to manage the large household where she lives with Shakespeare's parents, his siblings, and her three children. Mendelson and Crawford's comprehensive study of women's lives in early modern England describes how complex and demanding the management of a household was for rural and urban women at every socioeconomic level. Women in what we would now call "middle-class" households, such as Anne Shakespeare's,

had kitchen gardens, so they and their servants were involved in both growing and preparing food and medicinal herbs. Urban probate inventories show an increasing range of household goods in middling level households, much of which was the product of female labor, and all of which required further female labor to maintain.

(307)

In *Hamnet*, this cultivation of plants for food and herbology and the constant cleaning and upkeep of the household occupies Agnes, along with an exhausting list of other daily activities: baking bread, brewing, maintaining her beehives, sewing, caring for her children. Beyond tending to the immediate needs of her family, Agnes also serves the surrounding community as healer and wise woman. Young Hamnet is proud of his mother's skill—"people come from all over town, all over Warwickshire and beyond to speak with his mother through the window of the narrow cottage, to describe their symptoms, to tell her what they suffer, what they endure"—but Susanna is jealous of the attention her mother gives others (51). Agnes' mother-in-law also objects—"she doesn't know why Agnes carries on with this business because it's not as if she has need of money these days. Not ... that it ever brought in a great deal" (54). But Agnes is fiercely grateful that her ability to help and comfort others also strengthens her own selfhood.

Germaine Greer's biography, *Shakespeare's Wife* (2007), is a vigorous rebuke to the long tradition of dismissing or demonizing Anne Hathaway; O'Farrell cites it as one of the works that influenced her thinking about Agnes. Greer is intent on questioning much of the received wisdom surrounding Anne and restoring her to a central position in Shakespeare's life story, as well as her own. Greer claims that Anne was essentially her husband's steward and property manager, particularly after the purchase of New Place, which she imagines required considerable renovation under Anne's supervision. One of Greer's most compelling arguments is that Anne, like so many other Stratford women, was involved in malt-making:

> Within months of acquiring New Place Shakespeare is listed as a holder of malt; the malt was almost certainly made by Anne or under her supervision. If she was making malt, she was probably also brewing ale, and raising pigs on the spent malt, curing her own bacon, and baking bread, for all these activities were interdependent.
>
> *(217)*

Greer speculates that the level of malt-making activity that would have been possible at a dwelling as large as New Place would have resulted in a substantial profit, so that Anne could have also contributed significantly to the family income.

Orlin also suggests that "Anne may have trained young Stratford women in the business of brewing, as well as that of malt-making" and cites recent excavations at New Place that "have turned up stone pads, which, archaeologists suggest, may indicate an onsite brewhouse" (*Shakespeare Quarterly* 447). Orlin provides a detailed account of the industrious Elizabeth Quiney, a neighbor with close ties to the Shakespeares, and suggests it as "a cognate life to Anne Shakespeare's," which makes it

> possible for us to see Anne as a businesswoman of substance. And this, in turn, helps us explain another aspect of William Shakespeare's story that has haunted many biographers. How could he have afforded shares in the Globe? Purchased New Place and other properties in Stratford? The tithes? The Blackfriars gatehouse? Perhaps the answer lies with Anne, his partner in a two-earner marriage.
>
> (*Shakespeare Quarterly 448*)

In *Hamnet*, these are profitable activities that Anne began to engage in with the purchase of New Place, a year after Hamnet's death, and they may have also helped her to manage some of the heartache which further burdened a marriage already strained by separation. O'Farrell's attribution of the plague as the cause of Hamnet's death is not verifiable, but it is also quite plausible given its recurrent outbreaks throughout the early modern period. Like Emily St. John Mandel's *Station Eleven*, *Hamnet*, subtitled "A Novel of the Plague," was written before the Covid outbreak of 2019, but the parallels are again eerily resonant.

In *Station Eleven*, the pandemic is related to a modern lifestyle of globalization and human interconnection, but it also seems to strike with a harrowing randomness. Similarly, in *Hamnet*, humans are both responsible for and victims of a disease that is calculating but capricious. In a striking interlude mid-novel, O'Farrell traces the prolonged journey of the pestilence from a Murano glassmaker's packing materials to a pet monkey to a merchant ship's cabin boy in Alexandria and then through the many people who handle a box of glass beads with its stowaway infected flea. Eventually the package makes its way to Stratford to a local seamstress who ordered the Venetian beads for a wealthy client's gown and who then hands them over to the young neighbor girl who assists her: Judith Shakespeare.

The plague's many disruptions to Shakespeare's theatrical activities in London have become a familiar element in his biography, but O'Farrell redirects the focus away from its impact on his professional life to its effect on his family. When his young daughter misses her father, she thinks:

> If the plague comes to London, he can be back with them for months. The playhouses are all shut, by order of the Queen, and no one is allowed to gather in public. It is wrong to wish for the plague, her mother has said, but Susanna has done this a few times under her breath.
>
> *(56)*

The cruel irony is that her father will come home because of the plague, not because he is escaping its scourge in London but because it has killed his son in Stratford.

The plague, also called the Black Death or the pestilence, refers to the bubonic plague and its pneumonic variants. Two centuries before, between 1347–1350, the plague struck Europe and England, killing hundreds of thousands, and it cycled back repeatedly for the next several centuries with lesser or greater vehemence. In 1563, it returned mercilessly, killing almost 2000 people in London in just one week. By the next year it had spread to the countryside and in 1564, the year Shakespeare was born, one quarter of the Stratford population died from it. Thus, Shakespeare entered a world where the plague was both commonplace and terrifying. Other visitations would recur in the following decades, but none of these was "comparable to the violence of the pestilence that struck as Shakespeare's dramatic writing career was beginning in 1593. In one year at least 15,000 persons of a London population of 123,000 died—more than 12 percent" (Barroll 74). The plague returned in 1603, forcing the new monarch, King James, to postpone some of his coronation activities and close the theatres and other venues of large gatherings. Recurrent outbreaks in the coming decades would require repeated theatre closings and result in widespread poverty and fatalities. While the epidemiology of the disease was only minimally understood, the early modern assumption that the prohibition of crowds, social distancing, and quarantining could provide some control of a rampant disease has been proven in our own time.

Leeds Barroll has demonstrated that the plague did not just linger on the margins of Shakespeare's career—it was a defining factor. But if the plague marked his theatrical world and the lives of his fellow Londoners so profoundly, what about the rural and smaller urban areas beyond the city? A common trajectory of the disease was that it would first surface in more cosmopolitan London, usually through the traffic of imported goods and travelers, and then spread to the countryside. While we have many statistics about cases and fatalities, little is known about the effect on emotional lives, as James Shapiro points out: "the firsthand experience of these terrible visitations and their effects on families and neighborhoods went largely unrecorded. Most of what we know, then, comes from official documents, medical texts, plague pamphlets, sermons, and a few letters …" (*The Year of Lear* 274–275). And perhaps surprisingly, we learn relatively little about the plague from the theatre itself.

Given its relentless interruptions of playhouse operations, we could expect the plague to be a frequent topic in early modern drama. In Shakespeare's plays, there are numerous allusions: Lear maligns Goneril as "a plague-sore," Prospero conjures "the red plague" upon Caliban, and in *Romeo and Juliet*, Mercutio's famous damnation, "a plague upon both your houses," is set alongside Friar John's disastrous inability to deliver the warning letter to Romeo because he is in quarantine. But even as powerful as these invocations would have been, there is no portrayal of actual suffering or death by plague. That it was a notoriously horrifying way to die was surely no deterrent given the other violence—beheadings, mutilations, rapes—that Shakespeare staged. The omission may be precisely because the contagion and the theatre closures were so enmeshed. Shapiro argues that it would have been economically unwise and traumatic to remind theatregoers packed together of a transmissible disease: "Imagine writing a play about the transmission of coronavirus set in a subway car and then inviting people onto a subway car to see it. We'd all be a little nervous" (*Octavian*).

O'Farrell addresses the absence of personal writing about the plague with her piercing descriptions of Hamnet's suffering and the sorrow of his loving family who cared for him. Agnes' own anguish is particularly acute as she blames herself for the failure of her healing skills, and even more because she is torn between gratitude that Judith has been spared and anger that Hamnet was not:

> Her son's body is in a place of torture, of hell. It writhes, it twists, it buckles, it
> strains. Agnes holds him by the shoulders, by the chest, to keep him still.
> There is, she is starting to see, nothing more she can do. She can stay beside

him, comfort him as best she can, but this pestilence is too great, too strong, too vicious. It is an enemy too powerful for her.

(209)

The sorrow is not Agnes' alone: Hamnet's sisters, uncles, grandparents, and neighbors are also devastated. Among the many unknowns in Shakespeare's biography is his response to his son's death in his emotional life and his art, and specifically, whether he returned to Stratford for his son's funeral. The primary argument against his presence is time: hasty burials were mandated in the case of plague, but regardless of the cause of death, it would have taken several days to notify him and then allow for his travel home. Others cite the evidence that Shakespeare's theatre company was performing in the country that summer, so he may have been able to return to Stratford more quickly. This is the scenario that O'Farrell adopts but with a variation: Shakespeare is with his fellow players in Kent but the message he receives is that Judith is gravely ill; he rushes home to find that it is instead Hamnet laid out for burial.

While there may be scant testimony about the personal impact of the plague in particular, there is considerable evidence of the emotional suffering following the death of loved ones in the early modern period. Ever since Lawrence Stone claimed in his monumental survey, *Family, Sex, and Marriage in England 1500–1800*, that "the omnipresence of death colored affective relations at all levels of society by reducing the amount of emotional capital available for prudent investment in any single individual …"—in other words, that parents were hardened by the high rates of child mortality—scholars were quick to challenge his arguments with examples of bereavement in letters, literature, and other testimonies (651–652). Families grieved deeply over the deaths of their children, and although the account of the Shakespeare family's mourning in *Hamnet* is fictional, it is consistent with the historical evidence about such loss.

Hannah Newton exposes two other assumptions about parental bereavement in the early modern period, both gendered: one, that sons were mourned more deeply than daughters and two, that mothers responded differently because women were more inherently emotional than men and more invested in the raising of their children. The first claim is that concerns about lineage and property transfer in a patriarchal society would have deemed sons more valuable than daughters, and while this may have obtained in individual cases, Newton demonstrates that "there is little concrete evidence to support this view: the sufferings and deaths of children of both genders provoked comparable expressions of distress in parents" (123). Still, the notion that Shakespeare felt the loss of his only son more deeply, and may even have harbored some resentment at the survival of Hamnet's twin sister Judith, has had remarkable tenacity, in spite of any supporting evidence. This belief is in the background of Bill Cain's play *Equivocation*, in which Shakespeare resents his daughter Judith's survival in place of his son's. O'Farrell raises this issue when Judith asks her sister in the year following Hamnet's death if she thinks that their father doesn't come home "because I resemble him so closely. Perhaps it is hard for Father to let his eye rest upon me," but Susanna quickly assures her otherwise (148–149). The second assumption, that fathers experienced the death of their children less acutely than mothers, is also challenged by Newton as well as Patricia Philippy, who argues that "Early modern diaries and autobiographies written by men leave no doubt that, generally speaking, fathers' affections for their children were as heartfelt as were mothers' in the period and that men were subject to grief as profound as their wives' at child-loss," even if their emotional lives were manifest in different, culturally determined ways (203).

At first, Agnes assumes her husband's abrupt return to London after the funeral suggests his indifference, while she remains in a state of disbelief and anger. When he returns home a year later, she is further undone when she fears he has been unfaithful: "She wonders how he will tell her all this, what words he will choose," but instead he asks her how often she thinks about Hamnet. He confesses that he is

> constantly wondering where he is. Where he has gone. It is like a wheel ceaselessly turning at the back of my mind … I look for him everywhere, in every street, in every crowd, in every audience. That's what I'm doing when I look out at them all: I try to find him, or a version of him.
>
> *(263–264)*

He then asks if she and their daughters would move to London, but when Agnes reminds him that it is safer for the girls to live in Stratford, he announces the purchase of New Place; the "enormous house and gardens" propel Agnes into renewed activity and draws Shakespeare home more frequently.

But still they lament Hamnet, and Agnes' sorrow is renewed a few years later when she hears that her husband has written a new play called *Hamlet*. Her stepmother, Joan, shows Agnes a playbill that a cousin brought from London. Agnes is shocked:

> How can her son's name be on a London playbill? There has been some odd, strange mistake. He died. This name is her son's and he died, not four years ago … He is himself, not a play, not a piece of paper, not something to be spoken of or performed or displayed. He died … She cannot understand.
>
> *(287)*

The fluid orthography of the time meant that the names Hamnet and Hamlet were virtually interchangeable, leading scholars to debate a connection between the death of Shakespeare's son and his famous tragedy. Shakespeare most likely wrote *Hamlet* between 1599 and 1601, a few years after Hamnet's death. There are contemporary references to an earlier revenge play of the same name but no text survives, so we do not know how much Shakespeare may have borrowed from it. But the story, a thirteenth-century tale recorded in Latin by the Danish writer Saxo Grammaticus, was well known; it had also been translated into French by Francois de Belleforest in 1570, whose tales were familiar to Shakespeare. Any of these versions could have provided the basic contours of the plot, though the greater character complexity, the meta-play, the ghostly father, and the moral anguish of *Hamlet* are Shakespeare's.

Stephen Greenblatt was not the first to propose a relationship between the death of Hamnet and the play *Hamlet*—along with other scholars and biographers, James Joyce's Stephen Dedalus had suggested it in *Ulysses*—but his argument is perhaps now the most well-known. Greenblatt points to *Hamlet*'s signature interiority as a pronounced shift in Shakespeare's oeuvre, and suggests that such a profound turn signaled "some more personal cause for his daring transformation of both of his sources and his whole way of writing" (307). Greenblatt cites Hamnet's death a few years earlier and John Shakespeare's imminent death as this personal cause, and argues specifically that part of Hamlet's despair over his father's death—and Shakespeare's over his son's—may have been the Reformation's elimination of Catholic rituals for honoring loved ones: "What does it mean that a ghost from purgatory erupts into the world of *Hamlet* asking to be remembered?" Furthermore, *Hamlet* is about the death of a father, not a son, but from a psychoanalytic perspective, the author's deep grief is displaced and projected onto the father, an argument that Freud had made earlier in *The Interpretation of Dreams* (283). Other scholars deny any notions that Shakespeare's play is related to the death of his son because it was obviously named after the old Danish tale: most recently, Laurie Maguire and Emma Smith dismiss the Hamnet–*Hamlet* equivalence as one of "30 Great Myths about Shakespeare" (80–85). But one claim need not preclude the other, for Shakespeare's works never rely exclusively on one source of inspiration: his plays are an amalgam of collective beliefs, current events, foundational narratives, literary works, and topical allusions—and it is unlikely that traces of personal experiences would not also appear, even if obliquely.

Even if we cannot prove correspondence between Hamnet's death and its impact on *Hamlet*, parent–child relationships and their emotional ties are a preoccupation in almost every play he wrote after 1596. Some critics point to the fact that in the years immediately after Hamnet's death, Shakespeare wrote not tragedies but some of his greatest comedies—*The Merchant of Venice, The Merry Wives of Windsor, Much Ado About Nothing, As You Like It,* and *Twelfth Night*—and four histories—*King John* and the three plays of the *Henriad* that feature Falstaff, one of his greatest comic creations. *Hamlet* did not appear until four or five years after Hamnet's death. The conclusion is that while Shakespeare himself may have been personally affected by his bereavement, the plays he wrote did not reflect such sentiment since he busied himself writing works other than tragedies. This argument mistakenly assumes that mourning proceeds according to a predictable timeline and that comedies and histories cannot accommodate grave subject matter.

Richard Wheeler's survey of the plays written between 1596–1601 asks us not to insist on direct correlations between art and biography but to consider the more nuanced inflections that the plays might register. Wheeler points out that in the comedies *The Merchant of Venice* and *As You Like*, the focus on the experience of youth and the movement towards unions and community is driven by "the quasi-magical power of a daughter to transform herself into a man," a means of resurrecting the young son (145). This movement intensifies in *Twelfth Night* with its restoration of the assumed dead male twin and preservation of the female twin; many others agree that "Shakespeare could [not] have avoided thinking of Hamnet and Judith in turning to this narrative" (Holland 250). Wheeler also argues that the history plays of this period are "marked by a group of situations in which a beloved son's or a young boy's death produces a volatile mix of parental grief, guilt, distraction, helplessness, recrimination, rage" (145). Perhaps the most heartfelt example comes from *King John*, the play assumed to be the one written most immediately after Hamnet's death. Constance's anticipatory anguish over the death of her son Arthur is so acute that she is driven to suicidal thoughts. When she is scolded for this indulgent excess of emotion, she describes her pain in heartbreaking detail:

> Grief fills the room up of my absent child,
> Lies in his bed, walks up and down with me,
> Puts on his pretty looks, repeats his words,
> Remembers me of all his gracious parts,
> Stuffs out his vacant garments with his form ...
> O Lord, my boy, my Arthur, my fair son,
> My Life, my joy, my food, my all the world ...
> *(4.2. 93–104)*

That Shakespeare's complex response to the death of his son frequently found its way into his work seems undeniable, even when direct correlations cannot be proven. His later works continue to portray mothers and fathers grieving for lost children. In this study alone, we have seen Lear utterly broken over Cordelia's execution; Leontes so overcome by the death of his son Mamillius that he accepts it as divine retribution and Hermione equally anguished by the loss of Perdita; King Alonso in despair over the presumed loss of his son Ferdinand; and Pericles driven to self-destruction when he hears that his only daughter, Marina, has died. Again and again, parents are brought down by the assumed or actual loss of their children, and whether Shakespeare enacts those deaths, as with Arthur, Cordelia, Hotspur, and Mamillius, or restores them to life, as with Sebastian, Perdita, and Marina, parents are not allowed to take for granted the precious fragility of their child's life.

For Agnes Shakespeare in *Hamnet*, the thought that her husband translated any of their personal sorrow into art seems an act of betrayal, not homage, but she comes to understand it as a parallel to her own form of grief. Agnes describes the impulse parents experience when they witness the illness and imminent death of their children as a desire to take on their suffering, to exchange places with them: "She would try anything, she would do anything. She would open her own veins, her own body cavity, and give him her blood, her heart, her organs, if it would do the slightest good" (209). In the daring final pages of *Hamnet*, Agnes makes the difficult trip to London for the first time in her life, bent on confronting her husband. She finds her way to the theatre and into the front of the audience, and as she watches the play her husband has written and in which he is performing as Hamlet, the father, she begins to understand. Agnes sees that this Hamlet

> is two people, the young man, alive, and the father, dead. He is both alive and dead. Her husband has brought him back to life, the only way he can. As the ghost talks, she sees that her husband, in writing this, in taking the role of the ghost, has changed places with his son ... done what any father would wish to do, to exchange his child's suffering for his own, to take his place ... so that the boy might live.
>
> *(305)*

This is the confluence O'Farrell imagines between Hamnet and *Hamlet*, but what is finally significant is her generous portrayal of a man who loved his family deeply, even if his art also kept him away from them for long periods of time. How then is *Hamnet* talking back to Shakespeare? O'Farrell firmly repudiates the centuries of historiography that portrays Shakespeare's family as an unwanted burden, his wife as a scheming harridan, his daughter Judith as an object of resentment, his son as someone he barely cared for because they lived apart, and she does so without facile sentimentality. She portrays the famous bard as a flawed but ultimately compassionate man, lifting him down from his pedestal and restoring him to humanity. She renders dignity to the life of an early modern mother and wife whose contributions to her world, however local, were valuable to family and community.

And not incidentally, O'Farrell collapses the conventional divide of Shakespeare's two lives, the personal and professional, represented by the distance between Stratford and London. As Paul Edmondson and Stanley Wells claim, "Life in Stratford is too often hived off in Shakespeare biographies" (330). Shakespeare did not, in contrast to what some narratives suggest, flee his provincial hometown for the bright city lights only to return 25 years later as the small-village success story. His engagement with his life in Stratford was ongoing and, as O'Farrell imagines it, it is quite possible that he completed some of his research and writing during his visits home before returning to London. If the final journey in *Hamnet*, in which Agnes is the one on horseback from Stratford to London, seems a little preposterous, a small footnote in the Shakespeare biographical record tells us that in 1625, just two years after the publication of the First Folio, Susanna Shakespeare Hall travelled from Stratford to London with her sixteen-year-old daughter, Elizabeth. We do not know the reason for their visit, but perhaps we can indulge ourselves in thinking that while they were there, Elizabeth was able to take in one of her grandfather's plays.

References

Barroll, Leeds. *Politics, Plague, and Shakespeare's Theatre: The Stuart Years*. Ithaca: Cornell University, 1991.

Bloom, Harold. *The Western Canon: The Books and School of the Ages*. New York: Riverhead Books, 1995.

Brooks, Geraldine. "Shakespeare's Son Died at Eleven." *New York Times.* July 17, 2020: 1–16.

Burgess, Anthony. *Nothing Like the Sun: A Story of Shakespeare's Love-Life.* New York: W. W. Norton, 1964.

Burgess, Anthony. *Shakespeare.* London: Jonathan Cape, 1970.

DeGroot, Jerome. *The Historical Novel.* New York: Routledge, 2009.

Duncan-Jones, Katherine. *Ungentle Shakespeare: Scenes from His Life.* London: Arden, 2001.

Edmondson, Paul and Stanley Wells, eds. *The Shakespeare Circle.* Cambridge: Cambridge UP, 2015.

Freud, Sigmund. *The Interpretation of Dreams.* Trans. James Strachey. New York: Basic Books, 1955.

Greenblatt, Stephen. *Will in the World: How Shakespeare Became Shakespeare.* New York: W. W. Norton, 2004.

Greer, Germaine. *Shakespeare's Wife.* London: Bloomsbury, 2007.

Holderness, Graham. *Nine Lives of William Shakespeare.* New York: Continuum, 2011.

Holderness, Graham. "His Son Hamnet Shakespeare." In *The Shakespeare Circle: An Alternative Biography*, eds. Paul Edmonson and Stanley Wells. Cambridge: Cambridge UP, 2015: 101–109.

Holland, Peter. "Shakespeare and Biography." In *Shakespeare in Our Time*, eds. Dympna Callaghan and Suzanne Gossett. London: Bloomsbury, 2016.

Lackey, Michael. "Locating and Defining the Bio in Biofiction." *a/b: Auto/Biography Studies* 31. 1 (2016): 3–10.

Maguire, Laurie and Emma Smith. *30 Great Myths About Shakespeare.* Hoboken: Wiley-Blackwell, 2013.

Mendelson, Sara and Patricia Crawford. *Women in Early Modern England: 1550–1720.* Oxford: Clarendon Press, 1998.

Newton, Hannah. *The Sick Child in Early Modern England 1580–1720.* Oxford: Oxford UP, 2012.

O'Farrell, Maggie. *Hamnet.* New York: Knopf, 2020.

O'Farrell, Maggie. "Interview with Barbara Bogaev." Folger Shakespeare Podcast. August 4, 2020.

O'Farrell, Maggie. "Interview with Mary Louise Kelly." NPR. July 20, 2020.

Orlin, Lena Cowen. "Anne by Indirection." *Shakespeare Quarterly* 65. 4 (2014): 421–454.

Orlin, Lena Cowen. "Shakespeare's Marriage." In *The Oxford Handbook of Shakespeare and Embodiment: Gender, Sexuality, and Race*, ed. Valerie Traub. Oxford: Oxford UP, 2016: 39–56.

Philippy, Patricia. "'I Might Have Againe Have Been the Sepulchre': Paternal and Maternal Mourning in Early Modern England." In *Grief and Gender: 700–1700*, ed. Jennifer Vaught. New York: Palgrave Macmillan, 2003: 197–213.

Potter, Lois. "Biography v. Novel." In *Shakespeare In Our Time*, eds. Dympna Callaghan and Suzanne Gossett. London: Bloomsbury, 2016.

Sanders, Julie. *Adaptation and Appropriation*, 2nd ed. New York: Routledge, 2016.

Scheil, Katherine West. *Imagining Shakespeare's Wife: The Afterlife of Anne Hathaway.* Cambridge: Cambridge UP, 2018.

Shapiro, James. *A Year in the Life of William Shakespeare: 1599.* New York: Harper Collins, 2005.

Shapiro, James. *The Year of Lear.* New York: Simon and Schuster, 2015.

Shapiro, James. "A Pox On All Our Houses." Interview. *The Octavian Report.* Fall 2020.

Shapiro, James. *Shakespeare in a Divided America.* New York: Penguin, 2020.

Stone, Lawrence. *Family, Sex, and Marriage in England 1500–1800.* London: Weidenfeld & Nicolson, 1977.

Wheeler, Richard. "Deaths in the Family: The Loss of a Son and the Rise of Shakespearean Comedy." *Shakespeare Quarterly*, 51. 2 (2000): 127–153.

AFTERWORD

That *Women Talk Back to Shakespeare* is not comprehensive is cause for celebration: it means that there are many other adaptations and appropriations of Shakespeare from the last decade that deserve consideration but simply could not be accommodated within these pages. Even over the course of working on this book, new entries kept appearing on my radar, further confirmation that women still have much to say to Shakespeare, and scholars still have much to say about these creative responses.

These works remind us that this adaptational dialogue takes place across a variety of genres and media. Meme Garcia's Salvadoran-American adaptation of *Hamlet*, called *house of sueños*, appeared as a five-episode podcast from the Seattle Shakespeare Company in the spring of 2021. *Ophelia*, the 2018 film directed by Claire McCarthy and written by Semi Chellas, is an adaptation of yet another *Hamlet* adaptation, Lisa Klein's 2006 young adult novel of the same name. Alena Smith's wildly subversive television series on Hulu, *Dickinson*, talks back to the legacy of Emily Dickinson but devotes considerable attention to the poet's engagement with Shakespeare's work, especially *Othello*. And as of this writing, *Station Eleven* is itself being adapted by HBO as a mini-series, again evidence that the adaptive cycle is dynamic and ongoing.

In literature, Naomi Miller's *The Imperfect Alchemist* appeared in 2020; it is a historical novel about Mary Sidney Herbert, Countess of Pembroke, and her possible influence on Shakespeare's *Antony and Cleopatra*, and is the first in Miller's projected series of works about other early modern women writers. Two other highly anticipated novels of 2021—Mona Awad's *Alls Well* and Gillian Flynn's *Hamlet*—promise further contemporary updates to the conversation with Shakespeare. Dahlia Adler's anthology of 2021, *This Way Madness Lies: Shakespeare's Most Notable Works Reimagined*, is a rich collection of retellings by well-known young adult authors.

Intertextual allusions to Shakespeare also continue to pop up in various works by women. Claudia Rankine's 2014 book of poetry, *Citizen*, incorporates words from

DOI: 10.4324/9781003166580-9

Shakespeare, along with James Baldwin and Homi Bhaba, in her meditations on individual and collective racist behaviors in contemporary life. In a recent film that has garnered much critical attention, *Nomadland*, the character played by Frances McDormand finds solace in recalling Shakespeare's sonnets and sharing that love with the next generation. In Marilynne Robinson's novel, *Jack*, the latest addition to her Gilead series, the courtship of a doomed interracial couple begins with their shared experience of *Hamlet*. The point is not to catalogue every cultural Shakespeare sighting but to keep in mind that women artists continue to refashion, repurpose, reshape, and retell his work in innovative and unexpected ways.

The conversation between women and Shakespeare discussed in each chapter of this book is not meant to be exhaustive but to provoke further explorations. My wish is that this book encourages students and interested readers to explore new ways of thinking about Shakespeare, and other works we have so long considered canonical, by way of the many excellent works that not only talk back to him, but claim their own worthwhile place in our literary world.

INDEX

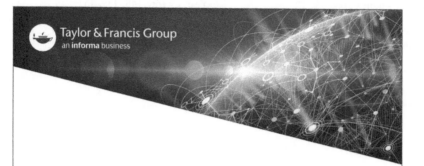

Taylor & Francis Group
an **informa** business

Taylor & Francis eBooks

www.taylorfrancis.com

A single destination for eBooks from Taylor & Francis
with increased functionality and an improved user
experience to meet the needs of our customers.

90,000+ eBooks of award-winning academic content in
Humanities, Social Science, Science, Technology, Engineering,
and Medical written by a global network of editors and authors.

TAYLOR & FRANCIS EBOOKS OFFERS:

A streamlined
experience for
our library
customers

A single point
of discovery
for all of our
eBook content

Improved
search and
discovery of
content at both
book and
chapter level

REQUEST A FREE TRIAL
support@taylorfrancis.com

 Routledge
Taylor & Francis Group

 CRC Press
Taylor & Francis Group